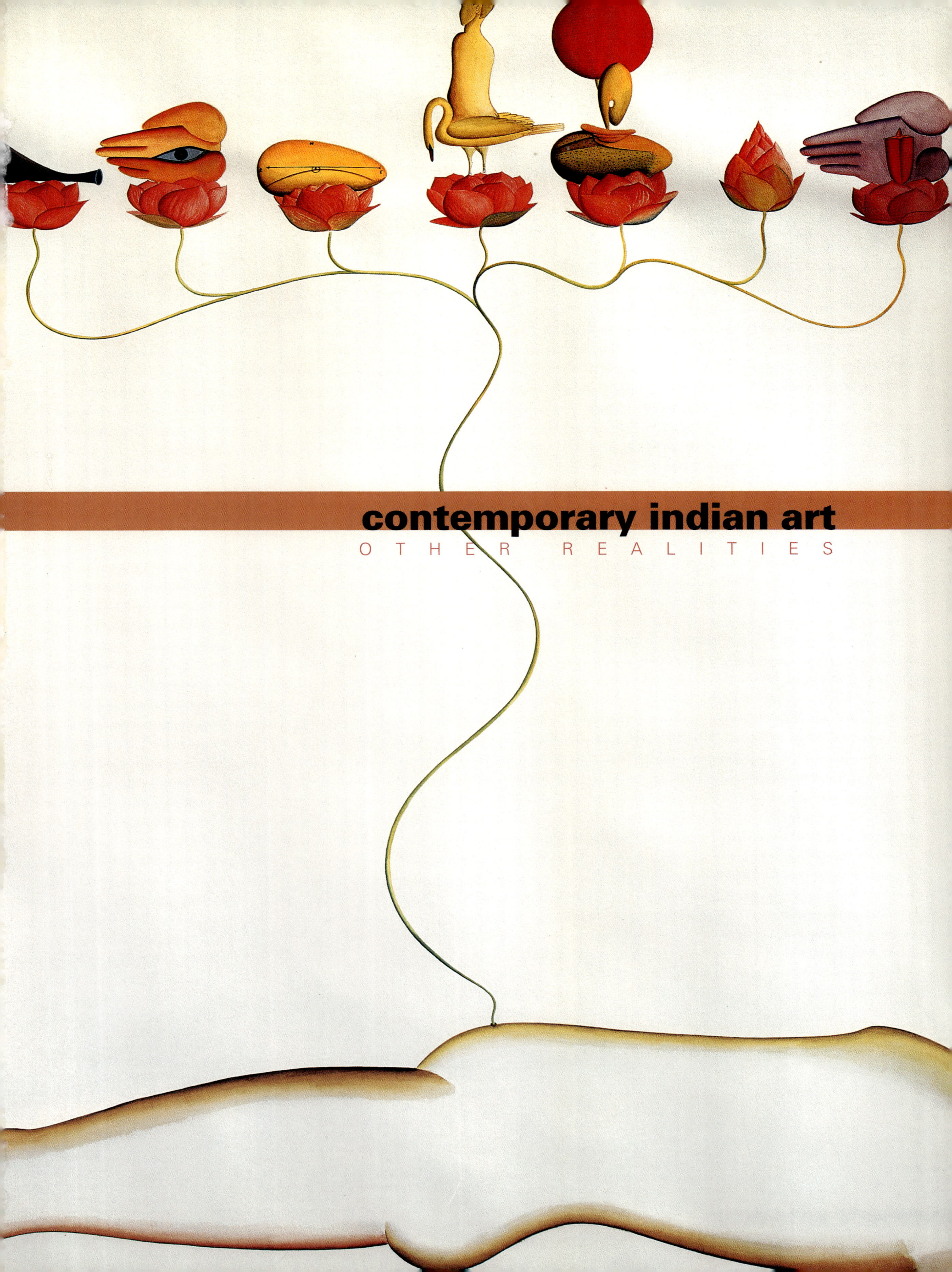
contemporary indian art
OTHER REALITIES

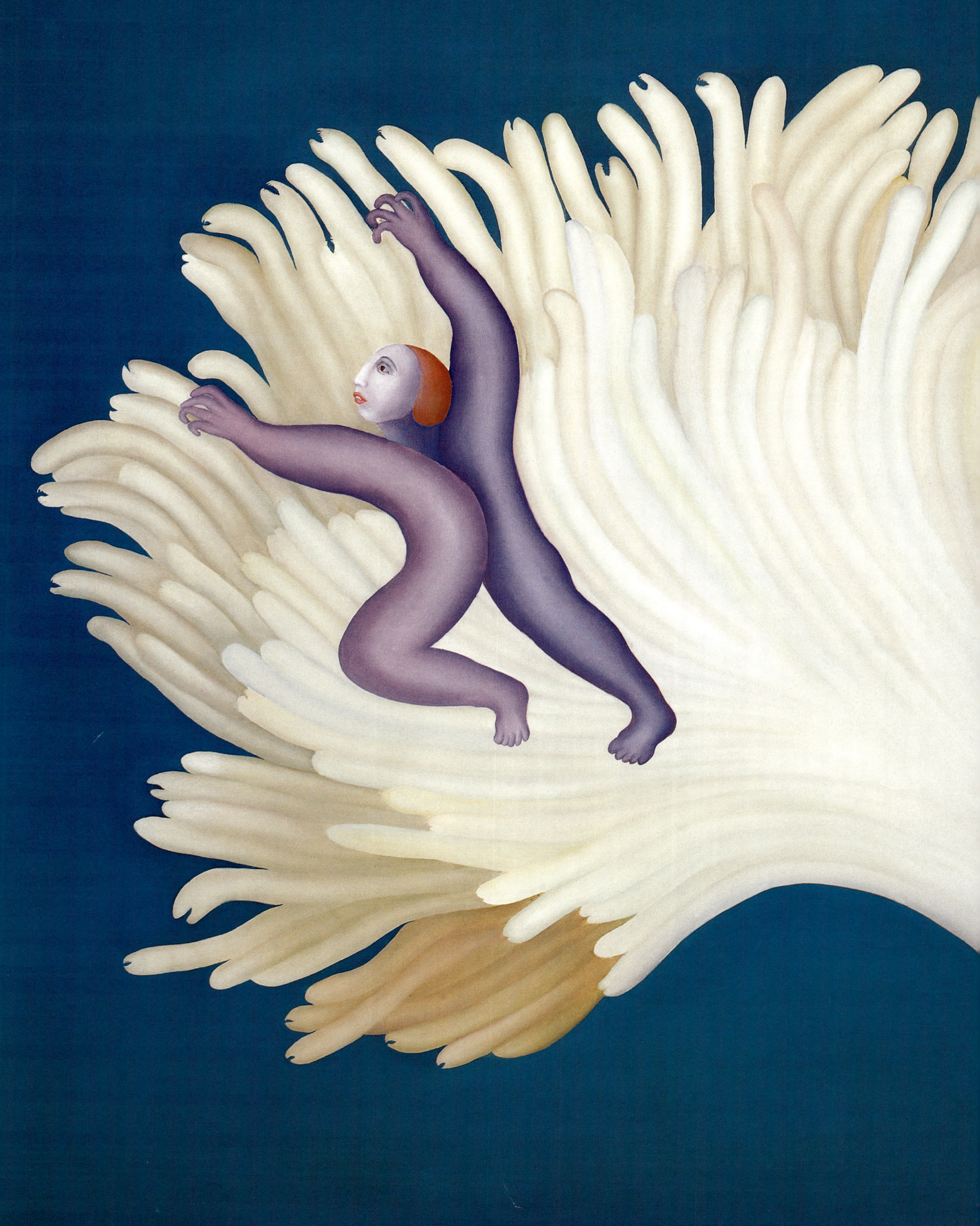

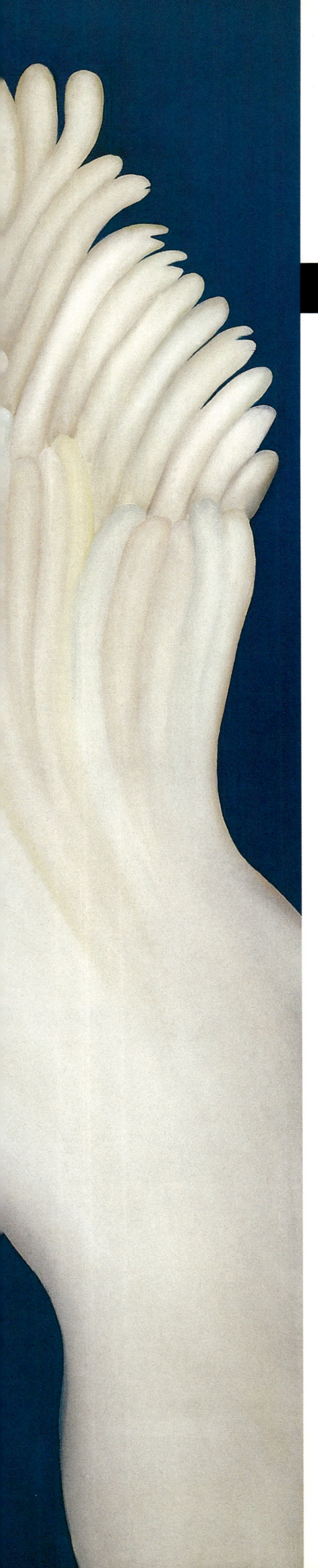

contemporary indian art

OTHER REALITIES

edited by
Yashodhara Dalmia

Márg publications

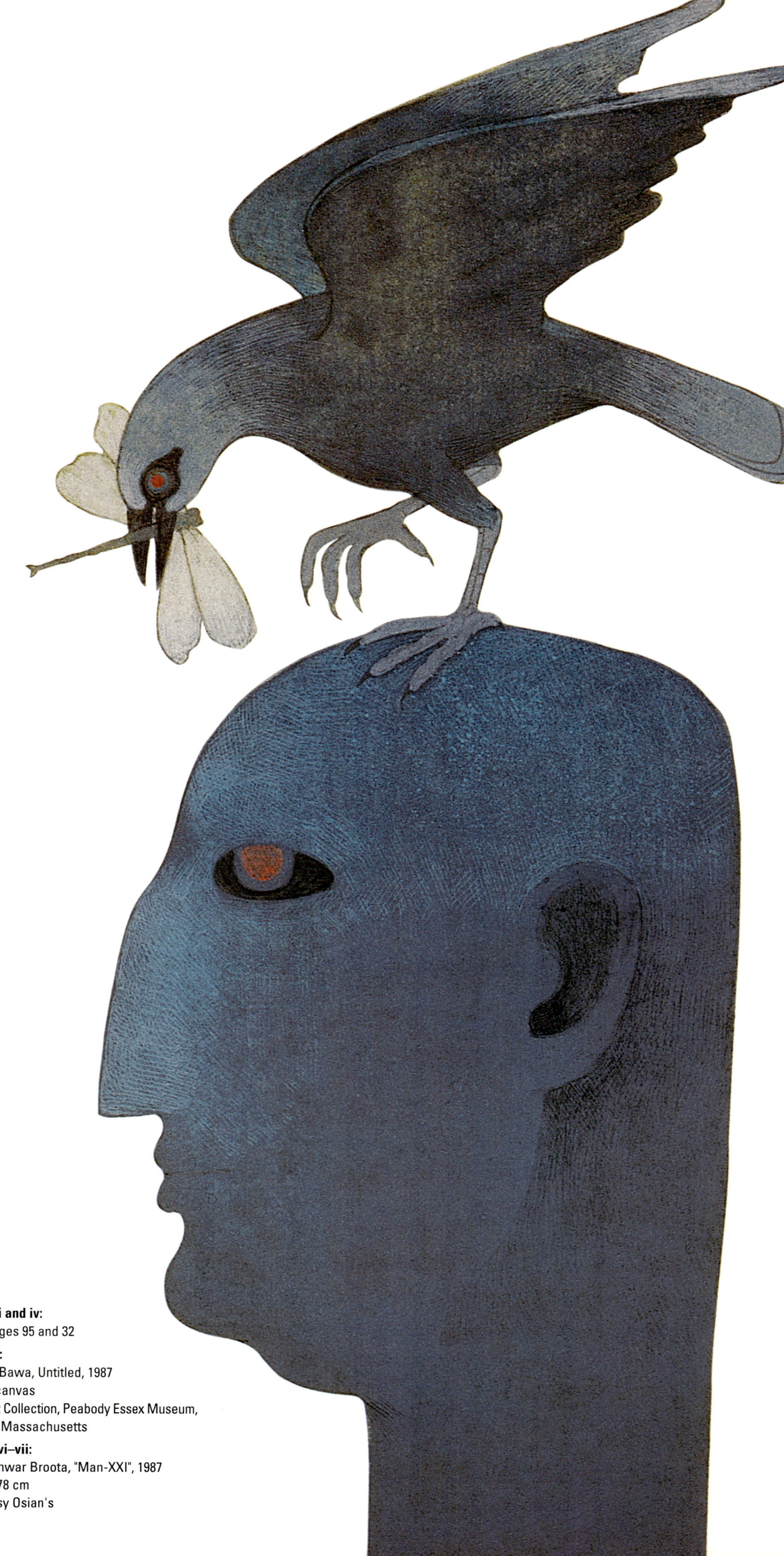

Vol. 53 No. 3
March 2002

Price: Rs 2250.00 / US$ 66.00

ISBN: 81-85026-55-6

Library of Congress Catalog
Card Number: 2002-285000

This book has been designed by Naju Hirani based on the design and layout concept of Kirti Trivedi.

Published by J.J. Bhabha for Marg Publications on behalf of the National Centre for the Performing Arts at 24, Homi Mody Street, Mumbai 400 001.

Colour and black and white processing by Reproscan, Mumbai 400 093.

Printed by A.S. Vadiwala at Tata Infomedia Limited, Mumbai 400 025, India.

Pages i and iv:
See pages 95 and 32

Page ii:
Manjit Bawa, Untitled, 1987
Oil on canvas
Herwitz Collection, Peabody Essex Museum, Salem, Massachusetts

Pages vi–vii:
Rameshwar Broota, "Man-XXI", 1987
127 x 178 cm
Courtesy Osian's

contents

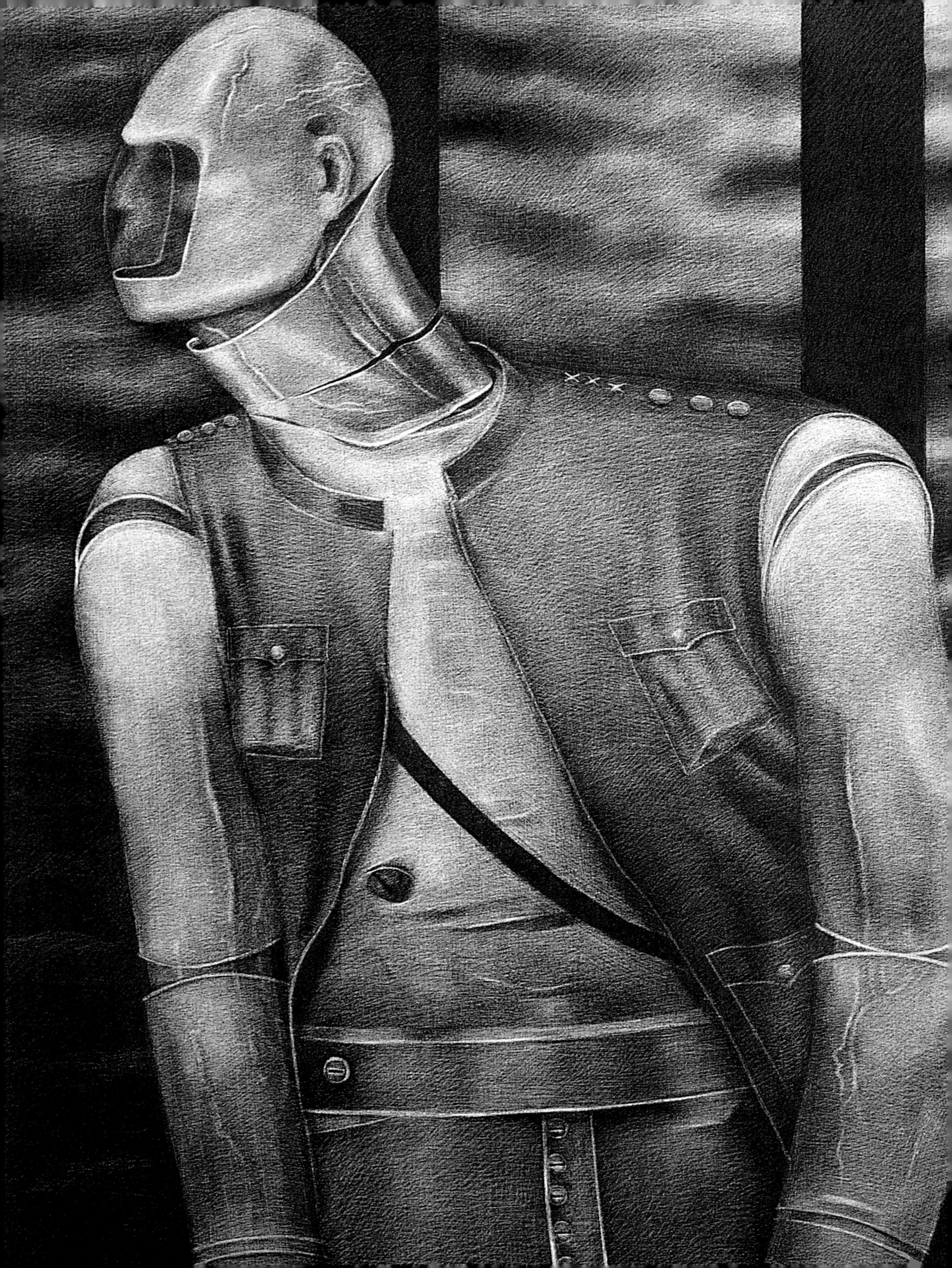

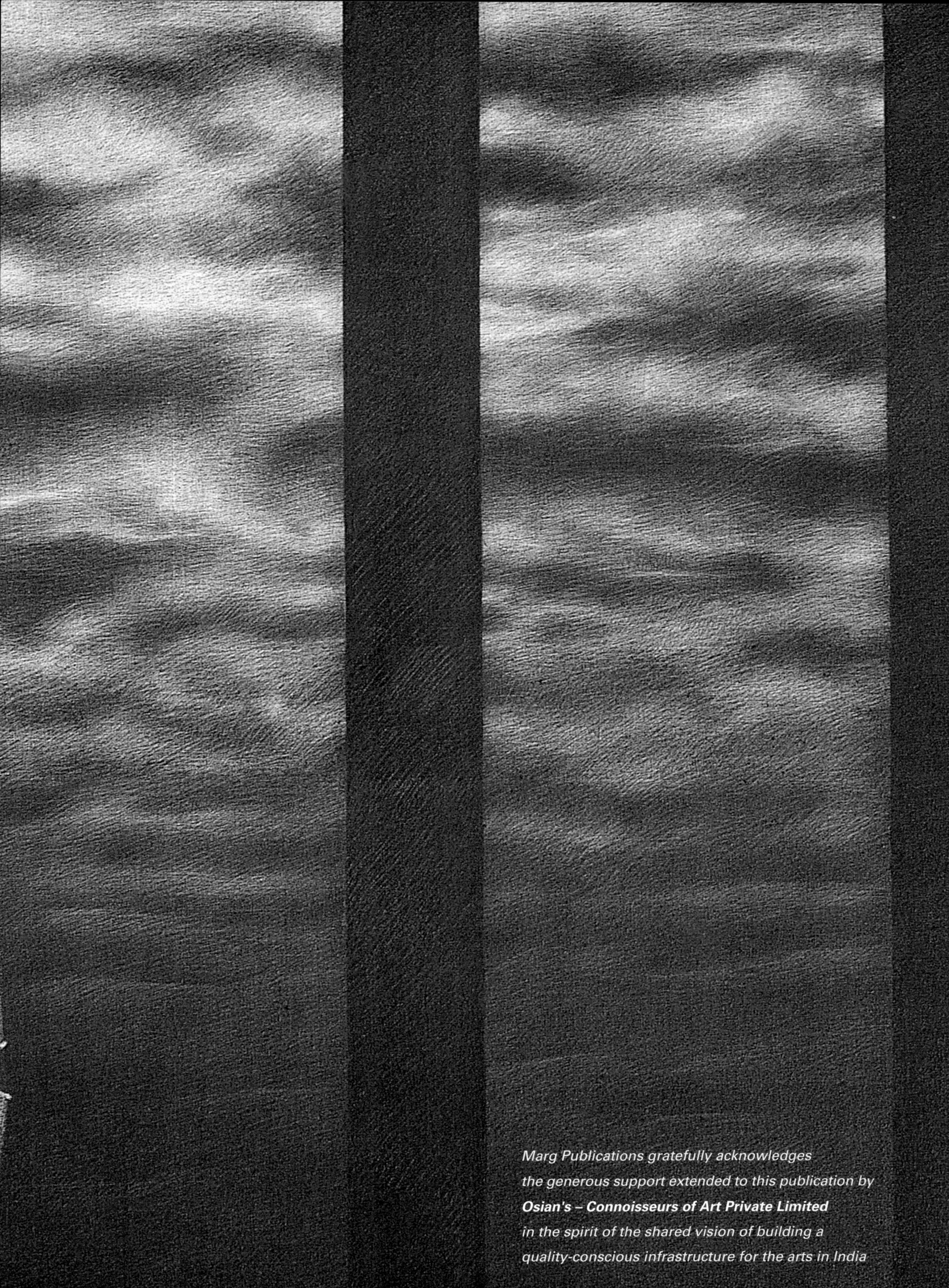

Marg Publications gratefully acknowledges
the generous support extended to this publication by
Osian's – Connoisseurs of Art Private Limited
in the spirit of the shared vision of building a
quality-conscious infrastructure for the arts in India

1
Ravi Varma
"Galaxy", 1893
Oil on canvas
Collection:
Jagan Mohan Palace, Mysore

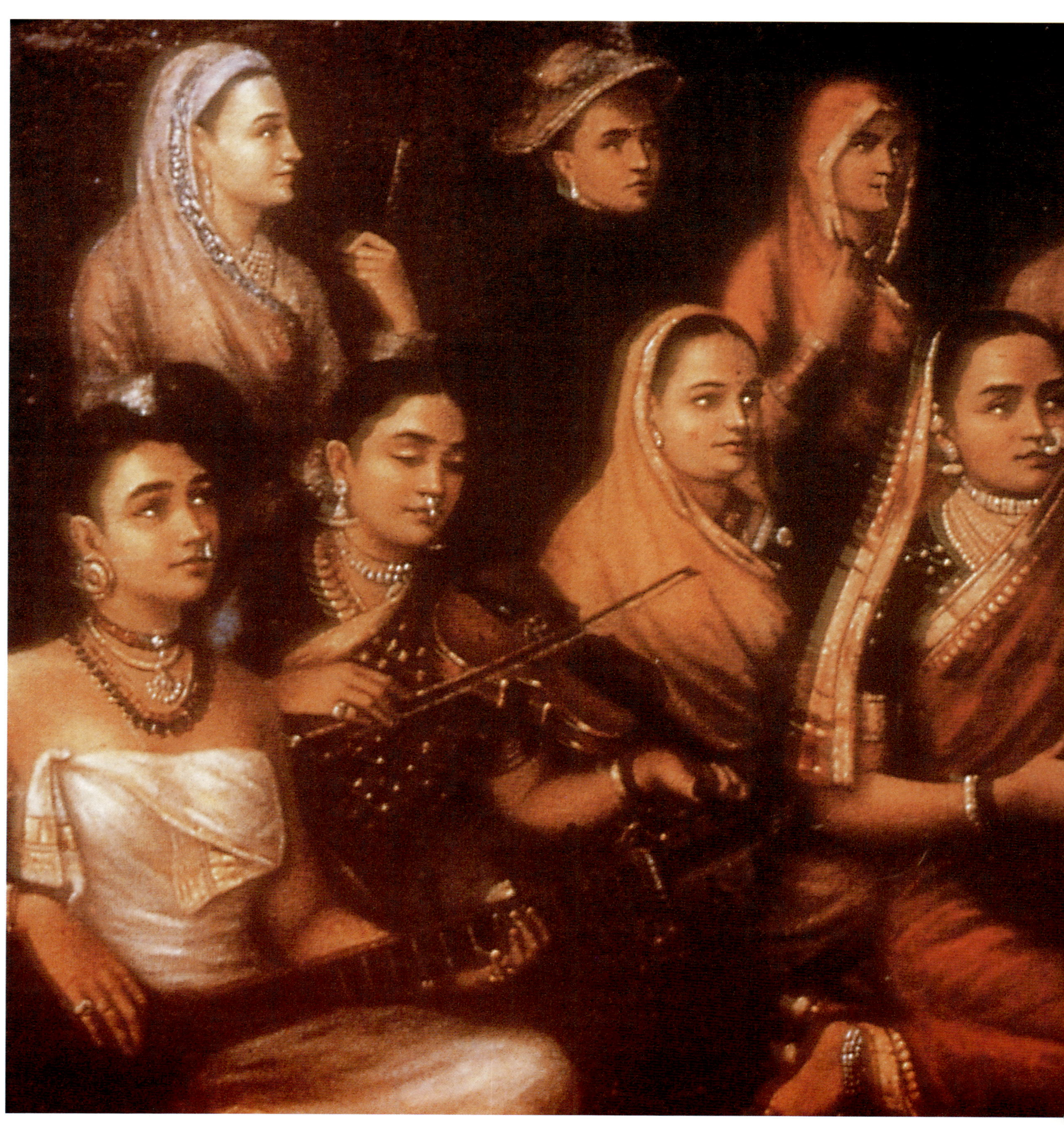

Yashodhara Dalmia

introduction

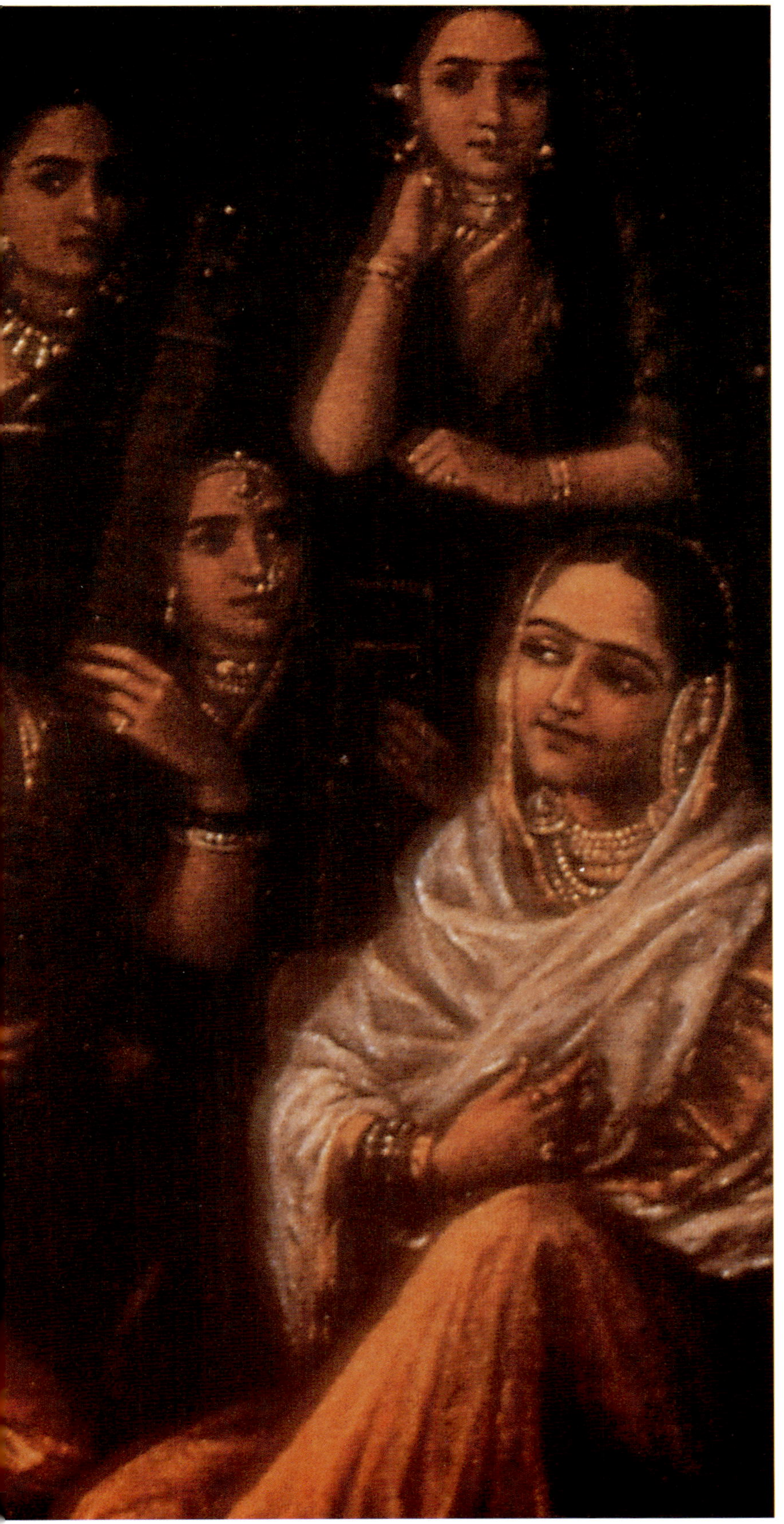

Even as the definitive contours of contemporary Indian art begin to get formed, it is worth noting that there is a constant gestative friction which it has to contend with. It is an art which, linked with the uneven course of history on the one hand and on the other with hybrid international influences, leads at its best to successful negotiations with the "other". The period of birth itself was fraught with ambivalent intent. The art institutions established by the British by the mid-19th century facilitated a knowledge of Western neo-classical art albeit through the backdoor with the initial attempt being to develop the "craft" tradition. This was to lead to an even greater ambiguity as the students were on the one hand taught to "imitate" reality and on the other to adhere to their own indigenous techniques and finally to achieve a successful fertilization of two contrary modes. The J.J. School of Art in Bombay for instance submits in its annual report of 1857–58:

> Another point is to bring Indian designers face to face with nature. Their tendency is to repeat traditional compositions which have come down to them from a distant age without refreshing or even glancing at real life. Hence they degenerate instead of improving. The grotesque images with the shapes of men and animals in all parts of the Hindu temple are unredeemably bad. Their sculptured foliage is purely abstract in character. It seems that the safest way of attempting to regenerate this defective and artificial manner of design without destroying what it has inherited from European schools of art is to set the student to copy faithfully the objects of nature, men and women, the beast, vegetation, the mountains that surround him and to leave him to digest the knowledge thus acquired. Thus, a school of design would in time arise, native in the best sense, owing its sense of accuracy, truth, and natural beauty to European inspiration but moulding its material into purely Indian types.[1]

However, it was with Ravi Varma who used naturalistic means to paint subjects from his own environment that European academic art began to make an impact on the Indian imagination. Ravi Varma (1848–1906) was not the product of British academies, but had taught himself the art of oil painting by watching the Dutch painter

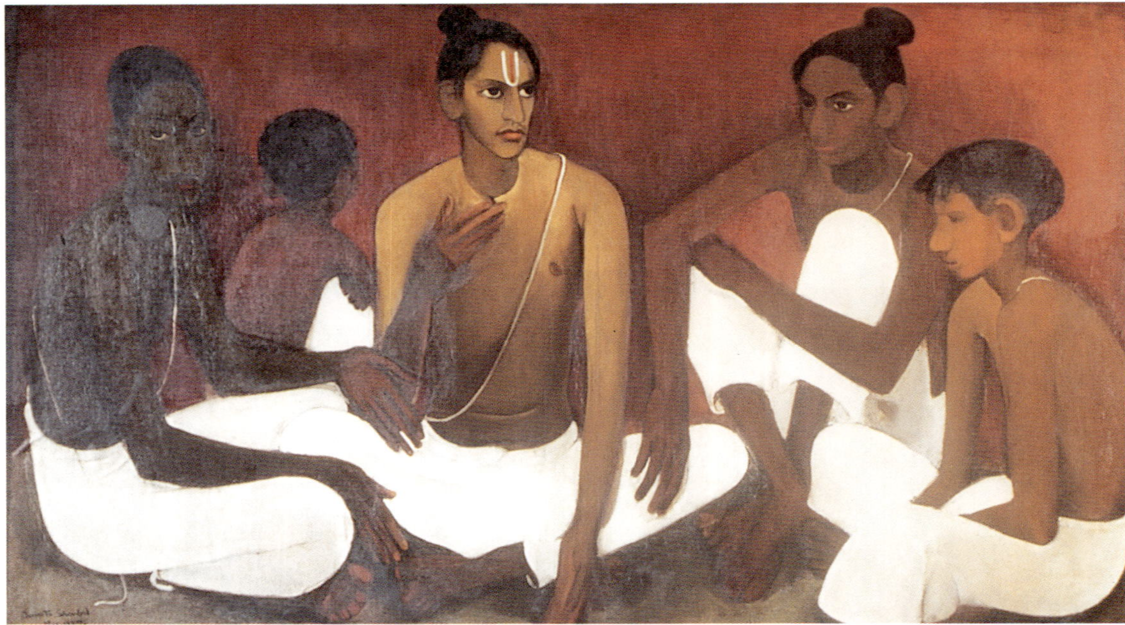

2
Amrita Sher-Gil
"Brahmacharis"
Oil on canvas; 86.5 x 144 cm
Collection: National Gallery of Modern Art, New Delhi

Theodore Janson in the Travancore court. He made paintings which depicted people from his surroundings dressed in their traditional costume. Their alluring quality and iconic stances met with popular success (figure 1). Even more in demand were his historical-mythological scenes which invoked a sense of national self-esteem.

Decrying the Western means used by Varma, a specifically indigenous method of painting was introduced by Abanindranath Tagore (1871–1951) and his followers. The Bengal School, as it came to be called, made rarefied pictures which drew from many Indian art-historical sources: Mughal miniatures, Ajanta murals, as well as the Japanese wash technique. The orientalist mode of the Bengal School had little to do with contemporary reality while romantic notions of a monolithic "Indian" past which was in some way heroic was itself a fallacy. The works however were beautifully crafted and exquisite gems in themselves. But recent research, as for instance by Ella Dutta in this volume, has shown that Abanindranath later not only geared himself to the existing reality but also the techniques developed by him significantly influenced artists like Ganesh Pyne and Lalu Prasad Shaw.

The earliest forbears of modernity in Indian art were artists like Rabindranath Tagore (1861–1941), Amrita Sher-Gil (1913–41), and Jamini Roy (1887–1972) whose work though very different from each other had a common aim: that of finding an authenticity of expression. In doing so each of them had to contend with the complexity of several languages of art existing at the same time and find a means of inventing or synthesizing one appropriate for the present. Amrita Sher-Gil, born of a Hungarian mother and a Sikh father, had left her bohemian Montmartre life in Paris and returned to India to find her roots as an artist. Paintings like "Hill Men" and the later "Brahmacharis" evoke all the gravity and dignity of the lives of people in India (figure 2). Deriving his impulse from the *pata* paintings as well as the painted terracotta and wooden toys and figures of Bengal, Jamini Roy used the simplicity of form and earthy colours while retaining a modernist stance. Rabindranath Tagore's brooding expressionistic portraits emerged from the depths of the unconscious and their distilled essence spoke of his own anguish. The Viswabharati University at Santiniketan established by Tagore was to inspire artists like Nandalal Bose, Benodebehari Mukherjee, and Ramkinkar Baij to create art related to the environment as well as to indigenous traditions and contemporary international movements as an expressive means. A form of contextual modernism as Siva Kumar would have it began to take shape with these artists which also focused on adopting and adapting traditional means such as the use of *wasli* and earth pigments (see his essay). It is Siva Kumar's contention however that these aims only reached a successful fruition with the later Santiniketan artist K.G. Subramanyan. Meanwhile Jyotindra Jain sheds light on the interventions of urban forms on folk art and the consequent creation of a hybrid, popular mode. More specifically, his focus on the Bengali *pata* style accounts for the easy assimilation of the modern within a well-rooted, lively tradition.

In the year of Independence, the Progressive Artists Group formed in Bombay and its influences on later art practices were significant. Artists like M.F. Husain, F.N. Souza, S.H. Raza, K.H. Ara, S. Bakre, and H.A. Gade rejected outright the revivalistic methods of the Bengal School. They also opposed the academic styles taught at the schools of art set up by the British. The artists made a strong thrust towards modernism, attempting to take historical reality fully into account and incorporating it into the present (figures 3 and 4). The emphasis on plastic values, rhythmic tonality, and pure hues was to gather force. The ranks swelled to include others like Tyeb Mehta, Akbar Padamsee, Ram Kumar, Krishen Khanna, V.S. Gaitonde, Bal Chhabda, and Mohan Samant. Much of the energy of the group however was depleted when Souza left for London in 1949 and Raza for Paris soon after. As practitioners of modernism these artists were forefronted on the national stage in the ensuing years.

While Paris was the Mecca of the art world at the time, some Indian artists turned for their inspiration towards Mexico in admiration of the heroic attempts of artists like Diego Rivera to forge a modernist movement. For instance, Satish Gujral returned from Mexico with a different expressionist fervour and combined it with his own pathos about Partition. J. Swaminathan, a personal friend of the Mexican poet Octavio Paz, spoke passionately against the technocratic, authoritarian culture of the West and for the magical potency and symbolism of folk and miniature artists (figure 5). In the south the Cholamandal group formed by K.C.S. Paniker mixed occult with grafitti to script anecdotal passages on the surface defying perspectival space (figure 6). The neo-tantrics like Biren De and G.R. Santosh invoked the ancient erotic symbols of tantra and attempted a reinterpretation of tantric diagrams and their associations with the cosmos. Meanwhile Ganesh Pyne, Bikash Bhattacharjee, and K.G. Subramanyan began to form independent interpretations of modernism. Pyne's shadowy figures reflected the Bengal School, Bhattacharjee used surrealism to depict his own milieu, and K.G. Subramanyan employed the wit and parody of folk

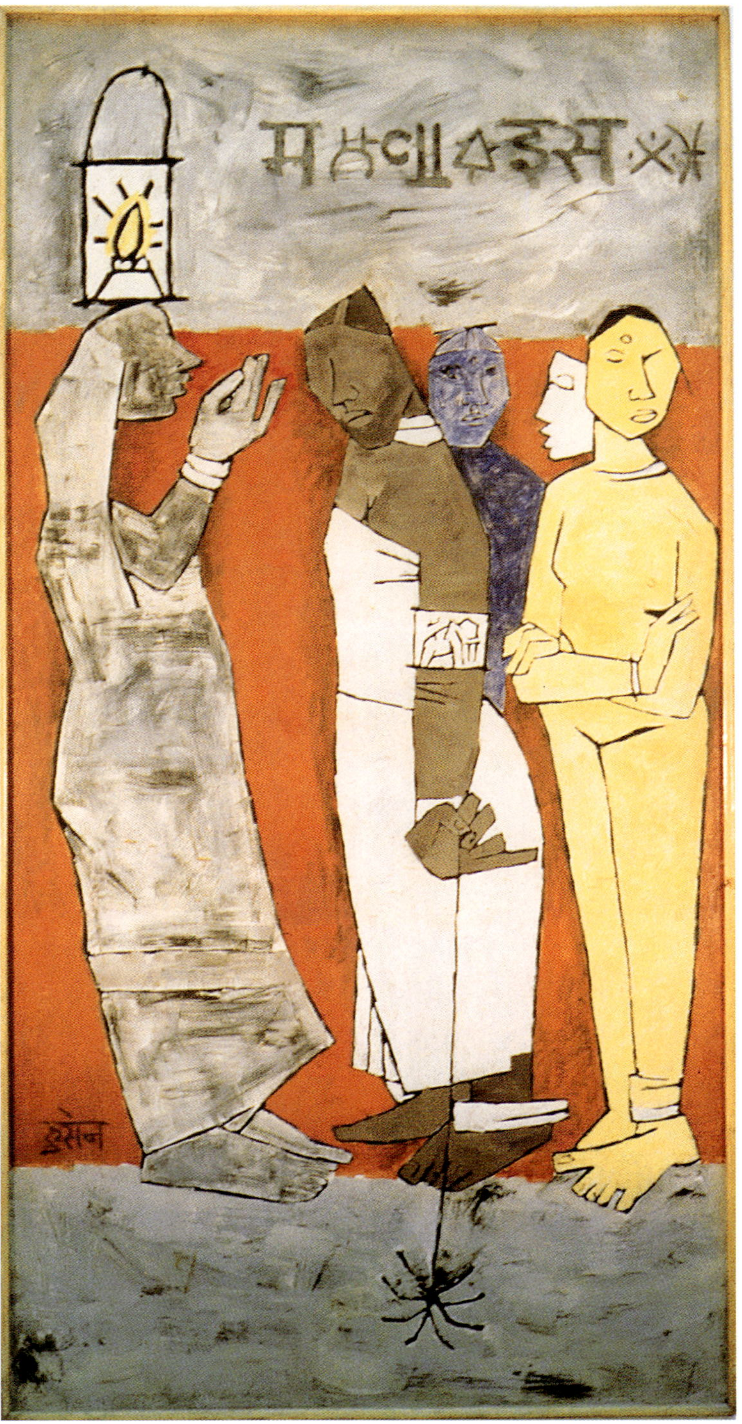

3
M.F. Husain
"The Spider and the Lamp", 1956
Oil on board; 229 x 125 cm
Collection: Artist

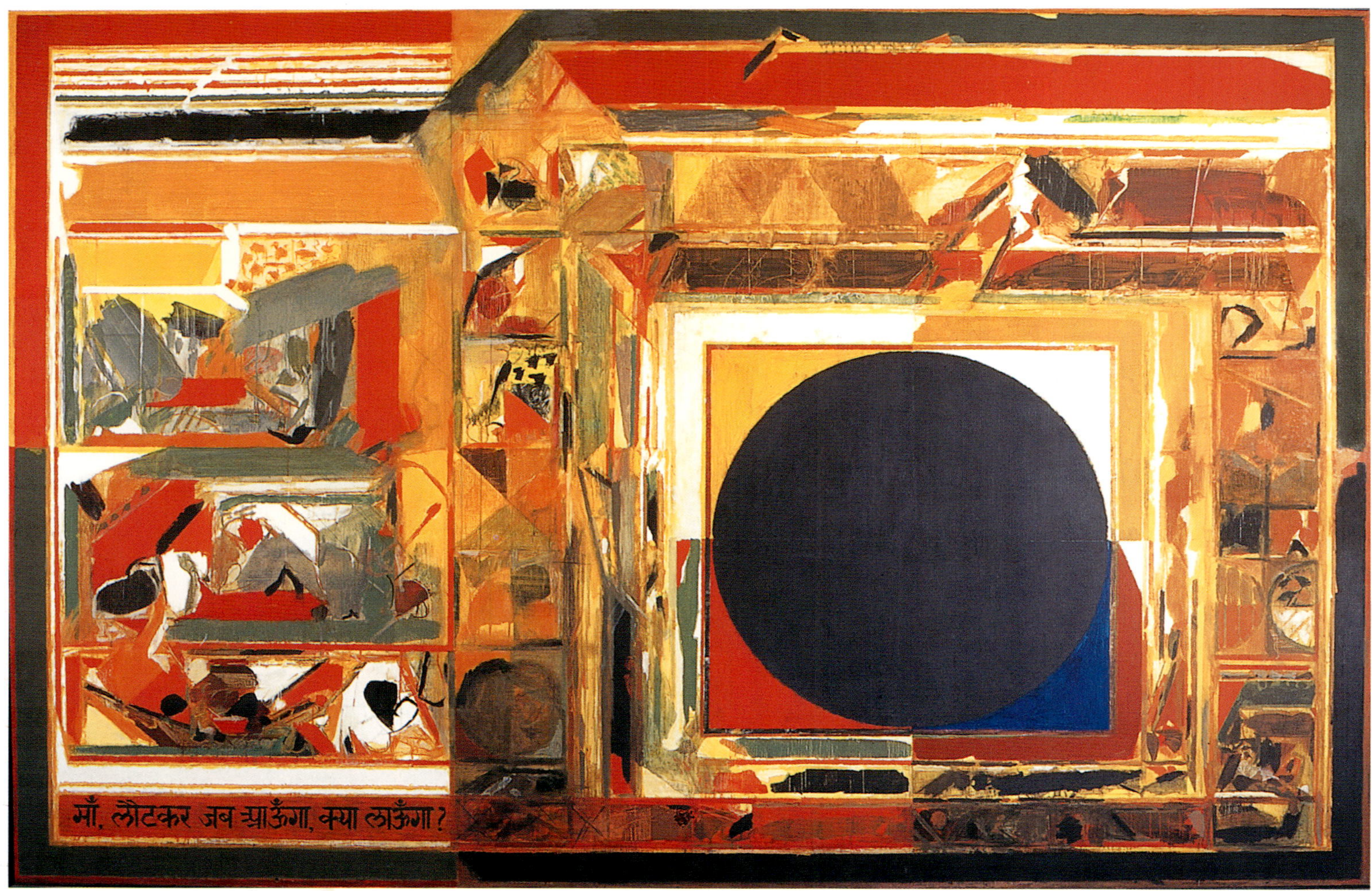

4
S.H. Raza
"Maa", 1981
Oil on canvas; 183 x 275 cm
Collection: Bal Chhabda and M.F. Husain

tradition, the bazaar, and 19th-century glass-paintings to make wholly inventive motifs. A towering figure Meera Mukherjee appropriated the lost wax method of the Bastar tribals to create works which were archetypal as well as contemporary. Many others were to contribute to the making of images in these fervent times.

By the '70s there is a move towards locating the works as artists begin to describe the life around them shorn of all mysticism. The language of modernism was considered pertinent only to signify and articulate the image. As the artist Gulammohammed Sheikh put it, "The various groups of artists are heterogeneous, as far as styles of their works are concerned and one could say that even ideological affinities are loose and liberal. But the most distinguishing feature of the art of the younger artist is the growing involvement with the local environment, its shift from generalities to specific areas of interest. This has led to an approach which is more realistic and intimate."[2] Consequently the figure is resurrected in the works of artists like Bhupen Khakhar, Gulammohammed and Nilima Sheikh and Vivan Sundaram in Baroda, Gieve Patel, Sudhir Patwardhan, Nalini Malani, Navjot and Altaf Mohamedi in Mumbai, Arpita Singh, Jogen Chowdhury, Manjit Bawa, A. Ramachandran, Anupam Sud, Mrinalini Mukherjee, Samshad Husain, Rameshwar Broota, and others in Delhi, and Laxma Goud and D.L.N. Reddy in Hyderabad. There is a burgeoning of forms which borrow from tradition as well as international pop art suggesting a tilt towards the outer world. Bhupen Khakhar with great pun and parody brings in the street and the common man with his contrary and myriad lives (figure 7). There is incessant invention and frequent crossovers.

A new internationalism emerged with the Festivals of India at London, Paris, and in the United States in the 1980s which spurred a greater awareness and opportunities for Indian artists to interact with other countries.[3] At this juncture it seems pertinent to consider the vexed question of the hybridity of art forms. If contemporary Indian art is really imitative of the West then is the praxis of Western art itself "pure"? The question is rhetorical since there is no such thing as "pure" art and in fact art can only evolve because of influences and implantations from other sources. As is well known, Picasso, Matisse, Gauguin, and many others had derived their inspiration from African, Persian, Oceanic, and Indian art and the incorporation of the "primitive" finally resulted in the modern. If in borrowing, art was not considered derivative as Thomas McEvilley is at pains to point out in his article, then why should it be so in lending? The hierarchical notion that only art from developing countries is imitative and not when the same process takes place in the West points towards an inherent bias. The paradigms of modernism in Asian countries are considerably different according to John Clark who observes here, "The difference of position derives ultimately from Euramerica's claim to have invented, and therefore to retain purchase on, modernity. This claim, whilst true in a rather simplistic developmental history, disappears the moment it is accepted that modernity invents itself everywhere it is required for a new relativization of the pasts of any given culture or group of cultures. The principal condition is that these cultures need to – and are capable of – carrying out this relativization."

In this volume some of the debates which have centred around contemporary Indian art in the past decade have been considered. Indeed there have been as many questions and counter-questions which have arisen around art in India as there have been diverse forms. Many of these have debated the contentious issues of modernism which to this day remain open-ended. Leaving aside the rather rhetorical question of whether there exists an Indian modernism, we have dwelt on three equally important issues. The form of modernism which is basically *Eurocentric* is seen as the norm, but as Thomas McEvilley argues it is essentially a Western concept. The second and related idea is that there are many modernisms and John Clark delves into the peculiarities of *Asian* modernism. R. Siva Kumar in his essay finds that *contextual* modernism given birth in Santiniketan is probably the most consequential and has strong roots in India, and Ella Dutta provides new perspectives on the

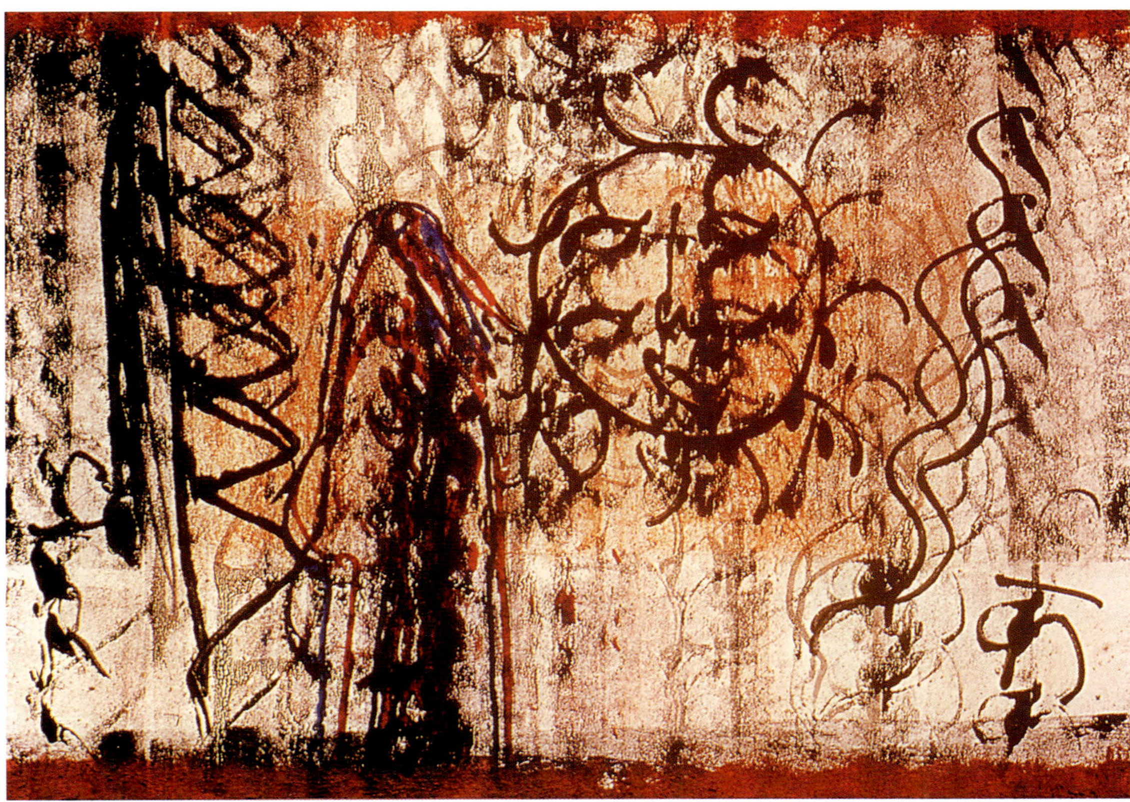

5
J. Swaminathan
"Untitled", 1991–92
Oil on canvas; 81 x 117 cm

contribution of Abanindranath Tagore in the socio-political context of the time. The conceptual basis for the present collection of essays is to foreground issues which have occurred around Indian art in its different phases rather than a mere chronicling of modes. Thus these are in the nature of debates rather than an elucidation of styles of art which are by now well known. While questions have often been asked about Indian art some of these are now consolidated to provide a perspective on prevailing modes. Thus the preoccupation with modernism in the 1950s gives way in the '80s to locating forms and generating a greater expressiveness about one's own reality. It is about this time that subalternism takes centrestage where the plight of the common man, the feminist, and the marginalized aim at altering consciousness. It is interesting to note in this context how notions of time are treated in Indian art. As Susan S. Bean points out, even when contemporary artists deal with the present moment there is a transcendentality which provides it a distinctive character. She states here, "While the time-situatedness of contemporary art applies to work created anywhere in the world, the temporal aspect of contemporary art in India is unusually rich because of the complexity and sophistication of co-present philosophical, theological, and scientific concepts." While dealing with a whole crop of women artists who have made their presence felt in India, Gayatri Sinha speaks of a "feminine space", rather than feminist art, whereby the feminine consciousness is applied to a whole plethora of political and social issues.

Notions of pluralism and multiculturalism infect the artists of the '90s, as there is a confident borrowing from all cultures and frequent crossovers. Free of any colonial hangover, the young have none of the self-doubt of the earlier generation as they resort to pluralistic modes – installations, earth-works, conceptual, performance, and video art. Ravinder Reddy, Dhruva Mistry, Sudarshan Shetty, Anita Dube, and Valsan Kolleri are some of the sculptors who resort to multiculturalism outside the precincts of the gallery, while Surendran Nair, Rekha Rodwittiya, Vasudha Thozur, Natraj Sharma, Atul and Anju Dodiya contend with hybridity, fragmentation, and pluralism within the frame of the canvas (figure 8). A whole host of younger artists like Shibu Natesan, N.S. Harsha, and Jitesh Kallat evolve an even more avant-garde vocabulary for the articulation of the new sensibility. Even as cyberspace opens out its super highway for interactive and modular art, the anxiety of passage can be sensed in many. Yet the leaps in consciousness also yield unexpected, perhaps forbidden zones which provide a new sense of freedom.

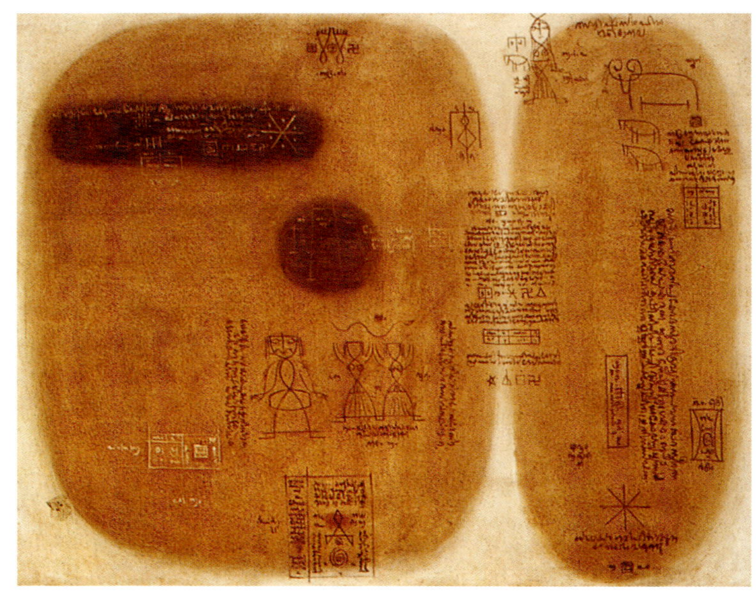

6
K.C.S. Paniker
"Words and Symbols"
Oil on board; 121.3 x 151 cm
Collection: National Gallery of Modern Art, New Delhi

7
Bhupen Khakhar
"Picture of their Thirtieth Wedding Anniversary"
Watercolour; 110 x 110 cm

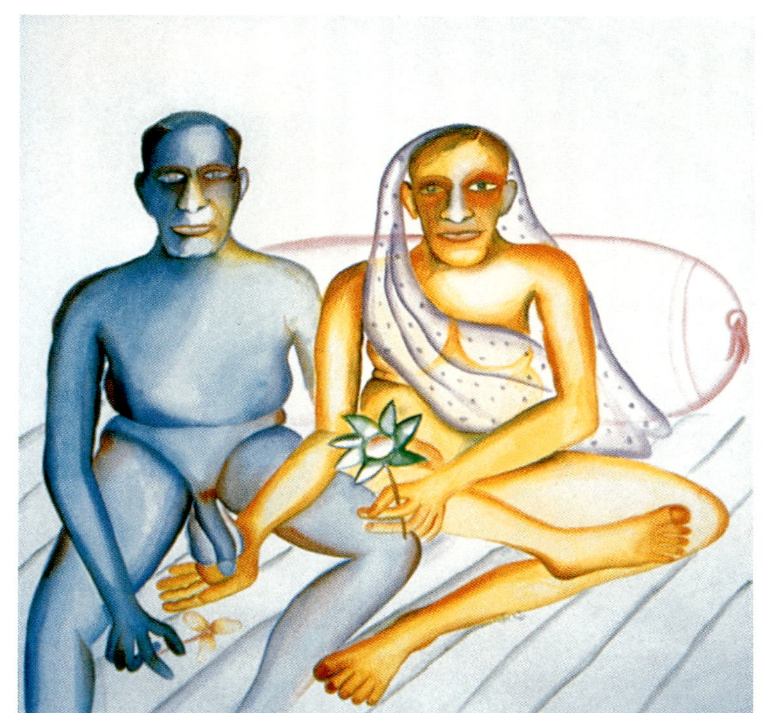

The new debates centre around pluralism and its consequence at the "receiving end" where the flux of forms often becomes inchoate. Is a possible subterfuge taking place where multiplicity is really a disguised ethnicity fitting the requirements of post-modernism as conceived in the West? Is there an authenticity of forms or a mere imitation of what is prescribed elsewhere? The changing parameters of post-modernism and their articulation in the works of some artists are reflected upon in my essay. Finally, diasporic art, an increasingly important component of art practices is considered by John Bowles.

8
Atul Dodiya
"Scapegoat", 1998
Oil, acrylic, and marble dust on canvas; 213 x 152 cm
Collection: Czaee Shah, Mumbai

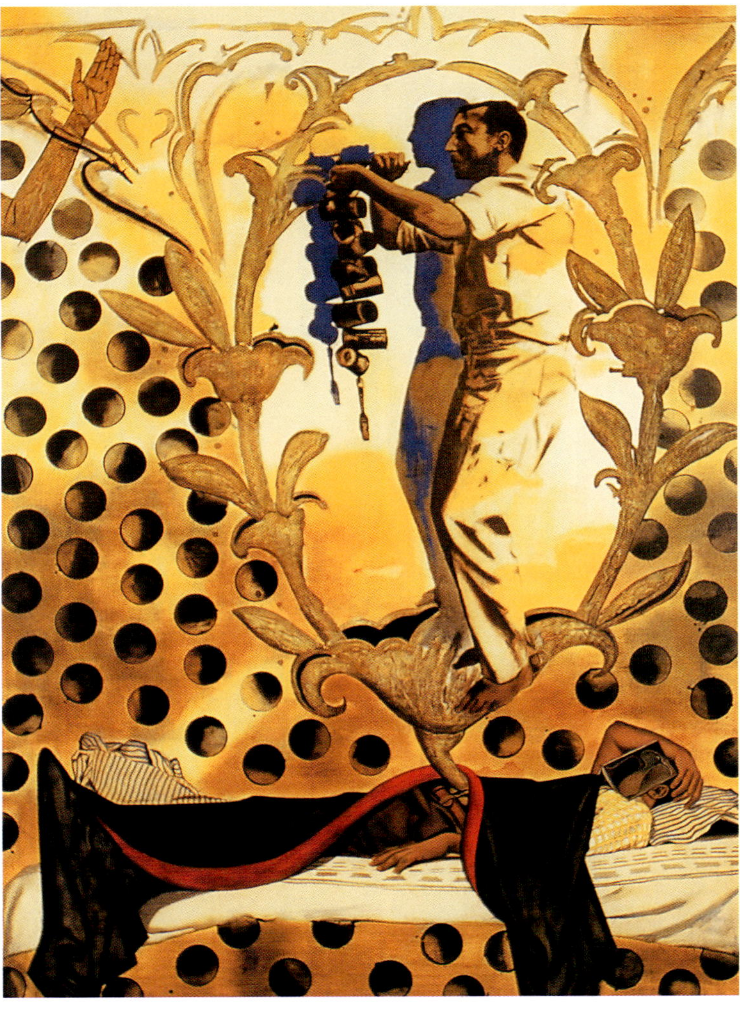

The last section of this book has extracts from significant writings which relate to the contentious issues of Indian art from its formative to its present stage. These will, hopefully, act as markers which register a different note from the one which has been conventionally stated. It is worth noting for instance that the earliest notion of the "modern" as delineated by Tapati Guha-Thakurta positions itself squarely in an imaginary Hindu past. The subalternism of the middle period is not without its problematic aspects as pointed out by John Clark. The transculturalism of the '90s can also be a carnivalesque affair and Ajay Sinha elucidates this. The processing of debates in this final section aims at sharpening an awareness of art and its related situations. This can then lead to further reflections on art practices in India.

NOTES

1. *The Sir J.J. School of Art Report*, Bombay, 1857–58.

2. Gulammohammed Sheikh, "New Contemporaries", *Marg* 31/2, March 1978, pp. 87–112.

3. The Festivals promoted Indian art and culture and were sponsored by a special commission headed by Pupul Jayakar. They were held simultaneously in London and Oxford in 1982, Paris in 1985, and in Washington DC the year after. They served to place Indian contemporary art among other forms on a wide platform.

1
Abanindranath Tagore
"Daughter of the Soil"
Wash and tempera on paper;
13.5 x 18.3 cm
Collection: National Gallery of
Modern Art, New Delhi

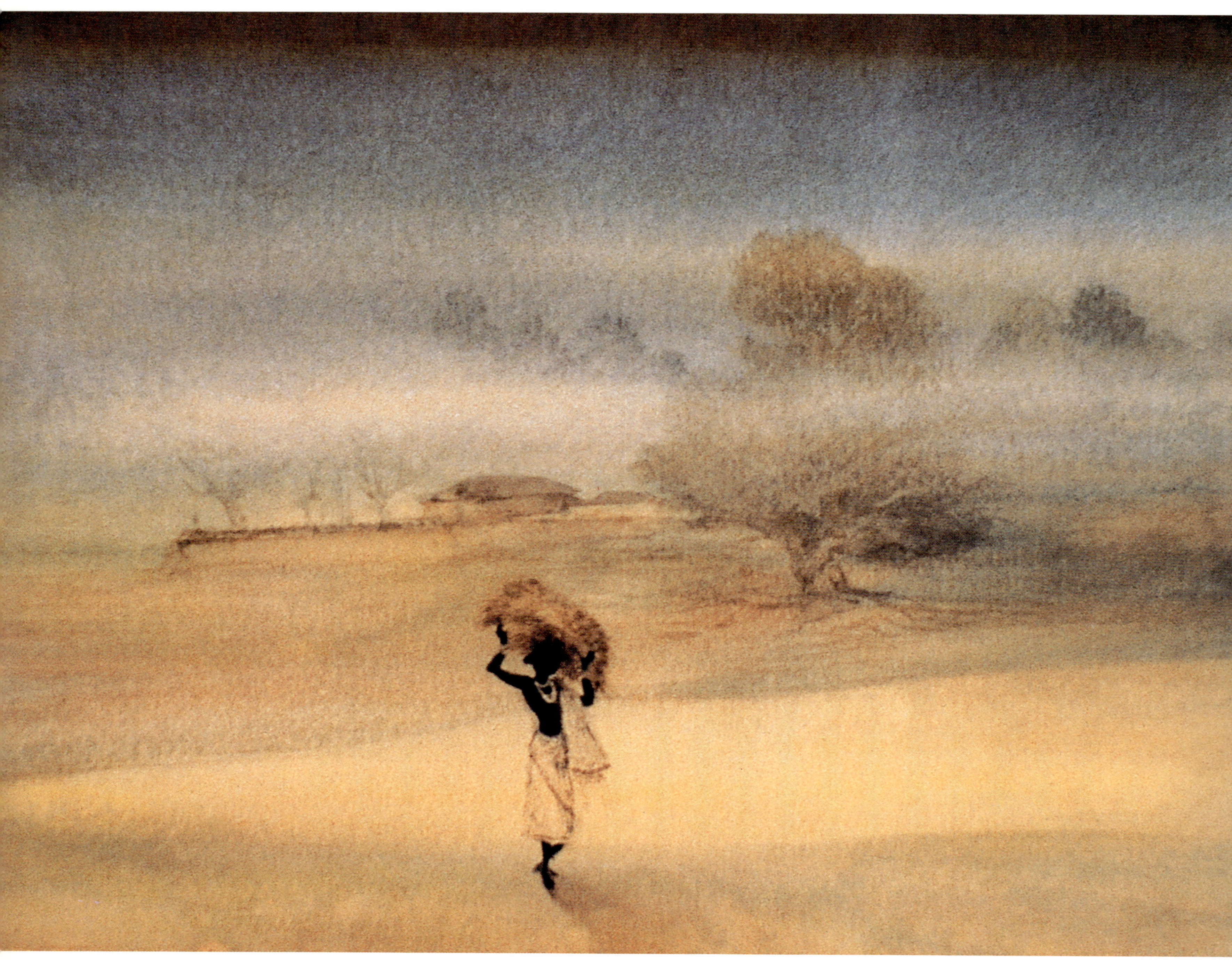

R. Siva Kumar

culture specificity, art language, and the practice of modernism

an indian perspective

The beginning of modernism in the West as well as in the East involved a review of traditional cultural antecedents in the light of cross-cultural encounters that opened up new experiential avenues and called for a restructuring of perception and language. This naturally led to the growth of forces that gravitated towards common values and others that pulled towards culture specificity. And the two were not mutually exclusive as the readings of modern art practices often suggest. Such pioneers of India's modern art movement as Abanindranath Tagore and Nandalal Bose for instance, even as they at times subscribed to nationalist rhetoric, were – like the nationalist leaders from Rammohan Roy to Jawaharlal Nehru – deeply committed to modernism. They understood modernism not as a stylistic shift but as a call for rethinking the larger issues of cultural practice, and saw cultural identity not as something that was complete and done with but as something that ought to be reconstructed and realized anew with each change in context. Similarly there are also post-nationalist modernists like K.G. Subramanyan who are involved with culture-sensitive modernist practice. Together they present a set of original and connected perspectives on the character and conduct of art practice, art language, and culture specificity in modernism. And the unfolding of these perspectives traced here through a brief discussion of the work and ideas of Abanindranath, Nandalal, and Subramanyan forms an important strand within the larger Indian discourse on modernism.

Abanindranath Tagore (1871–1951)

Abanindranath was the first Indian artist to openly commit himself to a culture-specific modernism. He saw himself at odds with Ravi Varma who had already attempted a combination of Indian themes with Western representational conventions and thus from the outset visualized culture-specific modernism as embracing the formal aspects as well. Committed as Abanindranath was to a new art with linkages to Indian antecedents, he made an effort to know what these were. But significantly he refrained from associating himself with the attenuated traditional practice of court painting, and decorative and functional arts that continued in isolated pockets. He preferred instead to see traditional practice as an area that has become history as a result of the cultural hiatus inflicted by colonial intervention. The discontinuity in tradition helped him to selectively appropriate the past, foregrounding what agreed with his sensibility. It also prompted him to be selectively eclectic, connecting up art practices temporally and culturally separated but addressing comparable problems and sharing similar values.

Although Abanindranath committed himself to modernism specific in form and content and took some interest in the work methods of traditional miniature painters, he did not quite reject the Western representational method in which he was initially trained. In fact in his picture of Indian traditional art, Mughal painting – which came closest to Western representational realism – took pride of place. He admired in Mughal miniatures the unique blending of object realism and compositional freedom. Later the same aspects attracted him to certain phases of Japanese and Persian art, and in both instances he avoided the more decorative aspects of those traditions. In turning away from the late academic version of Western representational realism to a removed realism that allowed detailing and wilful ambivalence he was – though working under the aegis of pan-Asianism – not unlike the early Western modernists who turned to East Asian painting for similar reasons. From these diverse sources he learned to combine representation of perceptual facts with personal response, or in other words to interweave reality and imagination.

He understood imagination as that which animates reality and gives character and identity to culture. He laid greater stress on continuity in imagination than on continuity in techniques and skills. He told his students that without the memory of Valmiki's description of the sea, the sea would be an expanse of brine, and without Kalidasa's *Meghadutam* the clouds would be mere dust clouds.[1]

But Abanindranath's own personal technique had nothing to do with those of traditional Indian painting. Indeed, the wash technique, though inspired by certain Japanese paintings he saw, was essentially a personal invention, a work process developed to suit his own sensibility and his predilection for a wholeness composed of intimate fragments.

Initially his pictures, with their small format and intimate scale adopted from traditional miniatures, were conceived as selectively focused images with considerable scenic unity. They present a figure, or episodic moment as a soft-focused cameo of experience. In them, style foregrounds the artist's sensibility in a symbolic fashion, but in his later paintings – as the subject matter shifted from personal response to representation of varied characters – styles too began to proliferate, transforming him into an artist endowed with a repertoire of forms. And in the finest of his mature work, the "Arabian Nights" series, as he moved from character-imaging to the narrativization of contemporary society, his paintings became complex collages of images and styles. And style became in them a narrative device.

Styles as an index of individual sensibility are an agent of particularization and demarcate individual from individual, class from class, or individual from class. Narrativization on the other hand begins with a recognition of differences and progresses towards the establishment of a social collective of voices by tracing the patterns of interaction between individuals and groups divided by sensibility, history, and power. Trying to narrativize a multipolar contemporary society through a collage of styles made Abanindranath look beyond the relation of style and sensibility and notice the correspondence between language and social levels. In the "Arabian Nights" series, besides the coexistence of different styles, sometimes within the same picture – invoking different associations, and marking different characters and social spaces – in a number of pictures the story itself gets narrated twice: once visually by the image, and a second time by the text inscribed on the painting. This simulates the use of texts in traditional miniatures but unlike in the miniatures they are not part of a literary device that anchors the image within the framework of a larger discourse or directs its reading (see Ella Dutta's article, figure 2). The text/image juxtaposition operates, even more than the stylistic collage, on the plane of social difference. The image exhibits a painterly dexterity of very

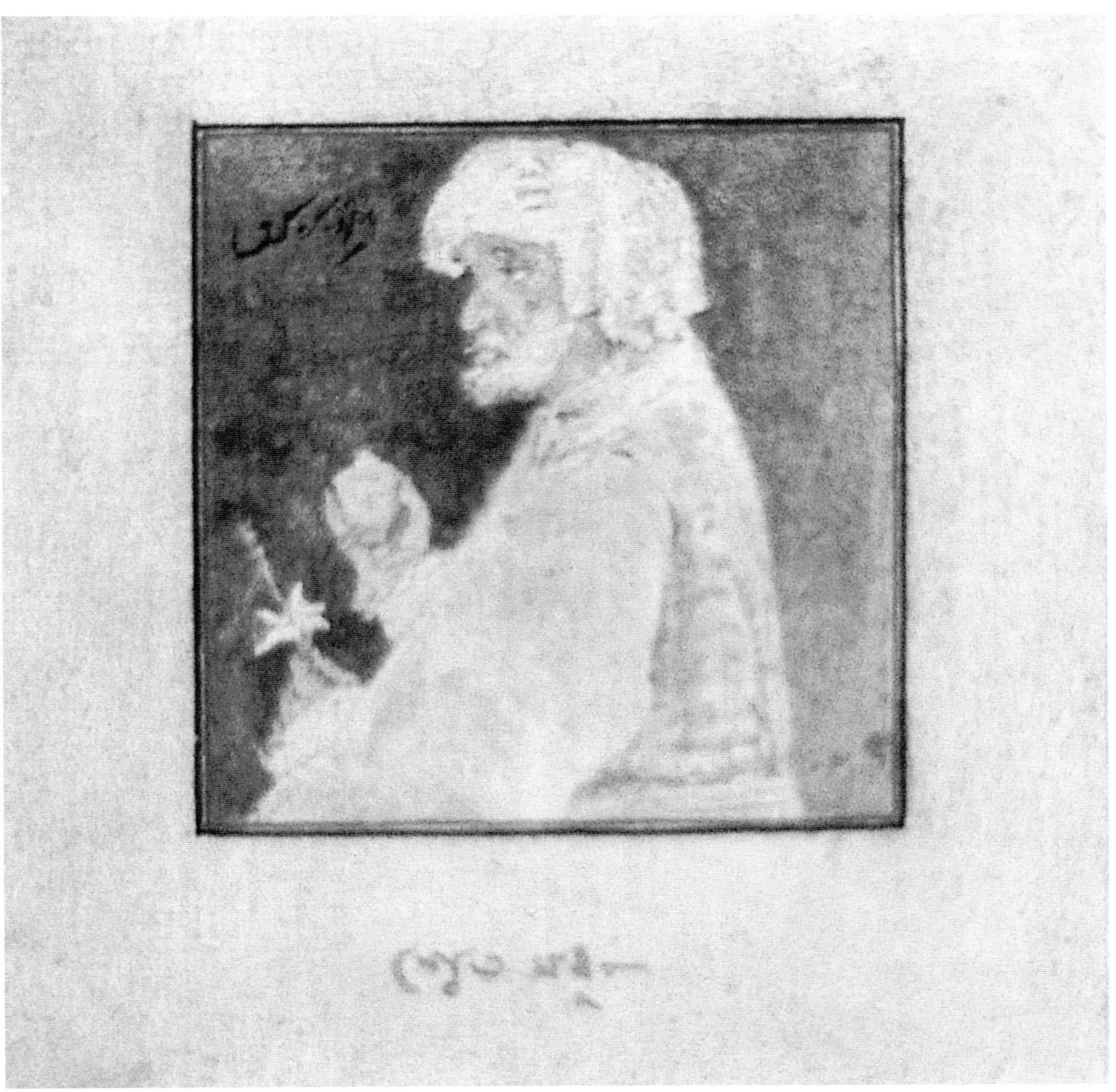

2
Abanindranath Tagore
"White Honey"
Wash and tempera on paper; 6.3 x 6.3 cm
Collection: National Gallery of Modern Art, New Delhi

high order and presents Abanindranath as a representative of "high" culture; the inscribed text, written with calculated irony in a fine calligraphic manner, by contrast re-narrates the pictured episode at a more subaltern level. The language of the inscribed text is always impure, and a product of much cultural and linguistic hybridity (partly because these were written and copied by calligraphers who were not scholars, and partly because there is nothing like "pure" language). The image – a token of "high" culture but on fine view a collage of styles – and the inscribed text – a halting hybrid articulation and a token of "low" culture – taken together present an early example of variable and multilayered narration in modern Indian art.

Abanindranath was an aristocrat and a dandy who cultivated refinements, but he was also an admirer of the folk and the popular. In his juxtaposition of different narrative voices there is not only a recognition of the multiple levels of culture and language but also an effort to draw them, and his divergent preference, together. It expresses his desire to go beyond the individual ego and achieve a new individuation by reconciling multivoiced narration with self-expression. In short he wanted multiplicity assimilated into a single idiom. As a writer it led him in his later years to structure his literary works like oral narrations rather than as written descriptions. The *jatra*s (plays) he wrote freely mixing different languages and dialects, folk and elitist diction, but all done with a calculated complexity and refinement bearing the unmistakable stamp of his cultural sophistication, exemplify what he aspired for. His last paintings modelled after folk antecedents were perhaps an effort in the same direction, but unfortunately they remained an achievement that failed to arrive.

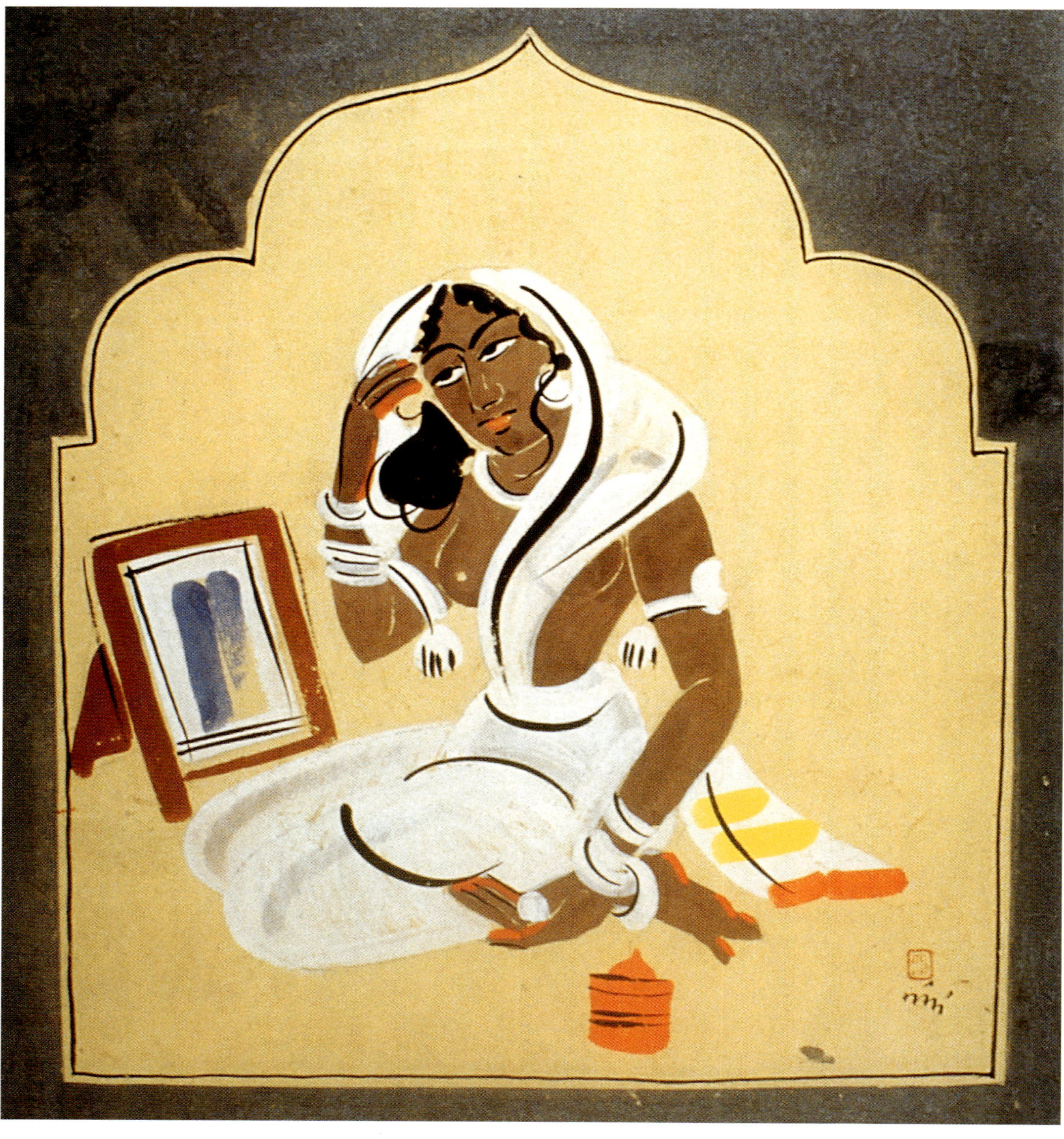

3
Nandalal Bose
"Toilet"
Tempera on paper;
64.3 x 59.5 cm
Collection: National Gallery of Modern Art, New Delhi

Nandalal Bose (1882–1966)

Nandalal, Abanindranath's foremost pupil, subscribed to the nationalist aspirations of his time more than his mentor. He too thought it was necessary to be aware of India's artistic antecedents to counter the colonial intervention and to re-establish a culture-responsive art practice. However, Nandalal's image of Indian tradition was different from Abanindranath's. Beginning his art education in the heyday of the Swadeshi movement, he subscribed more readily to the polemical opinion of the nationalist critics that realism was an exclusively Western value and in contradistinction Indian art was idealistic. In practice however this meant that he was drawn to Ajanta and Rajput painting and to Indian sculpture at large – precisely those areas that did not appeal to Abanindranath. His choices did not mark a stylistic preference except in the negative sense of each being anti-realistic. But they did lead him to read Indian art tradition as a spectrum of art forms running from the decorative to the representational, the abstract to the figurative, and from the symbolic to the narrative. His attempt to grasp Indian tradition in structural rather than stylistic terms was presumably influenced by his early contacts with Ananda Coomaraswamy. Coomaraswamy held that the separation of artists from craftsmen was alien to Eastern traditions and the final products were often the result of a division of labour amongst a group of artists and craftsmen bound by a common aesthetic. For Nandalal, Ajanta was a splendid example of this, and he conceptualized tradition as a total system comprising a hierarchy of functions and their corresponding levels of skills.

This view of tradition left its mark on his work both as an artist and as an art educator. The cultural hiatus that came with colonialism, Nandalal too realized, led tradition, as a total system, to an end even if some of its small segments did manage to survive. But Coomaraswamy's view that the best of traditional artists were "designers and themselves skilled in many crafts", and could be "at once...architect, jeweller, painter, and ivory carver",[2] suggested to him a model that the modern artist could profitably emulate, and he made a conscious pursuit of versatility central to his art practice and teaching. Thus even while the social conditions necessary to sustain a cohesive tradition are absent, individual artists, he believed, could work with a larger perspective. This led him to put communication and language above personal expression and style. And he made a concerted effort to explore the relation between visual communication and visual conventions in different traditions.

Though as an artist committed to nationalist anti-colonialism Nandalal did not pay enough attention to post-Renaissance and modern Western art, the traditional art forms he had studied – Indian, East Asian and West Asian, and pre-Renaissance Western – were numerous and varied enough for him to gain certain fundamental and incisive insights. He learned for instance that the different conventions operative in a given tradition are not always governed by the same linguistic rationale

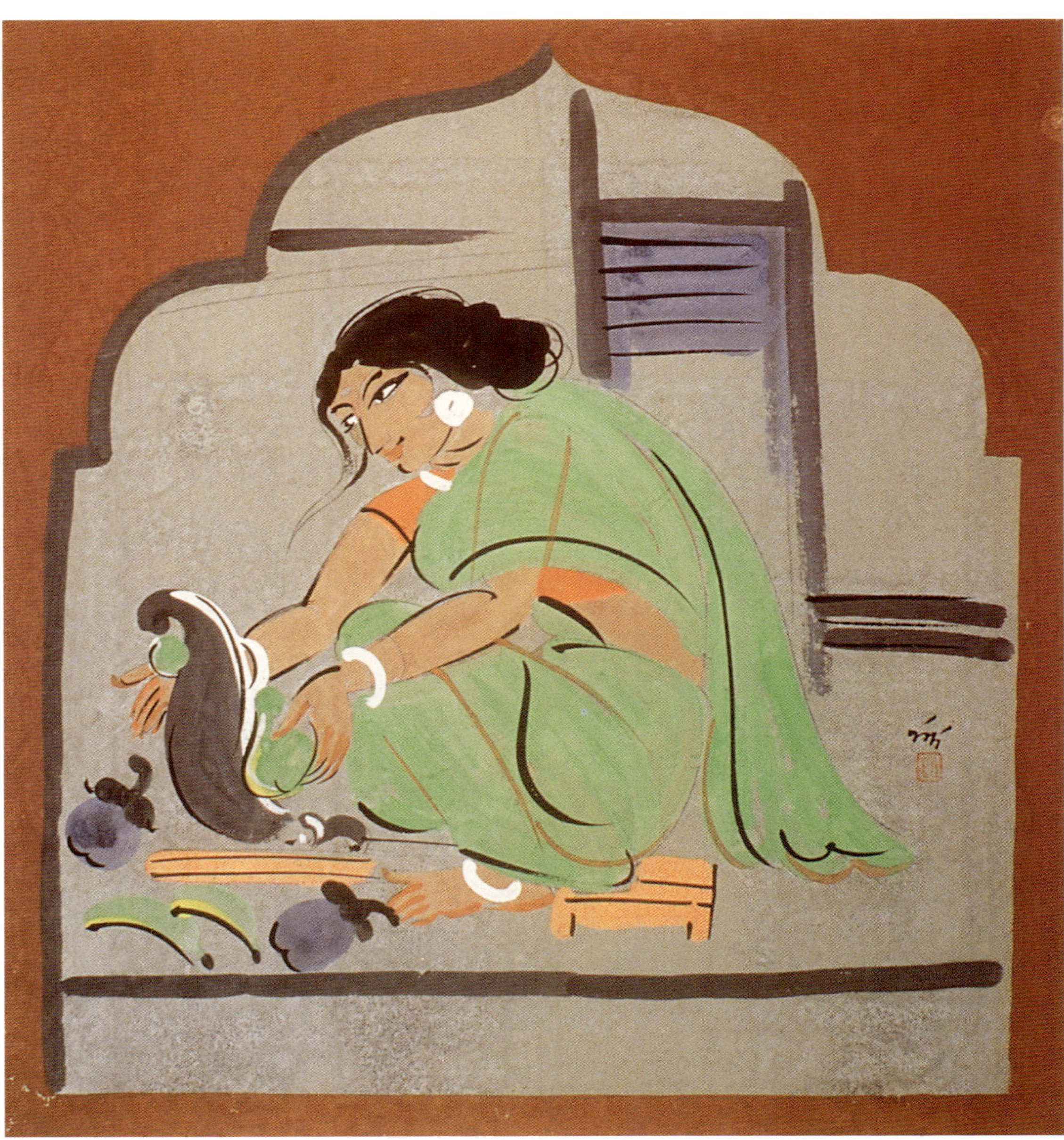

4
Nandalal Bose
"Cutting Vegetables"
Tempera on paper;
64.3 x 59.7 cm
Collection: National Gallery of Modern Art, New Delhi

and each convention connects up with a different phenomenal and perceptual experience. Conversely, he also realized that where communicational functions are similar or the underlying perceptions and experiences come close, the conventions could also come close and open up points of crossover between traditions. At another level it sensitized him to the relation between work-process and image. Unlike Abanindranath, Nandalal paid considerable attention to medium and techniques. His presentation of different traditional techniques in *Shilpacharcha* demonstrates how the choice of materials – supports, pigments, and brushes etc. – the format, the posture the artist assumes while painting, the work methods, and the artist's skills all contribute to the final image.[3]

The analytical study of traditional styles from an art language perspective and the blueprint for a versatile modernist practice were two of Nandalal's major contributions to Indian art; the third was paving the way for a modernism responsive to local reality. Though as a nationalist artist he began with a bias in favour of Indian tradition, as he matured both as theorist and artist he came to believe that in the final analysis it was not tradition but responsiveness to the social and natural environment that gave an artist's work its authenticity. Nandalal's involvement with the practice and support of crafts, theatre designing, book illustration, typography, interior designing, public art, and the aesthetics of social events and festivals underscore his social sensitivity as an artist. On the other hand his paintings from the 1930s, and more than that his large body of drawings, reveal his visual sensitivity to the varied environmental facts around him. As would be becoming of such an artist, "tradition", he came to believe, "is to the artist what capital is to the businessman. With its help, he can work with less effort and more profit." But tradition was not indispensable; if all cultural antecedents were to be

5
Ramkinkar Baij
"Gossip"
Watercolour; 19 x 27 cm
Collection: National Gallery of Modern Art, New Delhi

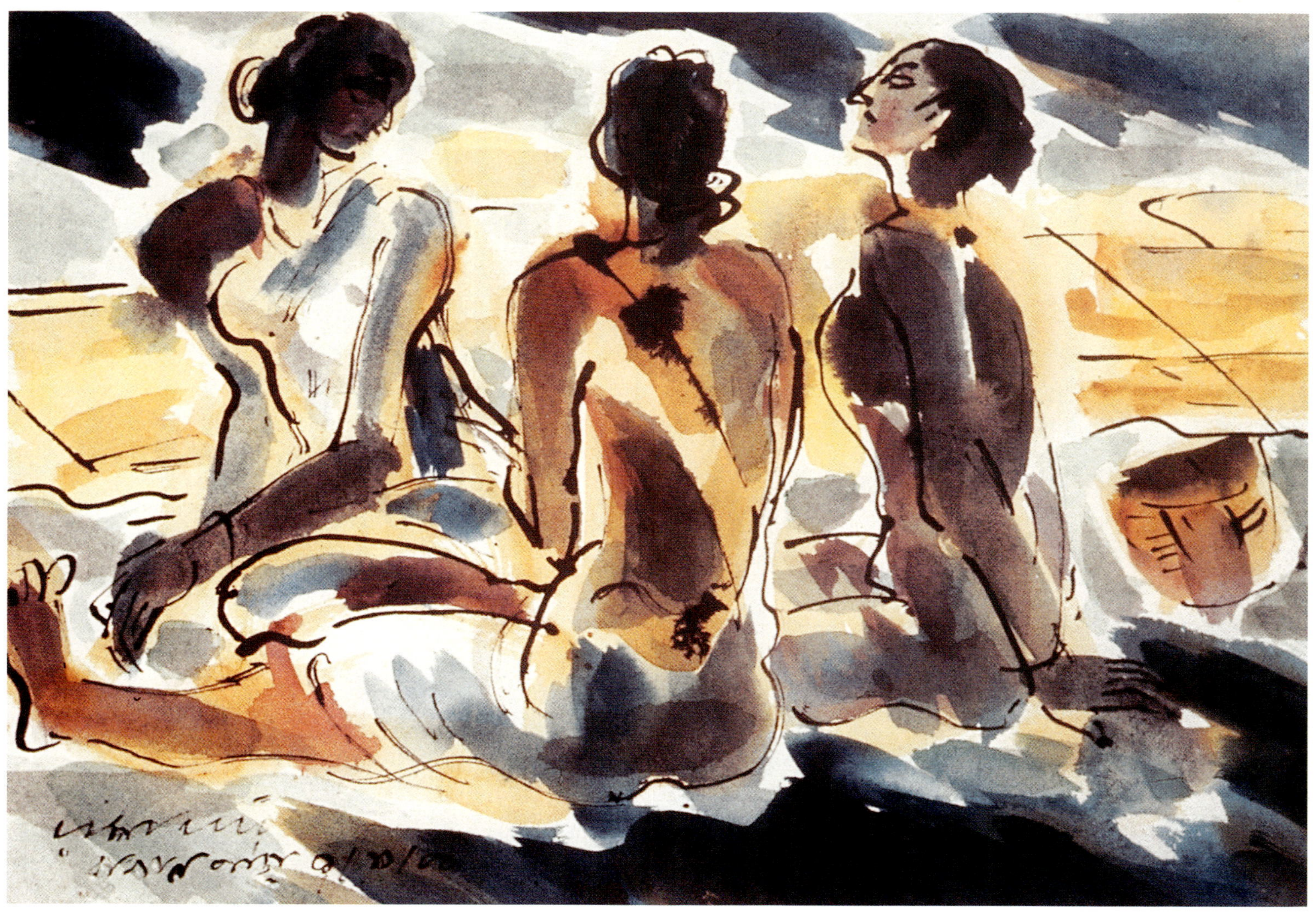

lost in some catastrophe, art would start anew like life after the deluge. As an artist who put communication and language above self-expression and style, for him originality was also not a sufficient source for authenticity. Cultural antecedents and the personality of the artist were important, but looking at his work it would not be difficult to see that for Nandalal they were incomplete without environmental inputs. It is only when tradition and individuality find an echo in lived reality that they become valid. He expressed this through the dictum: "For total development Art needs Nature, Tradition and Originality, all three."[4]

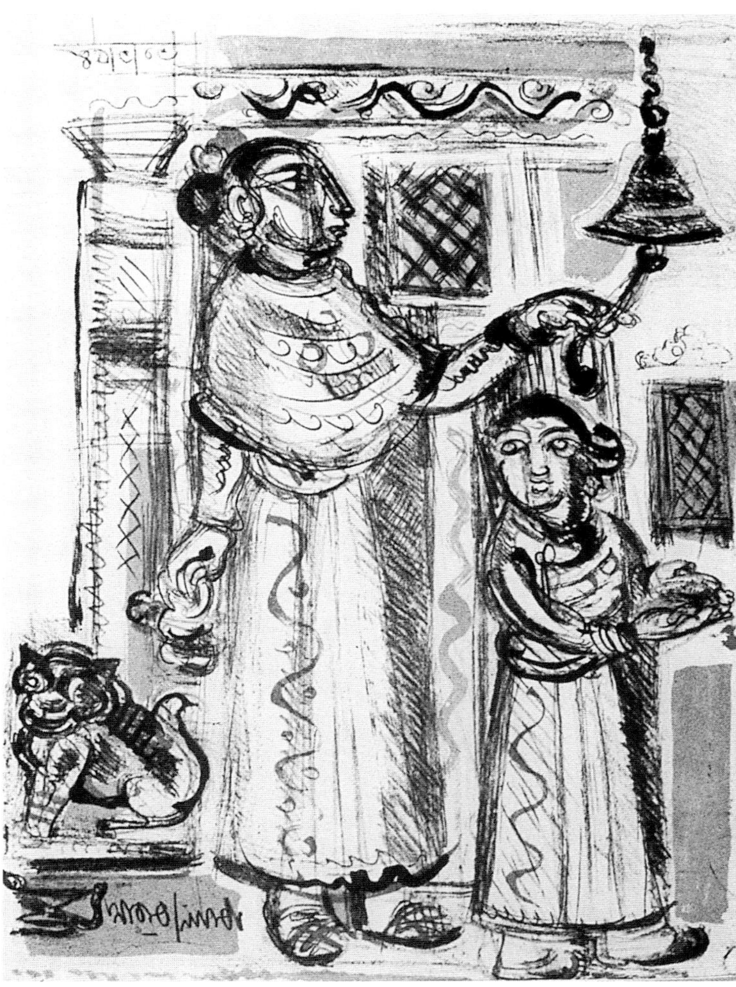

6
Benodebehari Mukherjee
"Temple – Nepal"
Lithograph; 38.4 x 28.2 cm
Collection: National Gallery of Modern Art, New Delhi

K.G. Subramanyan (b. 1924)

Most Indian artists who began their career in the post-independence years distanced themselves from culture-specific modernism and began to gravitate towards internationalist modernism, at least until the issue of cultural identity was revived in the early 1960s. Among the artists of this generation, K.G. Subramanyan belongs to the few who were more consistently exercised about the issue of culture sensitivity in modernist practice. He took to art only after an early stint as a nationalist activist, and he was familiar with the writings of Coomaraswamy even before he went to Santiniketan where he came in close touch with the ideas and work of Nandalal and Abanindranath. At Santiniketan he also came into intimate contact with Benodebehari Mukherjee and Ramkinkar Baij who were involved in extending Nandalal's analysis of traditions and the practice of a modernism emphatically responsive to local reality. They demonstrated to him that commitment to modernism and responsiveness to local experiences need not be antipathic. Their work also helped him to see that Nandalal's views on art language were not fundamentally different from those of the early Western modernists, and that both were exploring the contact points between visual conventions and visual experiences from a post-realist position. If there was a basic difference it was in their attitude to self-expression and individual style.

Subramanyan describes modern art as a post-industrial-revolution and post-traditional art. This makes it imperative for the modern artist to start from his sensibility and work towards a contact with the world and its cultural antecedents. In trying to do this Subramanyan realized, like Nandalal, that "No individual sensibility is exclusively individual; a civilized man's vision always carries a substructure of choices and ideas he shares with others."[5] Working in the post-independence situation he was more open to

Western traditions, and his own readings of Western modern art showed him how many of its innovations were shaped by cross-cultural encounters. Like Nandalal, he also realized that "if we line up the world traditions one after another we can see how they cover different areas of human sensibilities by accident or choice; taken together they can be considered different sectors of a total art language."[6] When an artist limits himself to exploring a single strand of human sensibility a personal style makes sense, but not when he is a man of varied sensibilities like Picasso or he is creative at varied levels like Nandalal. For them a personal vision and personal resourcefulness in the use of language becomes more meaningful.

Subramanyan began by representing local facts in a post-realist quasi-expressionist idiom in a manner reminiscent of Ramkinkar and to a lesser extent Benodebehari. He moved from this to a post-cubist idiom exploring the range of figural breakup and the reconfigurations it allowed and its syntactical overlaps with certain conventions of Indian miniatures. Around the same time he also became more exercised about regaining for modern art that additional resonance traditional artists derived from shared culture and language, experience and iconography. He moved closer to it as he became involved with weaving and textile designing, with toymaking, writing and illustrating books for children, and doing murals that worked with the architecture and yet were loaded with multiple meanings. These gave him an opportunity to break out of the narrow limits of high art and become operative at different levels of cultural production, to collaborate with skilled craftsmen and less

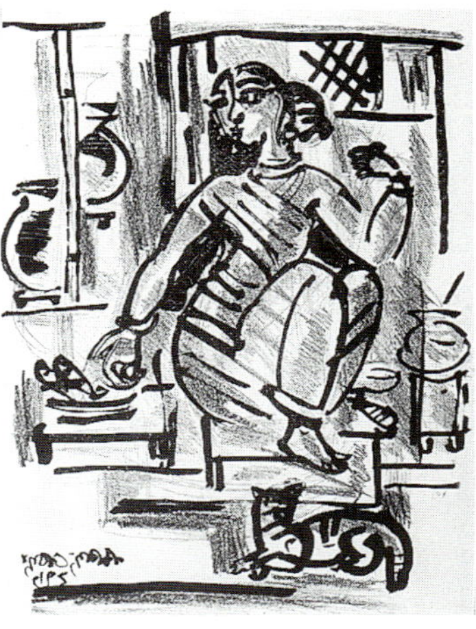

7
Benodebehari Mukherjee
"Kitchen"
Lithograph; 40.6 x 30.5 cm
Collection: National Gallery of Modern Art, New Delhi

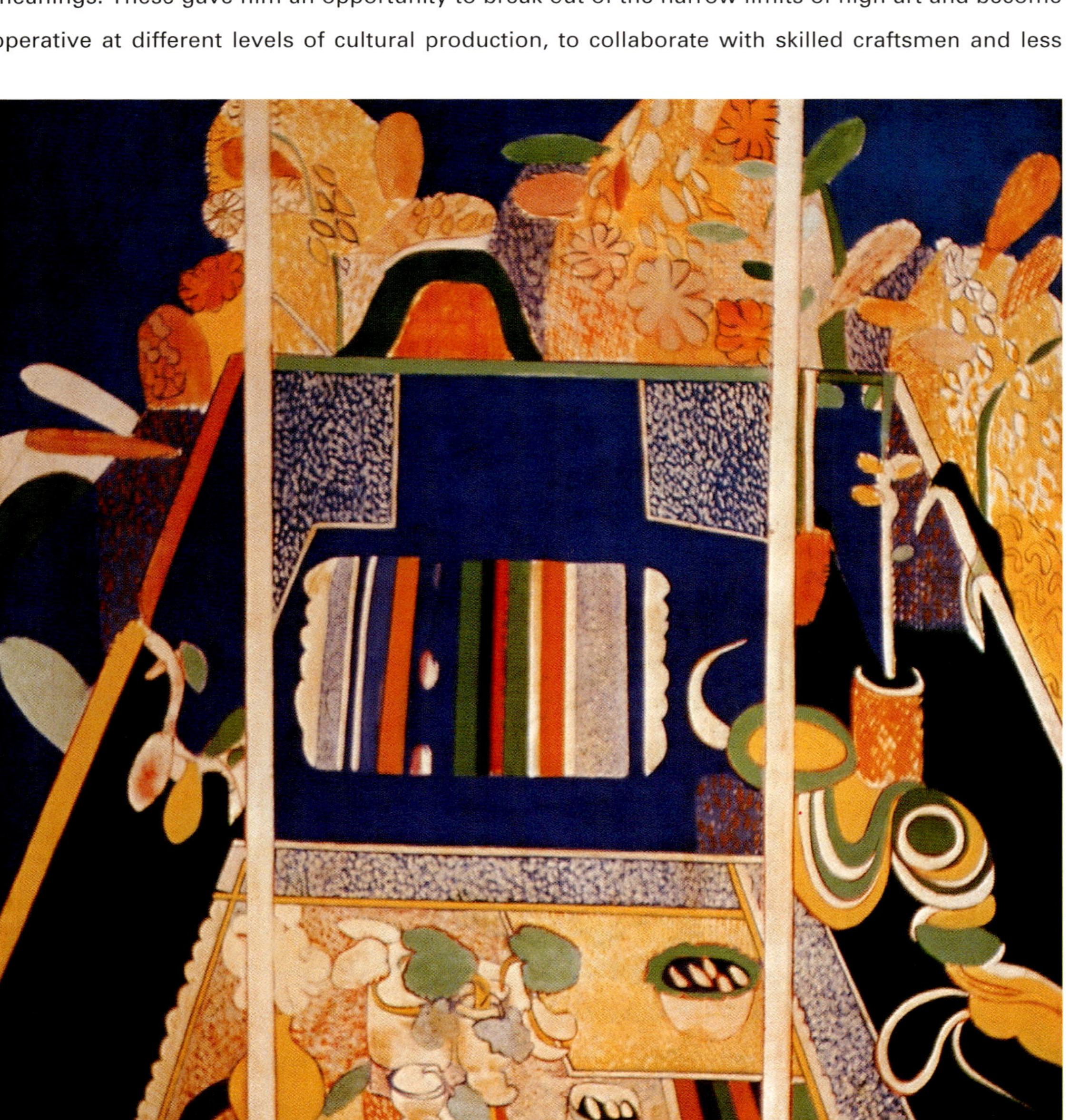

8
K.G. Subramanyan
"Terrace–2", 1974
Oil on canvas; 166 x 168 cm
Collection: National Gallery of Modern Art, New Delhi

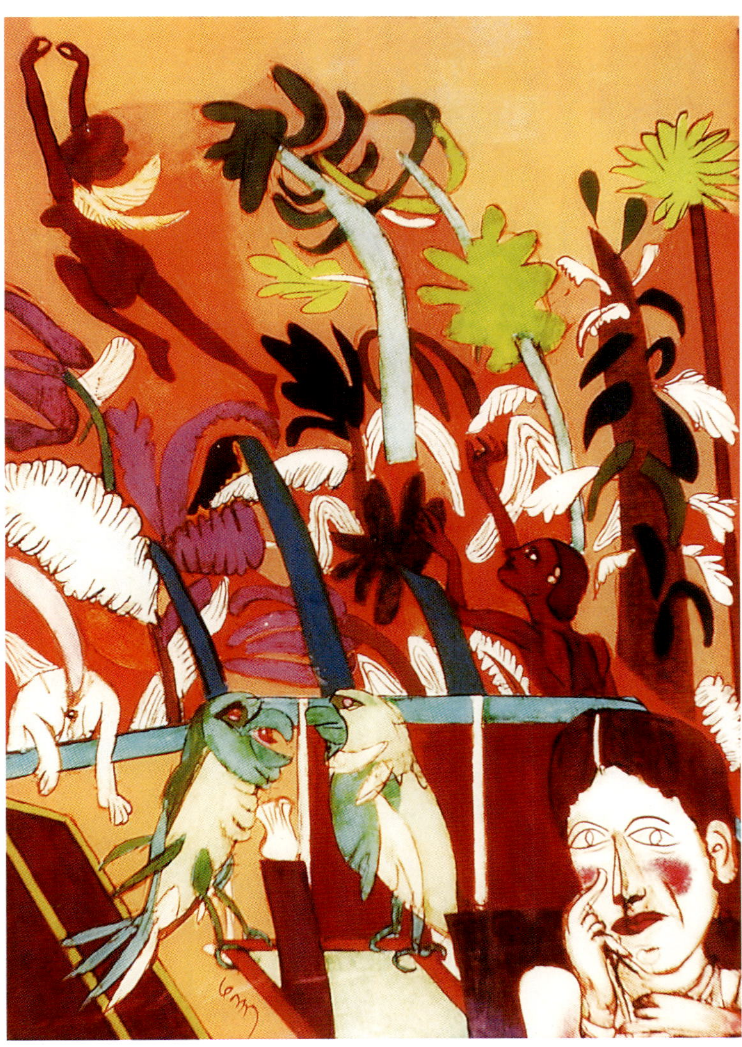

9
K.G. Subramanyan
"Woman Amidst Trees", 1980
Painting on acrylic sheet

endowed assistants, to take advantage of what is special to each medium, and to widen his understanding of the ethics of creativity and communication in the arts and crafts.

Like Nandalal he now became active at different levels and acquired new insights into eclecticism. For him eclecticism is not patchy hybridization, or the selective assimilation on the basis of stylistic similarities, sensibility overlaps, or convergence of work methods. Although all these have been profitably used in the past, the most meaningful form of eclecticism in our period of large-scale cross-cultural encounters, Subramanyan believes, is that which came from negotiating dissimilar cultural facts and images, and led to a widening of sensibility, vision, and expression. More importantly, while he wanted to gain from exposure to world culture he did not want to overlook his immediate environment, or lose his personal vision to become creative at many levels. Subramanyan believes that an artist's contact with alien cultures becomes beneficial only when he responds to it with his sensibility and cultural predilections, and his attempt to be versatile fructifies only when his personal vision breaks through the impersonal structures of language and work process. And when this happens the artist acquires a personal language rather than a personal style.

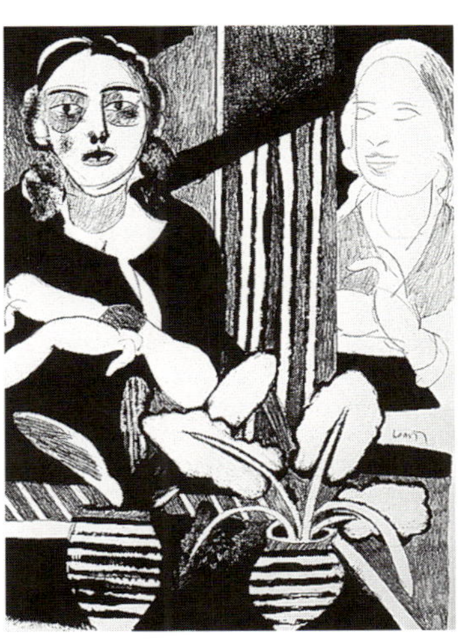

10
K.G. Subramanyan
Untitled
Lithograph; 38 x 27 cm
Collection: National Gallery of Modern Art, New Delhi

Through the concept of a personal language Subramanyan reconciles the counterpulls between communication and creation that separated Nandalal and Abanindranath, and their two kinds of versatility, one coming from the artist's ability to be multiprofessional and the other from his range of responses. The first he achieves in the 1960s and the second comes into prominence in the '70s. His subsequent works show how fully he realized that for an artist to be versatile at the highest level, on the one hand his emotional and perceptual responses to the cultural and natural environment had to

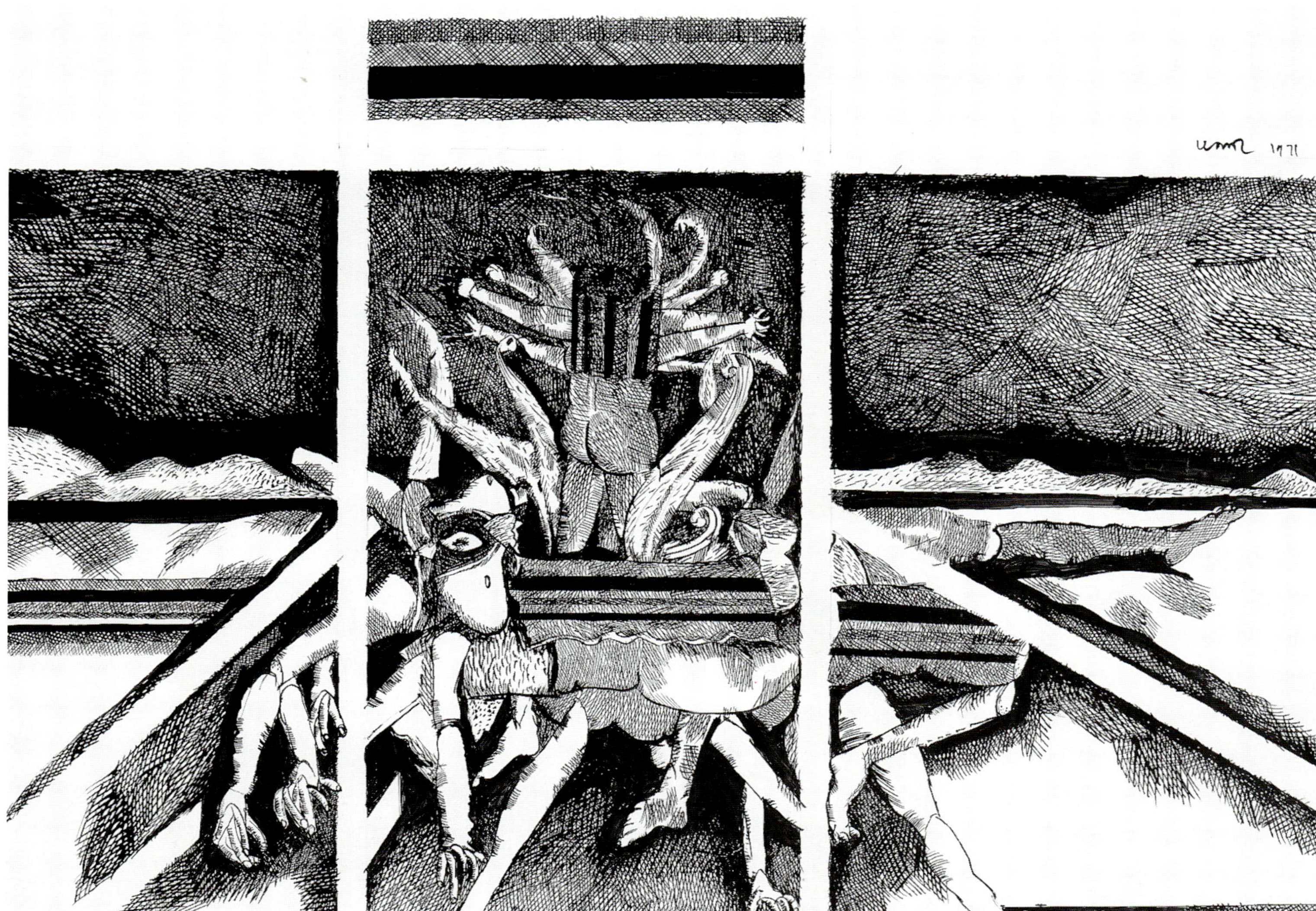

11
K.G. Subramanyan
Untitled
Lithograph; 55.9 x 71.1 cm

12
K.G. Subramanyan
"Figure 1", 1995
Oil on board; 45.7 x 35.6 cm

be meaningful and, on the other, his personal (visual) language should be as resourceful and flexible as any fully developed verbal language. And the resourcefulness and flexibility of such a language is proportionate to the formal reorchestrations that can be effected without any substantial change in syntax. While as a versatile artist in the sense of being a multiprofessional, he built upon the legacy of Nandalal, as an artist whose responsiveness and resourcefulness added up to a total spectrum he achieved what Abanindranath had set out to do in his last phase but could not achieve. In retrospect Abanindranath appears to have fallen short on two counts: firstly, he did not complete the necessary shift from personal style to personal language, and secondly, in spite of moderating the Western representational system he began with, through a series of eclectic assimilations, he remained somewhat circumscribed by realist aesthetics. Subramanyan, in contrast, began from a post-realist position, and further, taking cue from Nandalal, Picasso's post-cubist explorations and the primitive arts that inspired it, as well as from indigenous folk and popular arts, he developed a work process that begins from simple and often non-objective work units and through their variable orchestrations works towards different levels of perceptual and experiential correspondence. He also realized that the emotional resonance and semantic nuances of works do not all come from their syntactical structure; they also come from the cultural and experiential associations they invoke. The effortless oscillation between the abstract and the representational, the iconic and the narrative, the decorative and the expressive, the sensuous and the conceptual, the playful and the ironic, the real and surreal that he achieves in his recent work comes from this insight. And in them he takes the discourse on culture-specific modernism, versatility, and art language that began with Abanindranath to new heights.

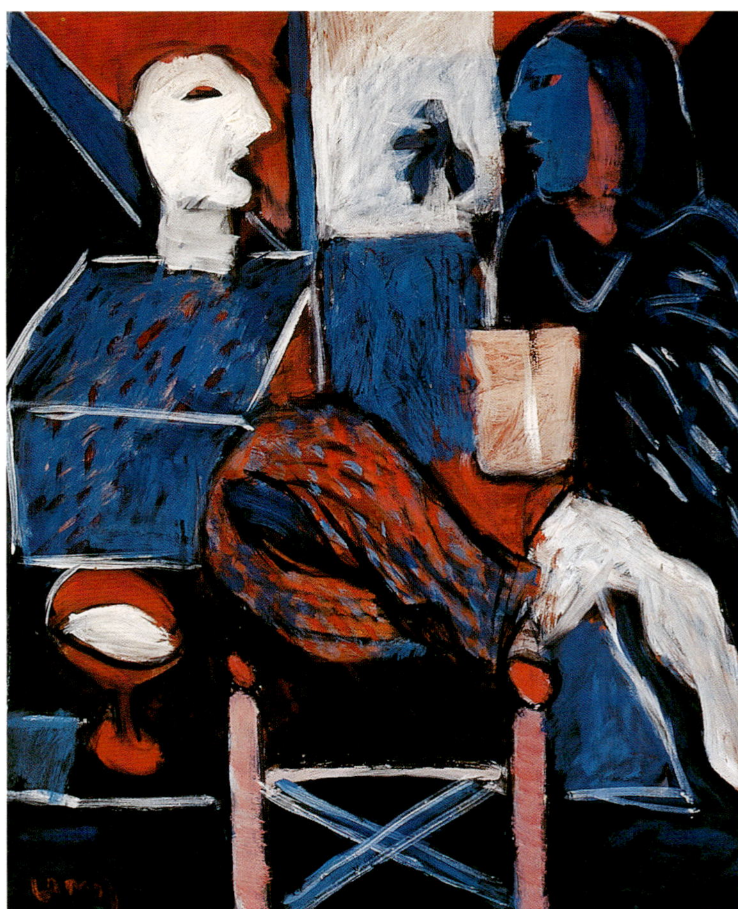

13
K.G. Subramanyan
"Man on Chair", 1995
Oil and gouache on acrylic sheet;
27.9 x 20.3 cm

NOTES

1. Abanindranath Tagore, *"Silper Devata"*, *Prabasi*, Kartik 1316 (1909), p. 483.
2. Ananda K. Coomaraswamy, *The Arts and Crafts of India and Ceylon*, London, 1913, p. 35.
3. For an English translation of *Shilpacharcha* see Nandalal Bose, *Vision and Creation*, Calcutta, 1999.
4. Ibid., p. 44.
5. K.G. Subramanyan, *The Creative Circuit*, Calcutta, 1992, p. 11.
6. Ibid.

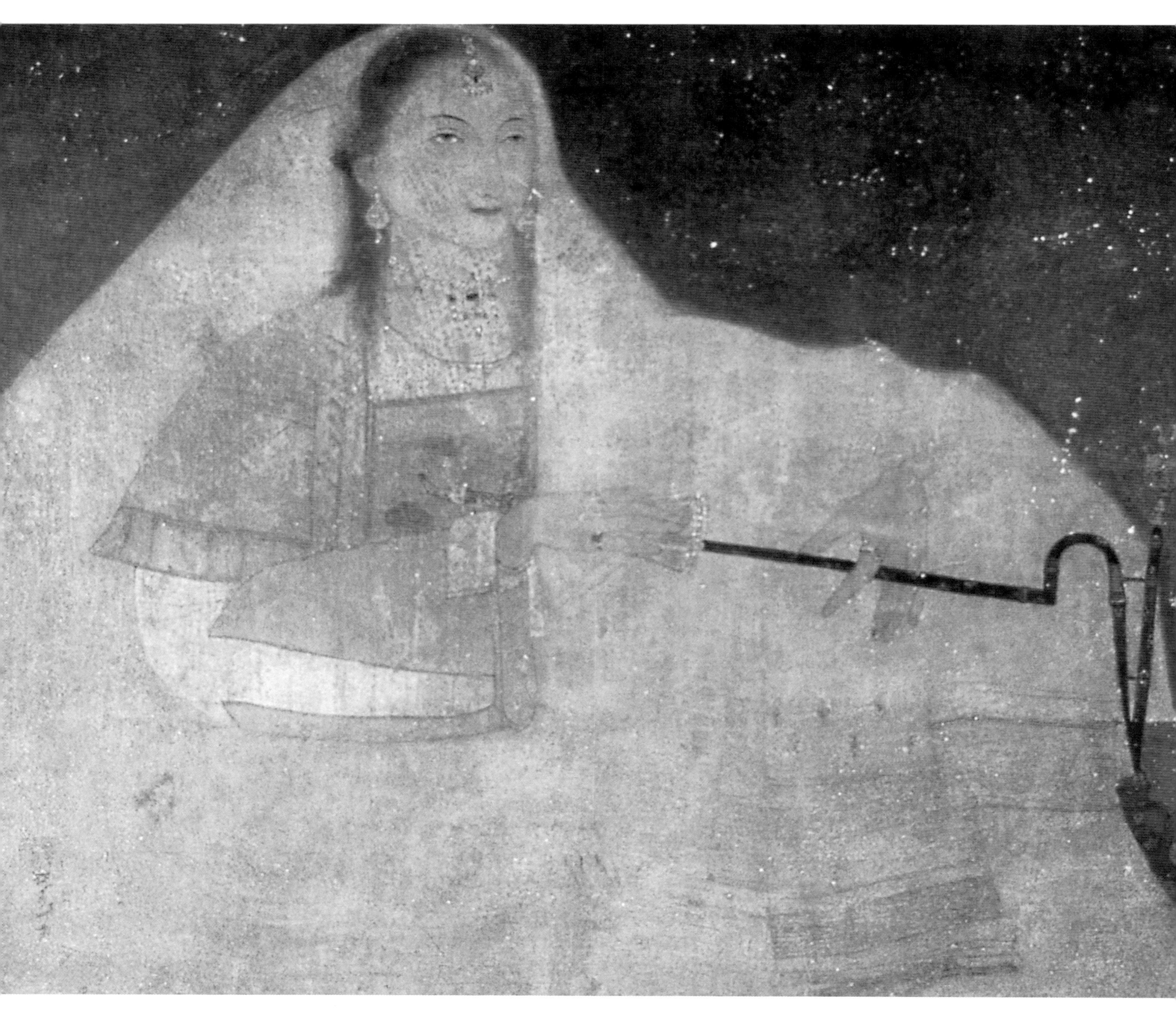

Ella Dutta

abanindranath tagore

a new context

Attempting a rethink on Abanindranath Tagore is a task riddled with ambiguity. Is he to be seen as the founder of a new school of painting, the Bengal School? Do we take into account his links with the nascent nationalist movement? Or do we only consider his achievements as an artist? These and several other questions, arising out of the particular socio-political context in which Abanindranath gave rein to his creativity, have to be answered.

The ambivalence pursued Abanindranath through his life and even after his death. In 1912, Queen Mary of England bought a painting by Abanindranath called "Tissa, Asoka's Queen". The well-known jurist and orientalist, John Woodroffe commenting on the activities of the Indian Society of Oriental Art said, "Its earliest and best product is to be found in the work of Mr A.N. Tagore.... The beauty of his work is a sign of what may be given to the world...."[1]

When an exhibition of Indian paintings was shown in Paris in 1914, a French paper singled out Abanindranath's work for its "intimate and symbolic idealism".[2] The painter was praised for the strength of his style.

Such praise and patronage were only one side of the coin. There was a flip side to the success and acclaim. Throughout his life Abanindranath faced flak for the art movement he originated, from the academic realists, from the apostles of international modernism, from a section of Bengali middle-class intelligentsia who were more drawn to naturalistic representations. The criticisms built up to a crescendo over the years.

In 1941, Amrita Sher-Gil dismissed the Bengal School as being entirely illustrative. She did not find any pictorial merit in them.[3] Mulk Raj Anand was another harsh critic. In a paper delivered at the Coomaraswamy Centenary Seminar in 1977, Anand stated scathingly about the works of Abanindranath, Nandalal Bose, Asit Haldar, and others, "Unfortunately, however, some of us who saw the actual works of these artists, found in them neither the substance of traditional sculpture, nor the poetical intuitions of Rossetti and pre-Raphaelites but mostly imitations of Mughal miniatures and some Ajanta figures, in surface prints, liquefied, so as to create an artificial ethereal atmosphere."[4]

Illustrative of more recent popular opinion, in the millennium issue of a news weekly identifying one hundred people who shaped Indian ideas in the 20th century, Abanindranath did not even find a mention. So where lies the truth between these polarities of approval and rejection?

1
Abanindranath Tagore
"Mumtaz"
Watercolour and wash on paper;
14 x 21 cm
Collection: National Gallery of Modern Art, New Delhi

His Artistic Vision

Before we analyse Abanindranath's position in 20th-century Indian art, a closer look at the so-called Bengal School will give us a clarity of perspective. The very term has a feel of the "other". Just

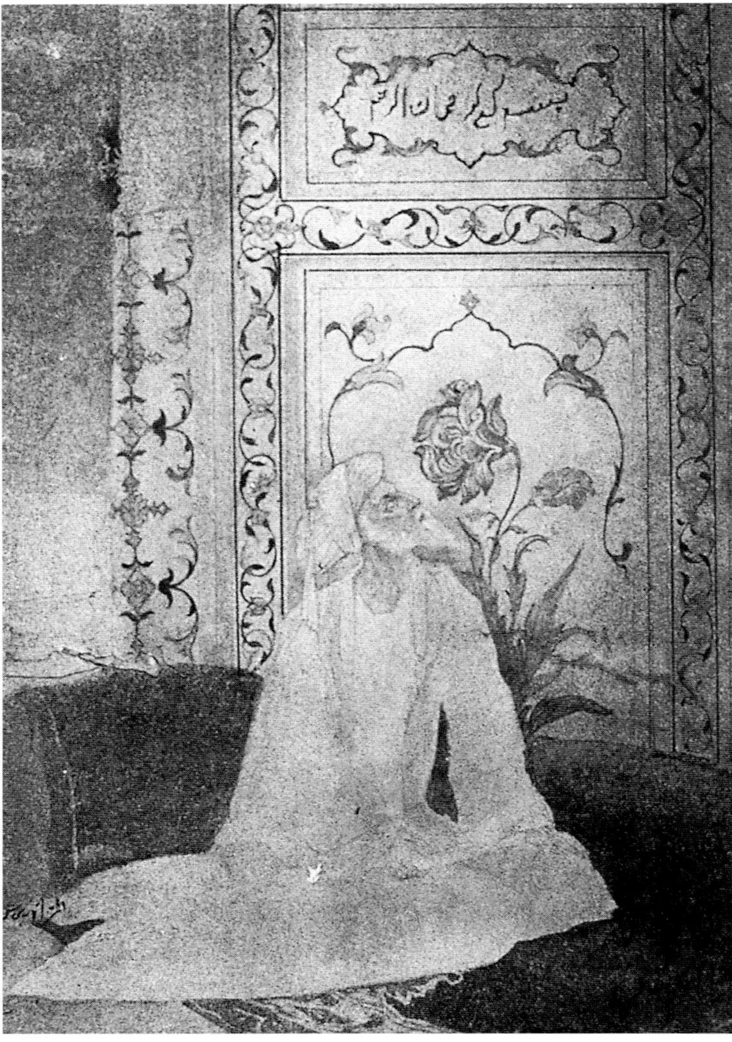

2
Abanindranath Tagore
"Badshah Shah Alam"
Wash and tempera on paper;
25.1 x 7.8 cm
Collection: National Gallery of Modern Art, New Delhi

as sweet shops all over India refer to two categories – Indian and Bengali sweets.

When Abanindranath pioneered a new style of painting, assiduously followed by a set of disciples, it was referred to variously as oriental art, a new style of Indian painting, and so on. The works of Abanindranath and his disciples were referred to also as New Calcutta School or Neo-Bengal School. The term Bengal School came into currency much later when the style of painting began to be practised throughout India and in the course of time was questioned and challenged by other artists.[5]

Abanindranath as an artist, aesthete, and writer was a man of rare sensibilities, imagination, and thinking. As an originator of a new style of painting, Abanindranath's contribution cannot be entirely judged in the context of the Bengal School. To get a measure of the artist one has to gauge his influence on a later generation of painters. There is also the fact that Abanindranath was a key figure in the debate between indigenism and internationalism that has been central to the development of modern Indian art.

Abanindranath was born in 1871 into the illustrious Tagore family of Jorasanko in north Calcutta. As a child, he did not show any interest in formal education, but he was fortunate in being part of a family which gave free rein to creativity and encouraged its expression.

The details of his life are very familiar by now. In 1891–92, Abanindranath began receiving lessons in the Western academic style of painting from O. Ghilardi, vice-principal of the Calcutta School of Art. After Ghilardi left, Abanindranath had another stint of lessons in oil painting from C. Palmer, a teacher trained at South Kensington, England. Palmer's lessons were rejected by Abanindranath when he was asked to draw from a human skull and was revolted by the idea.[6] These lessons in realistic painting left Abanindranath dissatisfied and frustrated and he began to look elsewhere to create another idiom. At about the same time, his search for a new language of expression was reinforced by some external stimuli.

One was an illuminated manuscript of Irish ballads in the art nouveau style that came into his possession. The other was a portfolio of miniatures of the Delhi *qalam* which was presented to him. The magnificent sense of design and fine craftsmanship in both the illuminated manuscript and the portfolio appealed to his sensibilities. He began to experiment and blend various elements to redefine a new way of painting for himself.

Towards the closing years of the 19th century and the beginning of the 20th, other meetings took place which spurred Abanindranath into even newer courses. In 1897–98 he met E.B. Havell who was then principal of the Calcutta School of Art, and through Havell he became acquainted with other orientalists.

These were momentous encounters. For Abanindranath, it meant support and approval of a refined and knowledgeable audience. For the orientalists among Havell's circle, Abanindranath was the ideal vehicle for reviving a glorified vision of India's past. A similar view of the worth of Abanindranath's work was held by the emerging nationalists.

On a different level, an encounter with Kakuzo Okakura in 1902 had a more critical influence on the evolution of Abanindranath's language of painting. Okakura, who was a strong advocate of a pan-

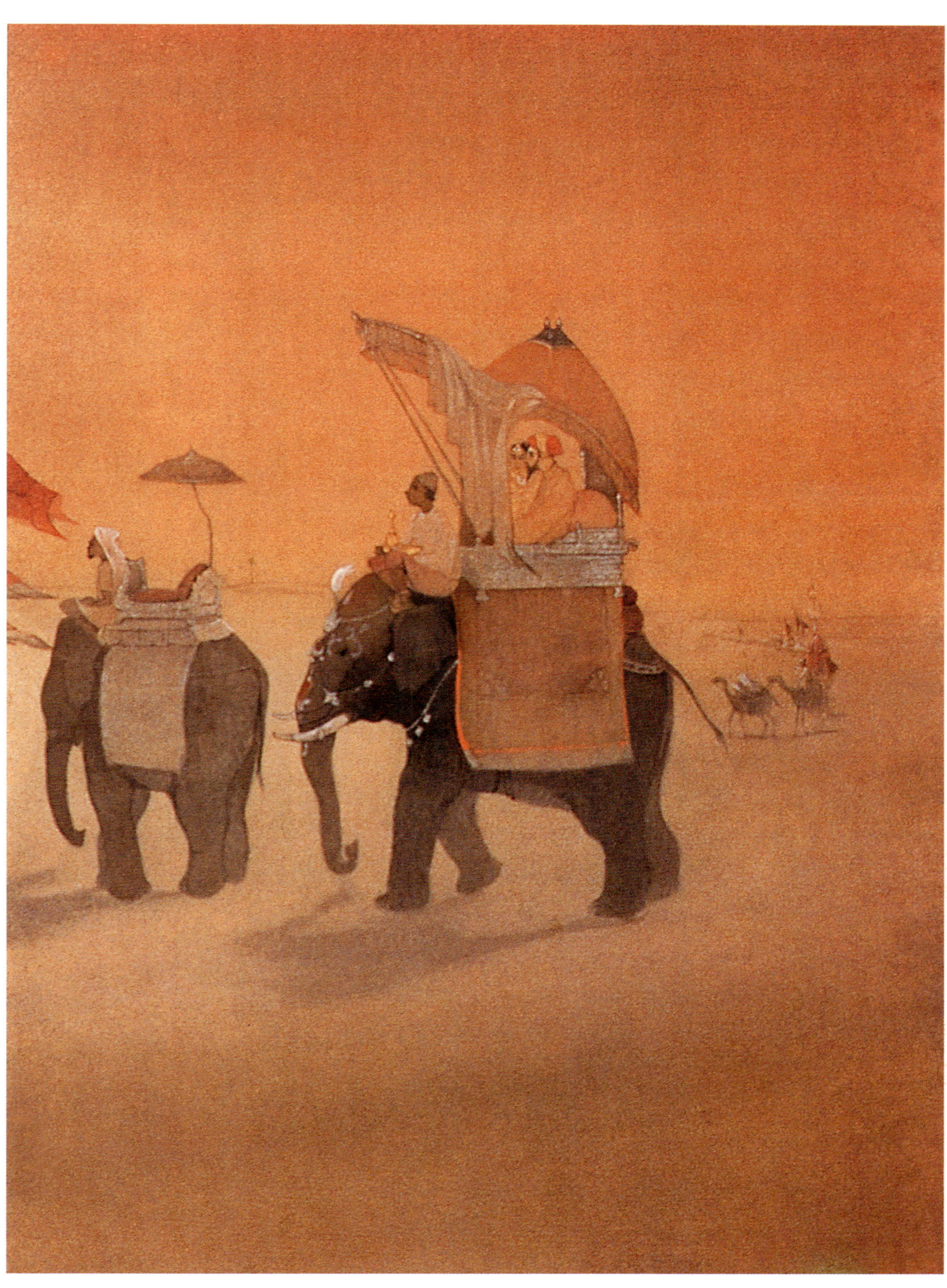

3
Abanindranath Tagore
"Emperor's March to Kashmir"
Watercolour and wash on paper;
24.5 x 27.5 cm
Collection: National Gallery of Modern Art, New Delhi

Asian aesthetic, offered Abanindranath the opportunity of experiencing the subtleties of Japanese painting. This marked the beginnings of the "wash" technique which became a hallmark of Abanindranath's style.

The development of Abanindranath's oeuvre will be discussed later. For the moment, some broad features of his style need to be mentioned. Abanindranath worked out a visual language marked by soft colours, delicate lyrical figuration with gracefully drawn elongated fingers, and rich decorative elements wherever there was scope. Abanindranath also referred to literary, mythical, or historical sources for the subjects of his paintings.

Over the years, a stereotype was created which spread throughout India and was eagerly appropriated by commercial artists. Whether it was the illustration of a dancing girl on a calendar or a scattering of jasmines on a tin of talcum powder, flashes of Abanindranath's evocations could still be seen in the 1960s/'70s. The reason behind such a spread was the first batch of Abanindranath's students at the Government School of Art. Abanindranath's work as a guru continued at his residence in Jorasanko through the Bichitra Art Club and later through the Indian Society of Oriental Art.

Nandalal Bose and Surendranath Ganguly were Abanindranath's very first students. Others who soon followed were Asit Kumar Haldar, Kshitindranath Majumdar, Sailendranath Dey, Samarendranath Gupta, Surendranath Kar, Sarada Charan Ukil, and K. Venkatappa. The students in their turn went on to head art schools all over India which then ensured the dispersal of Abanindranath's style of painting. But with the exception of Nandalal Bose, who tried to chart a new course at Kala Bhavana in Santiniketan, all the other disciples followed the master blindly. This resulted in a replication of Abanindranath's style without the spark of individual genius.

However, there is no question about the uniqueness and deep impact of Abanindranath's artistic vision. No matter what claims he made for nationalism in art in *Bharat Shilpa* (Calcutta 1909), art for him did not have to communicate a message. It was enough that it create a mood, express the artist's perceptions of the world around him, convey an emotional state.[7]

Both Benodebehari Mukherjee and K.G. Subramanyan have commented on Abanindranath's childlike sense of wonder with which he absorbed the world around him. Abanindranath himself mentions in his autobiographical writings some of the images which played on his sensibilities – moonlight seeping through

4
Abanindranath Tagore
"Surangama (From *King of the Dark Chamber*, a play by Rabindranath Tagore)"
Watercolour; 45.7 x 22.5 cm
Collection: National Gallery of Modern Art, New Delhi

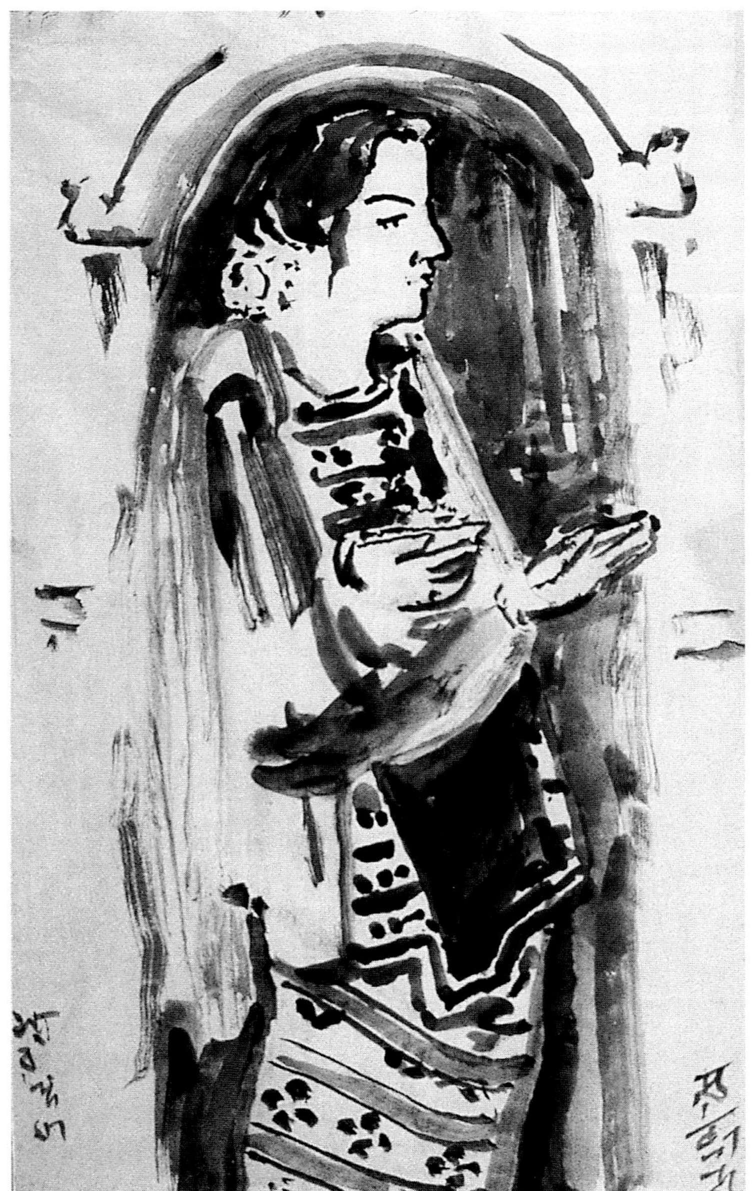

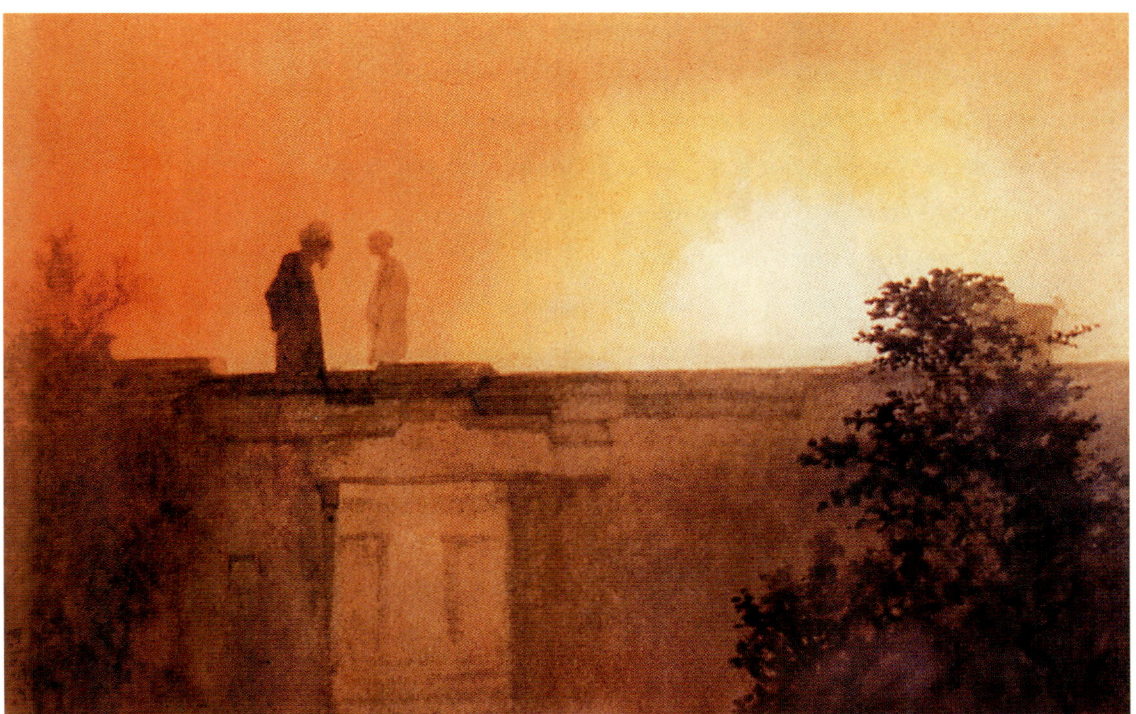

5
Abanindranath Tagore
"Stormy Night"
Wash and tempera on paper;
21 x 30.5 cm
Collection: National Gallery of Modern Art, New Delhi

shuttered windows, a pair of red slippers, a silhouette of his favourite maid projected on a whitewashed wall, a lotus carved from white marble reflected in a looking glass, and so on.[8]

Elaborating on this point, Subramanyan wrote that Abanindranath "was a born romancer; both in his painting and his writing he had an alchemy of touch, investing his actual descriptions with the far-awayness of dreams and his fantasies with a strange palpability, an ambivalence one associates with a child's imagination." Abanindranath recognized this quality in himself and made full use of it in the vivid, whimsical, playful stories he wrote for children.[9]

Even during ordinary conversations, Paritosh Sen once recounted to me, Abanindranath could slip into whimsicality suddenly. We note this in many of his works. Consider "The Goat" and "The Monkey" in wash and tempera. This quality of imagination is particularly manifest in the "Arabian Nights" series where the reality of the world, seen from the south verandah of his Jorasanko residence, mingled delightfully with the fantastic vision of an exotic Middle-Eastern cityscape.

Abanindranath's mature views on art are clearly enunciated in the Bageshwari Lectures instituted by the University of Calcutta (1921–29). Subramanyan refers to them "as the most authentic compendium of his views and methods of approach".[10] Beautifully written, the lectures are like a sparkling, gurgling stream spontaneously and effortlessly throwing up complex ideas. Translating the language replete with visual imagery becomes a Herculean task.

Nevertheless, I have attempted a rough translation of excerpts from his essay "*Jati o Shilpa*", the seventeenth lecture in the Bageshwari series, to illustrate his true feelings for art as a form of pure expression shorn of such baggage as nationalism.

Abanindranath says, "The nation cannot be the mother of art, nor can there be a union between nation and art. That always takes place with the artist. During springtime, flowers bloom on the shrubs in the garden. Seeing the blossoms, it would be a mistake to think of the owner of the garden as the creator of the flower. You must remember there are elements like the spirit of spring, mother earth, the gentle south breeze. The breath of life blown by the nation can spark national pride but cannot blow open a bud into a flower. Even in national parks created by the state, the flowers don't bloom at the nation's command."

He further goes on to emphasize in the same essay, "When a nation survives on the accruals of its past, it may continue to preserve its national identity, but it would be increasingly difficult to maintain the quality of its art and other creative expressions. Art thrives on its integrations with the present – not alienated from the past, but not entirely directed towards the past."[11]

So much for all the charges of revivalism hurled at him. The truth of the matter is that Abanindranath sought to give expression to the emotions and images that stirred his inner self. It is also equally true that his soul responded to some evocations in the visual languages of the past.

His aversion to Western academic realism with its accent on anatomical accuracy strongly articulated in oil comes through in the seventh Bageshwari Lecture, "*Shilpa o Dehatatwa*" (Art and Anatomy). Abanindranath describes the human body as standing erect between the two poles of sky and earth. He says, "Medical anatomy is like the wire tied taut between two pegs. But artistic anatomy is different. Its real description is like the different rhythms seen in the growth of trees, vines, flowers and leaves burgeoning and branching out sinuously with the caress of breeze and touch of light."[12]

His Works

To get a measure of the totality of Abanindranath's development, one must turn to Benodebehari Mukherjee's chronological catalogue of Abanindranath's paintings. The catalogue provides an invaluable guide to understanding Abanindranath's evolution as an artist. Except for some early drawings and pastel portraits, Abanindranath did not usually date his paintings. He signed his works variously and from 1913 onwards used a seal presented to him by Okakura. From around 1918, he also used a seal with a Ganesh icon. Both the signature and the seal formed an integral part of the composition.

Up to 1895, Abanindranath worked in European technique. Some sketches of landscapes and portraits of his family members belong to this period. In 1895, he received an album of miniatures of the Lucknow *qalam*. He did the "Krishnaleela" series between 1895–97 comprising twenty paintings. According to Mukherjee, this set shows the artist's interest in textures.

From 1897 to 1900, he developed an attraction for Rajput and Mughal painting. The period is marked by bright colours and decorative composition as in the paintings "Buddha and Sujata", "Building of Taj", and "Abhisarika". "Death of Shahjahan",

6
Abanindranath Tagore
"Rabindranath as Baul Mendicant"
Watercolour; 10 x 5 cm
Collection: National Gallery of Modern Art, New Delhi

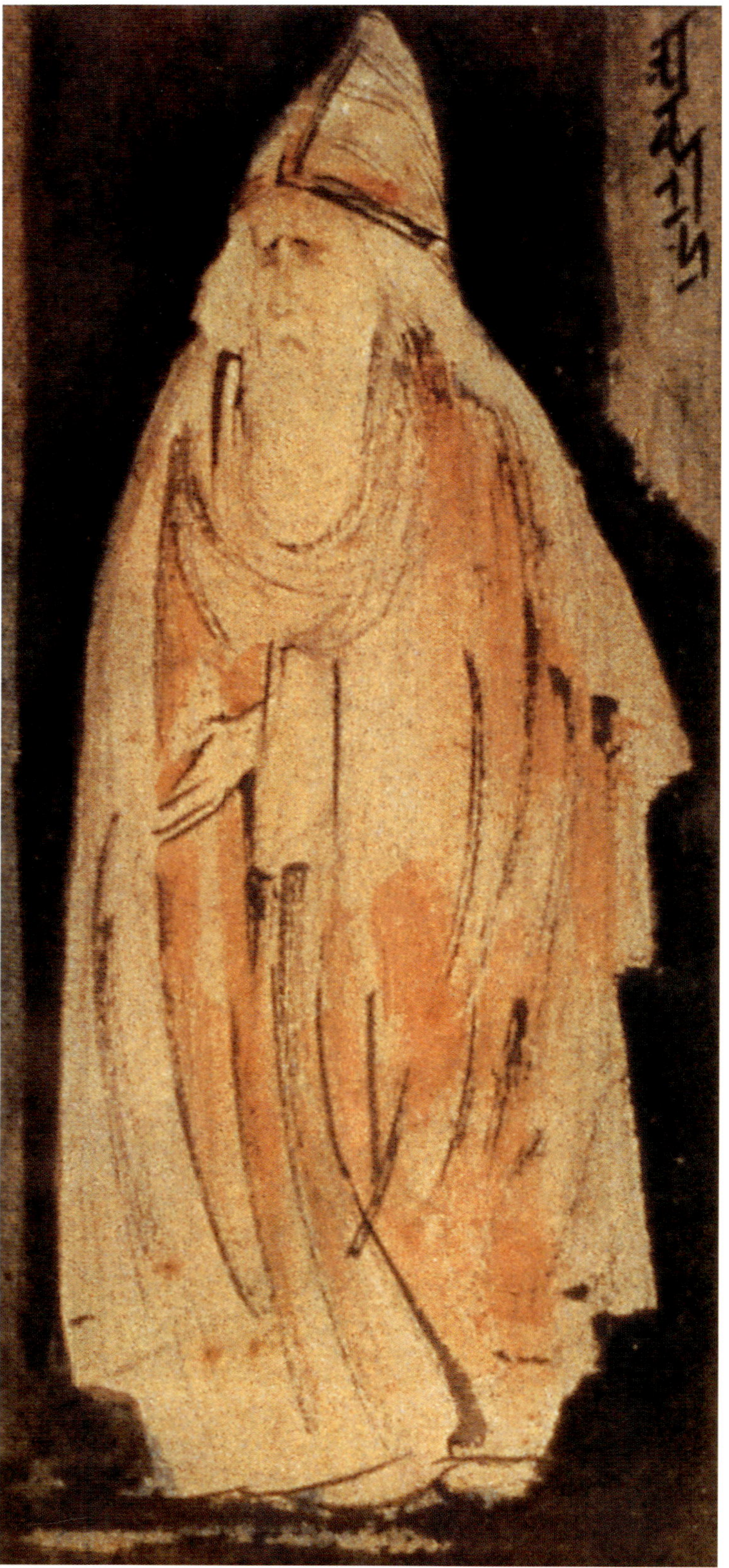

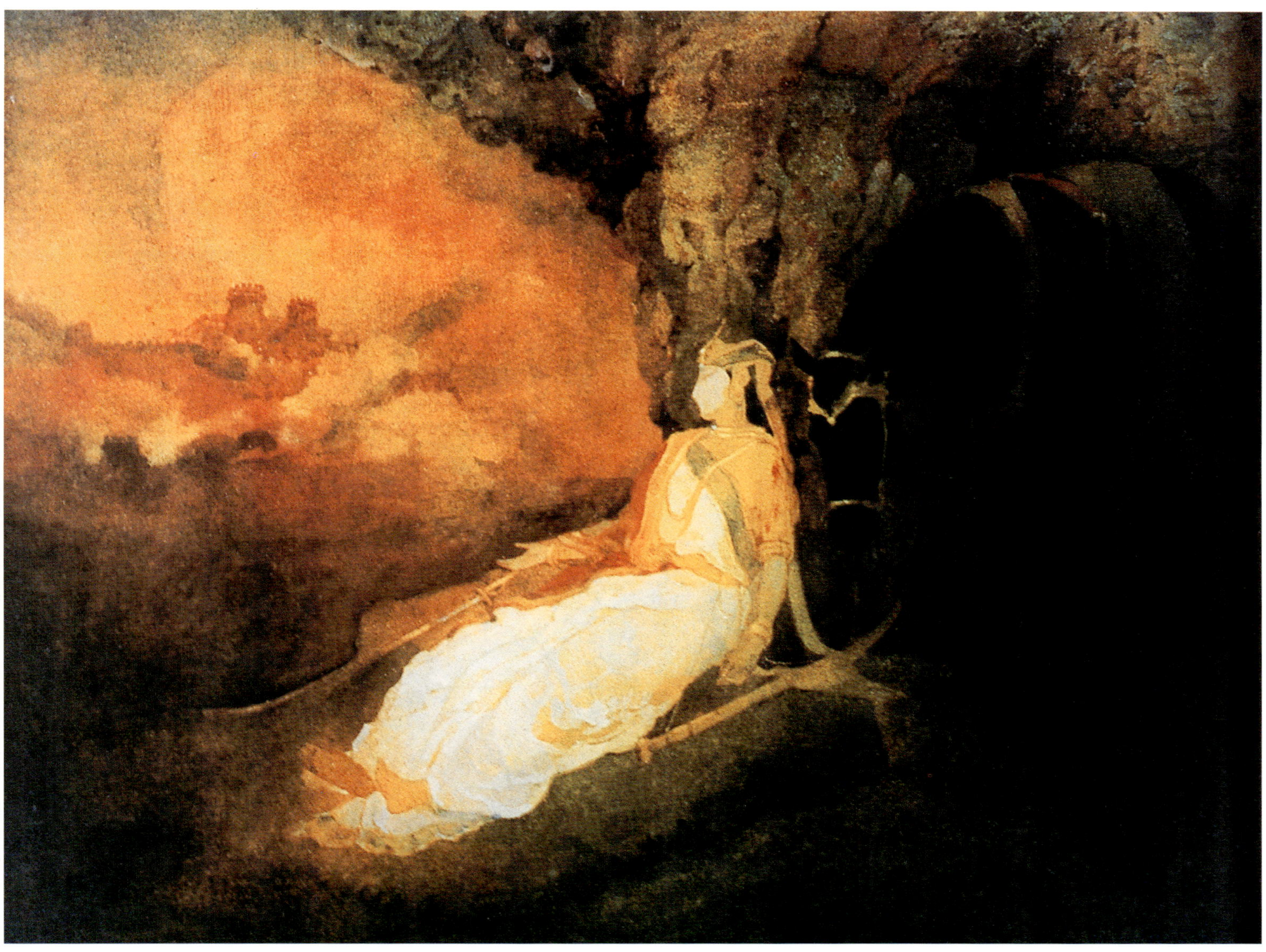

7
Ganesh Pyne
"Death of a Dream", 1957
Watercolour; 16 x 21 cm
Private collection

although painted in oil on wood at this time, belongs to a later period stylistically, says Mukherjee.

Between 1900 and 1911, his style underwent another transformation. Besides Kakuzo Okakura, who first came to Calcutta at the invitation of Swami Vivekananda, Abanindranath met in this period the two Japanese artists sent to India by Okakura, Yokoyama Taikan and Hishida Shunso. His encounters with the Japanese style of painting brought about a radical change in technique. "Bharata Mata", in which for the first time a secular figure was iconized, was typical of this phase.

During these years, Abanindranath also illustrated the *Rubaiyyat* of Omar Khayyam and the works of Kalidasa, drew portraits from Mughal history, and so on. The period is marked according to Mukherjee by "texture, atmosphere, deep interest in portraiture and dramatic expression". These are the qualities which shaped Abanindranath's distinctive style and influenced artists of a later generation.

Between 1911 and 1920, after a visit to Puri, although he continued to use the wash technique, his style changed to a heavier, opaque quality from the use of white in wash. This was one of the most fruitful periods of his career. He did several landscapes, a genre which had not interested him greatly earlier. Now a fuller female form with heavy ornaments appeared in his work. "Tissa, Asoka's Queen", bought by Queen Mary, belonged to this phase. He also painted a number of Bengali stage performers. The sensitive paintings "End of the Journey" and "Portrait of the Artist's Mother" are of this period. Both paintings are tinged with the melancholy that creeps into many of his works. Consider the earlier "Death of Shahjahan" or "Head of Dara", for example. He did many animal life paintings at

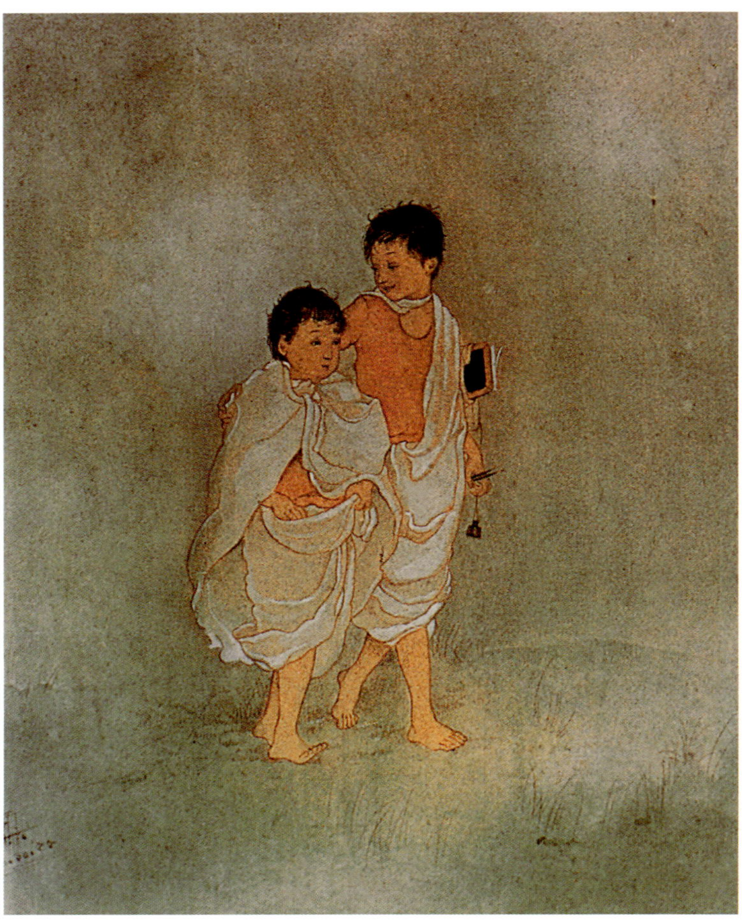

8
Ganesh Pyne
"Winter Morning", 1955
Watercolour; 19.5 x 14.5 cm
Private collection

this time. Also illustrations for Rabindranath Tagore's *Gitanjali*, as well as Puri and Darjeeling landscapes.

The next stage in the development of Abanindranath's art was witnessed between 1920 and 1930. These years were marked by attention to structural aspects of composition. The textural quality had disappeared and the treatment of the figures was flat. The palette was bright. He did many portraits in pastel towards the end of this period. There were quite a few landscapes of the Bengal countryside done during this phase. There were also many paintings of fauna including the "Playmate" series to which the well-known "The Monkey" and "The Goat" belong.

The culmination of Abanindranath's creativity was the "Arabian Nights" series done in 1930. The inventiveness, the imagination, the decorative elements, the wash technique, all contributed to making this an outstanding phase in his oeuvre. Here he invested the distant shores of his imagination with a reality with which he was familiar – a reality that was nonetheless mysterious and alluring. According to a list compiled by Mukherjee from Abanindranath's family members, there were 45 paintings in the series.

Abanindranath stopped doing any important painting after "Arabian Nights". Instead he wrote *jatra*s based on mythological themes. In 1938, he once again experienced the urge to paint and

9
Ganesh Pyne
"Rakta Karabi", 1957
Watercolour; 42.5 x 28 cm
Private collection

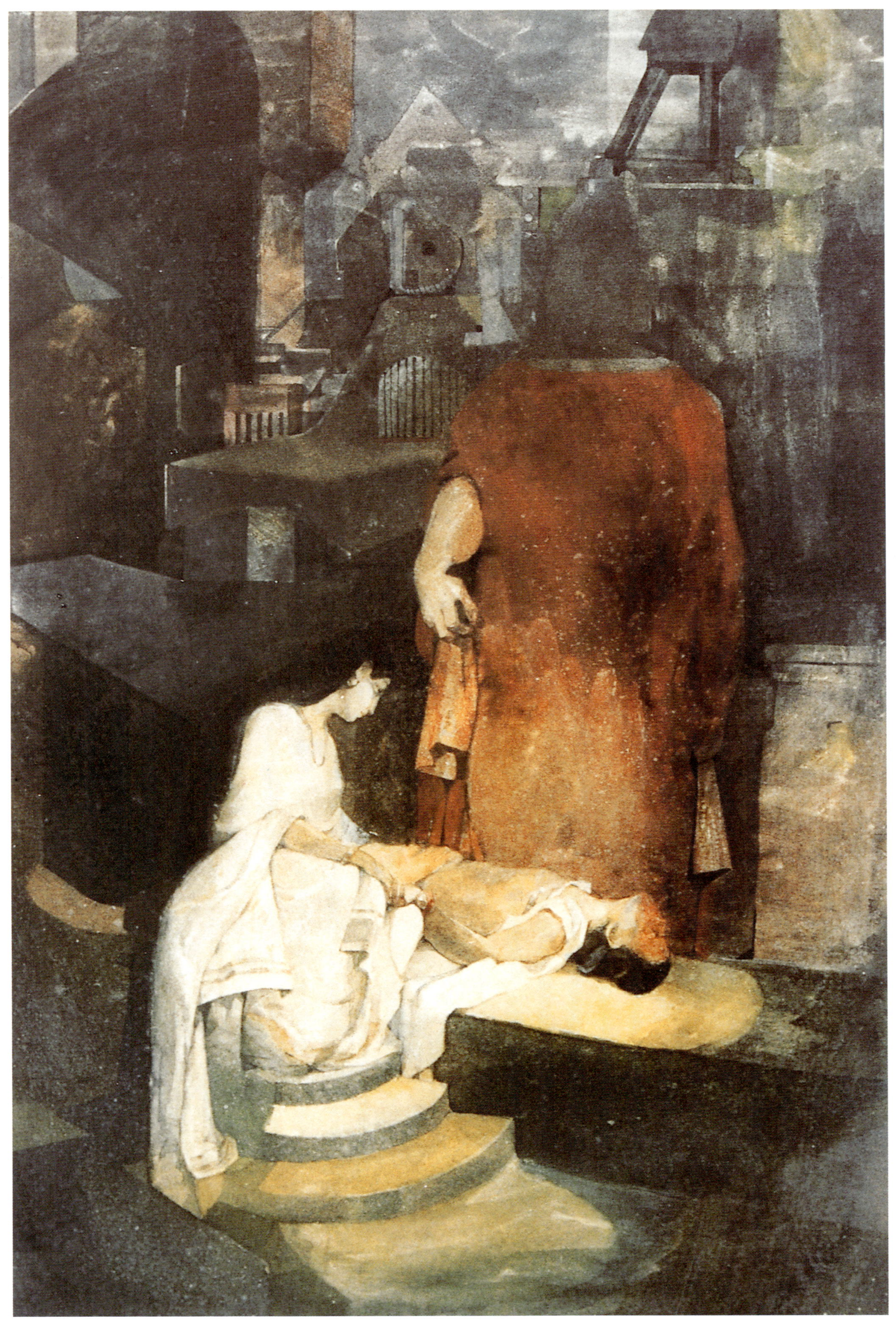

did a large body of folk-style *pata* paintings. These works were characterized by a generous use of black, which Abanindranath generally did not employ, and a carefree feeling. The two prominent series of this period are "Kavikankan Chandi" and "Krishna Mangal".

From 1940 onwards, Abanindranath began to make toys or what he called *katum kutum* with twigs, bark, driftwood, and other found objects. His fondness for texture and whimsical forms saw full expression in these works.[13]

Both Mukherjee and Nandalal Bose have recorded Abanindranath's wash technique. Mukherjee divides the development of Abanindranath's technique into two periods. He writes, "First Period: drawing in pencil; space is filled in mostly with transparent colour; the whole surface is laid over with a colour-wash; the colour-wash is allowed to dry; the paper is dipped into water and taken out to dry; the colour is now fixed. After this another coating of colour...may be given. This process may be repeated indefinitely.... The purpose of this kind of colour-wash is to make the object hazy and break the surface of the paper....

"Second Period: The colour coating in his wash became more and more complex and he began to use opaque colour and transparent colour alternately for wash...."[14]

Nandalal Bose paints an even more intimate portrait of Abanindranath's technique in his Bengali book *Shilpacharcha*, where he details techniques, mediums, and material. Bose describes Abanindranath's fondness for English transparent watercolours. He would open the flat box of watercolours and touch his brush delicately on the pigments much like a master pianist would the keys of a piano. No one would make out over which notes the fingers had flitted. Bose also noted that Abanindranath liked some of the cool toned blues and red hues like French blue, indigo, neutral tint, mauve, crimson, and carmine. Abanindranath used white in his wash in such a way that it created the effect of a good tempera. This is particularly visible in the "Omar Khayyam" and "Arabian Nights" series.[15]

His Legacy

As mentioned above, with the exception of Nandalal Bose who led the Santiniketan school into new experiments with visual language, most of Abanindranath's immediate disciples followed the master mechanically. In the process, they lost out on his crispness, tonal variations, and expressions of atmosphere. Among the artists of Bengal who were not his followers, there was a lot of criticism of his worldview.

It was not till the end of the '50s that Abanindranath's vision inspired a young artist in the Government College of Art in Calcutta. The fledgling artist was Ganesh Pyne. Pyne had once described Abanindranath's paintings as "softly-intoned soliloquies". From the mid-'50s onwards, the figuration and colouring in his paintings were deeply influenced by Abanindranath. One could see the same finely-drawn, lyrical, sometimes sinuous lines. In such paintings as "Death of a Dream", the colour palette had the same resonance.

It was in the early '60s that Pyne began to change his figuration using stiff, angular lines. The colour tones also became darker and he turned predominantly to the opaque medium of tempera. But Pyne shared with Abanindranath a common goal. The painting became a vehicle to convey mood, emotion, atmosphere; and not so much social comment or intellectual ideas. It was a surface on which fleeting flashes of remembered images could be recorded and textures could be created.

Spanning generations, it is not difficult to understand why Abanindranath and Pyne shared such a spiritual kinship. Both artists have a profoundly poetic sensibility. The melancholy in Abanindranath's works deepened into angst in Pyne's temperas. Both are masters of line capable of great lyricism. Most importantly, both bring to their view of the world, a child's sense of wonder and innocence.

It was Pyne's declaration of Abanindranath as a source of inspiration that forced many to re-examine Abanindranath's visual language minus such contexts as the Bengal School and nationalism. It brought to the fore an artist who had evolved a unique, sensitive, personal style.

The course charted by Abanindranath once again came centrestage when some of the younger Bengali artists of the '50s and '60s turned to a miniature format. There were Dharmanarayan Dasgupta's playful temperas done from the '70s onwards. But Dasgupta also showed the influence of folk styles.

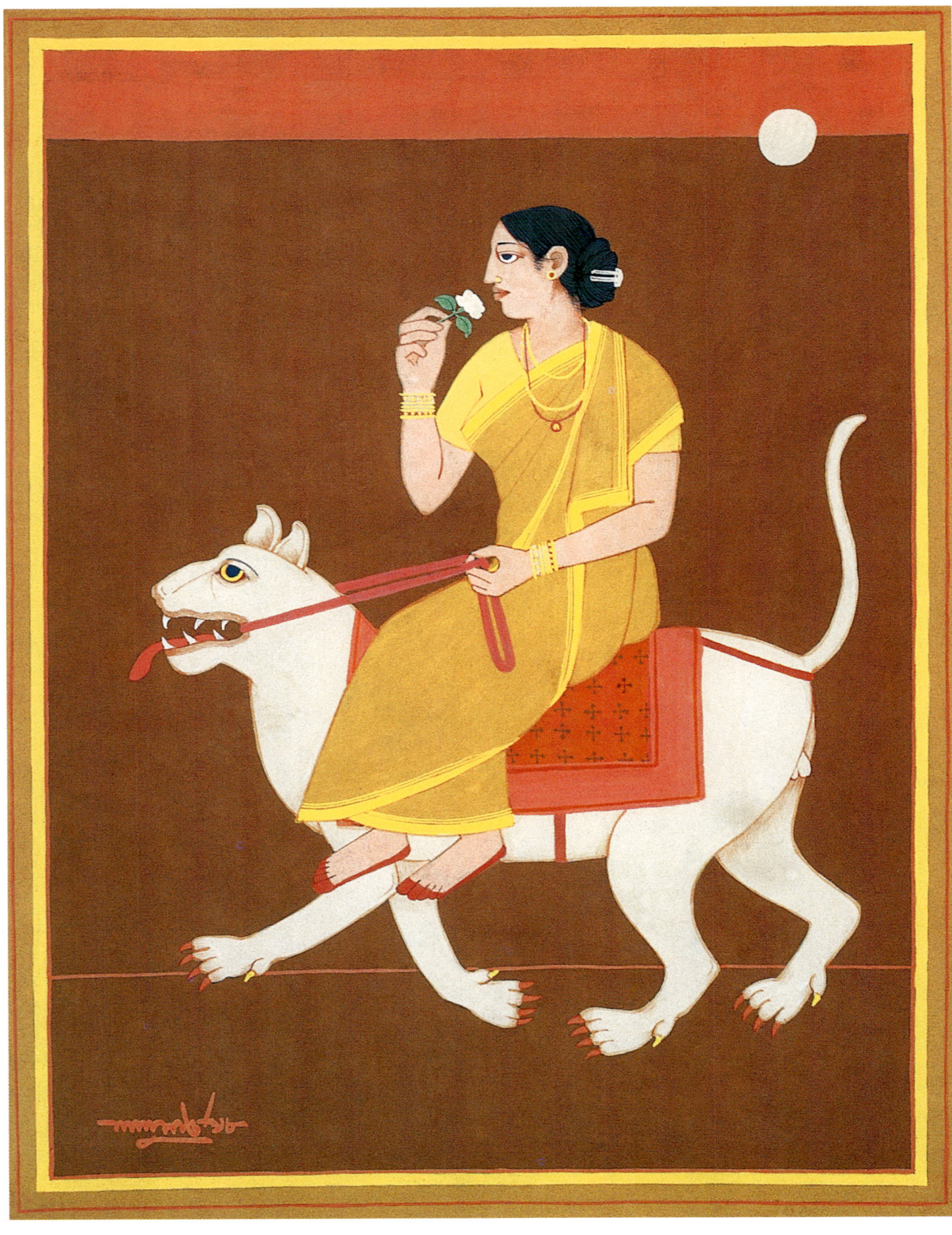

10
Lalu Prasad Shaw
"Rai Baghini", 1998
Tempera
Private collection

Lalu Prasad Shaw, a contemporary of Pyne at art college, was known for his modernist, abstract, monochromatic lithographs. He began to paint miniature style temperas from the '80s onwards. Shaw says that in his youth Abanindranath's paintings stirred him. One developed a sense of kinship with the works from repeated viewings. The wash paintings attracted both his mind and his eye. He tried to paint in the medium but not being fully conversant with the technique, the works suffered from some weakness. He gave up using pure wash technique.

Shaw sees one area of aesthetics which he shares with Abanindranath: a sense of Indian identity. Apart from some indirect flashes of the Bengal School in his works, Shaw says his style of painting also has a blend of styles from Rajput, Mughal, and Kalighat schools. Abanindranath's wash technique was distinctly his own. When Shaw uses wash with tempera, it is only to create atmosphere. Shaw

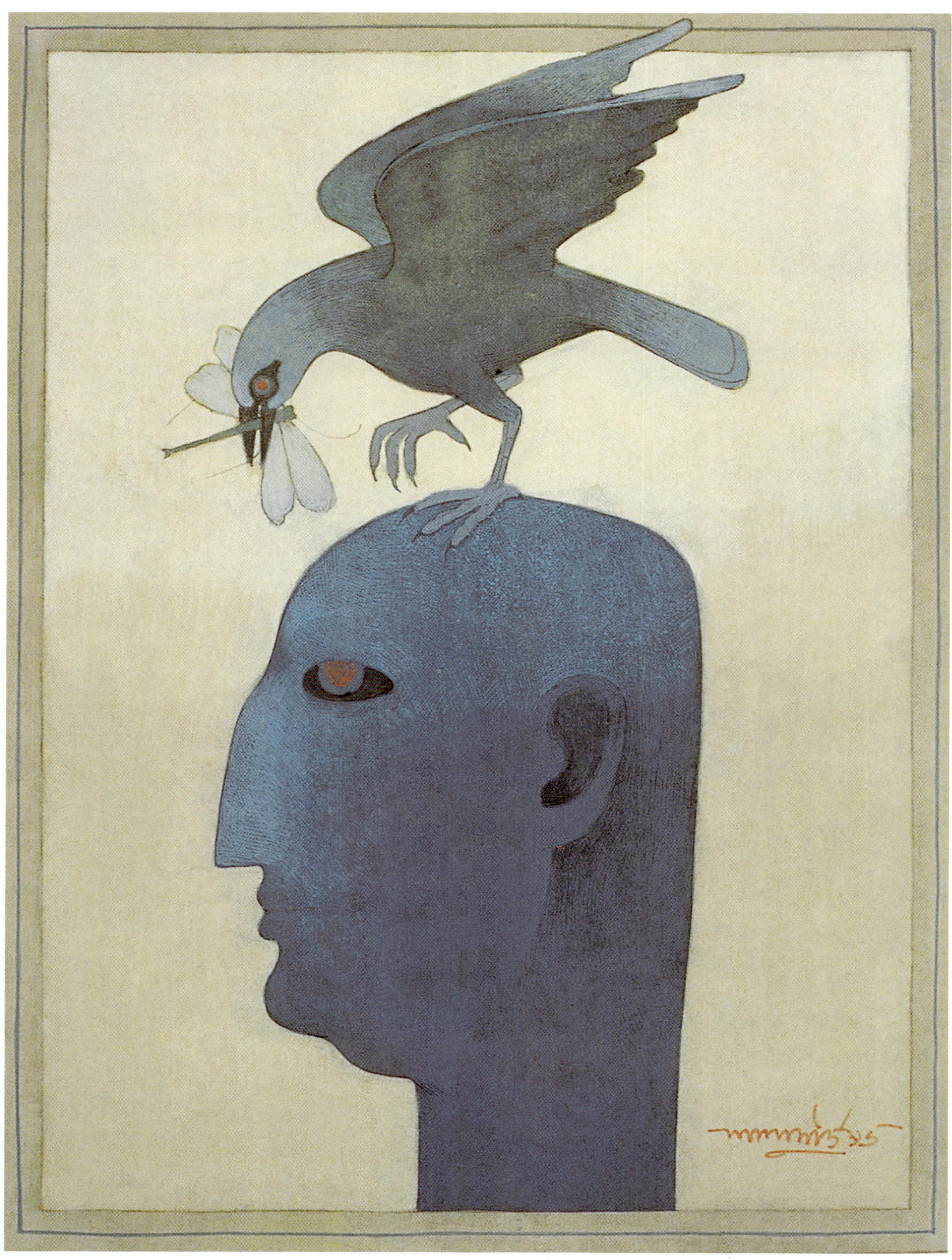

11
Lalu Prasad Shaw
"Untitled", 1996
Tempera and wash
Private collection

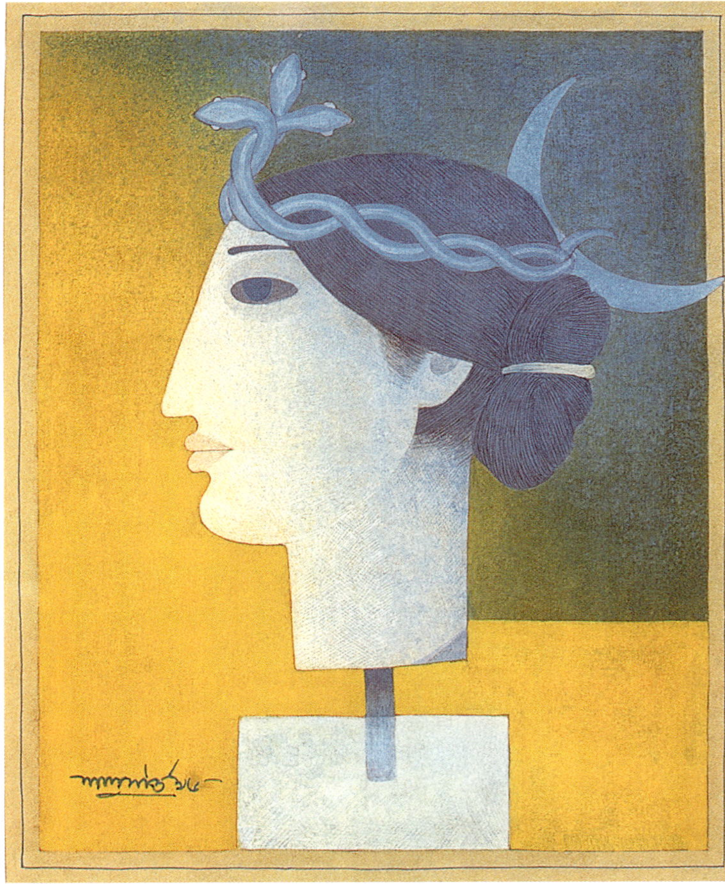

12
Lalu Prasad Shaw
"Queen", 1996
Tempera and wash
Private collection

asserts, "If Abanindranath had not arrived in the world of Indian art, a bridge between traditional art and contemporary Indian art would not have been created."

According to Paritosh Sen, the charges of revivalism against Abanindranath are not important. They have to be seen in the historical context of the times. Shaw also feels that Abanindranath has to be seen against the socio-political backdrop of his time. And finally, as Subramanyan writes, other artists may have greater vocabulary or powers of expression, but few could create a new language like Abanindranath did.[16]

NOTES

1. Partha Mitter, *Art and Nationalism in Colonial India 1850–1922*, Cambridge, 1994, p. 315.

2. Ibid., p. 325.

3. Ibid., p. 380.

4. Mulk Raj Anand, "Coomaraswamy Darshan", in Gulammohammed Sheikh et al., eds, *Paroksha: Coomaraswamy Centenary Seminar Papers*, New Delhi, 1984, p. 11.

5. Tapati Guha-Thakurta, *The Making of a New 'Indian' Art*, Cambridge, 1992, p. 3.

6. Ibid., p. 231.

7. Benodebehari Mukhopadhyay, *Abanindranath Tagore* (NGMA catalogue), New Delhi, 1988, p. 34.

8. Ibid.

9. K.G. Subramanyan, *Moving Focus, 'The Phenomenon' of Abanindranath Tagore*, New Delhi, 1978, p. 61.

10. Ibid., p. 59.

11. Abanindranath Thakur, "*Jati o Shilpa*", *Bageshwari Shilpaprabandhabali* (in Bengali), Calcutta, 1962, pp. 210–11.

12. Ibid., p. 96.

13. Benodebehari Mukhopadhyay, "A Chronology of Abanindranath's Paintings", *Chitrakatha*, Calcutta, 1984, pp. 361–78.

14. Ibid.

15. Nandalal Basu, "Wash", *Shilpacharcha* (in Bengali), Calcutta, 1986, p. 106.

16. Subramanyan, *Moving Focus*, p. 62.

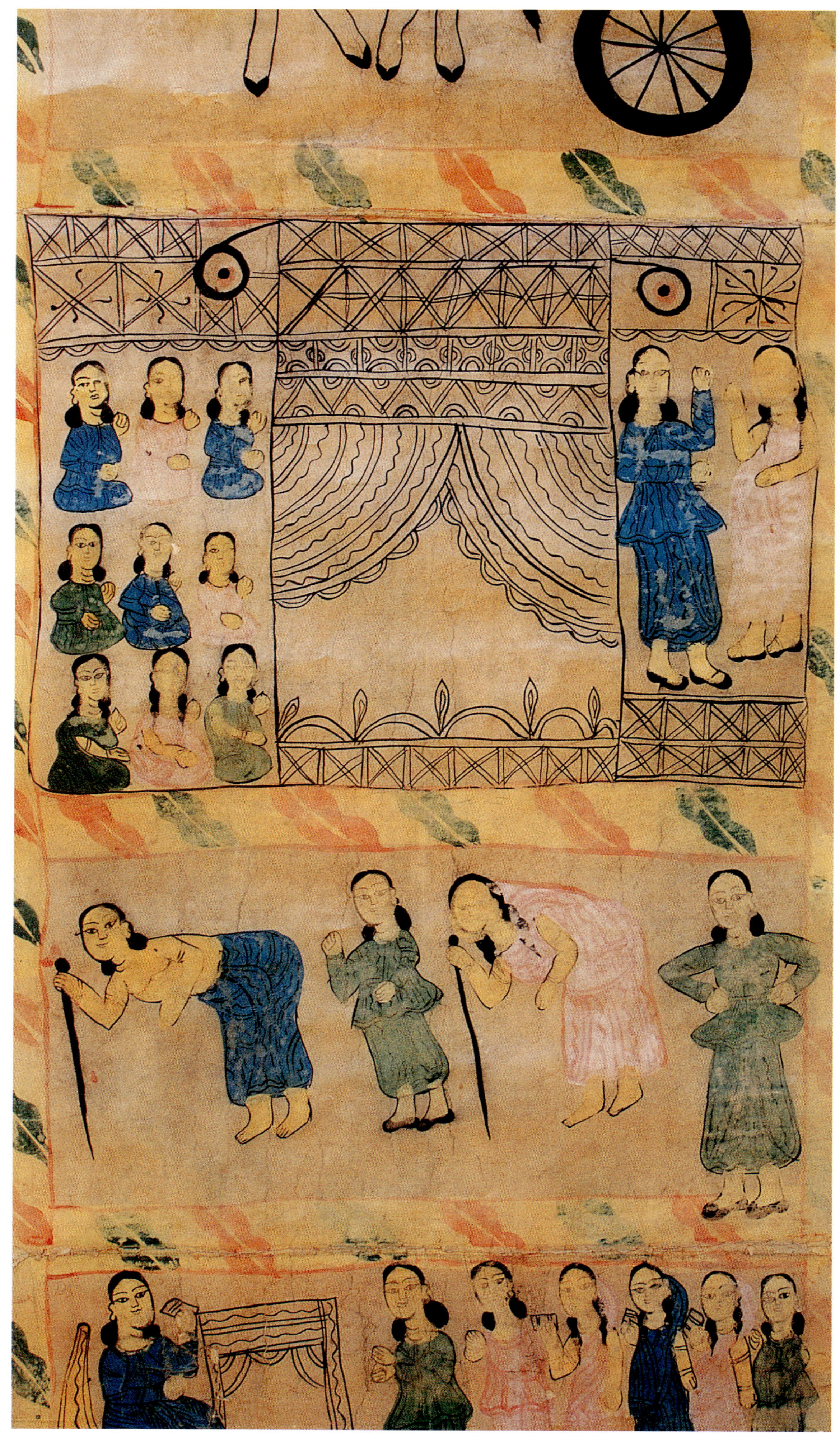

Jyotindra Jain

folk artists of bengal and contemporary images

a case of reverse appropriation

The second half of the 19th century and the first half of the 20th coincide with Bengal's "age of mechanical reproduction" and its immediate aftermath: woodcuts, lithography, oleography, printing, photography, and cinema. For the first time the common man had access to a range of images through printed pictures of gods, goddesses, and renowned personalities of the time ("suitable for framing"); through postcards, calendars, and product labels; through photographs, newspapers, and textbooks. Grappling with this new onslaught of mass proliferation of reproduced imagery with its reduced or enlarged scales and proportions, realistic but frozen gestures and postures, and severely edited and fragmented figures, the first-generation audiences of the age of mechanical replication had to decipher the new "pictorial" script, eventually to be able to "read" it and communicate through it. Bengal's response to this new vocabulary was twofold – on the one hand resisting the change, often with sarcastic ridicule, and on the other adopting many of its features in professional practice (including the idioms of visual communication through image making), even to the extent of using it as a tool for more effective expression and a wider outreach. While savouring the transition, the urban middle-class and rural Bengal were developing a taste for the new visual culture. The bazaar painters of Kalighat, the rural *patua* scroll painters and storytellers, and the village women embroiderers of the *kantha* quilts not only survived these major technological and cultural transformations but imbibed and appropriated these changes in the pictorial conceptualization of their images. In a manner of speaking, they not only became the first contemporaries of Indian art, but anticipated the popular culture of the 20th century that was to follow. In this article I examine how the rural storytellers, scroll painters, and embroiderers confronted the media and the media-based imagery, how they saw in the process of transformation the essence of expression, and how as image makers they recalibrated their pictorial language after their exposure to the replicated pictures proliferating at that time.

Not having been involved in the debate on the orientalist or nationalist aesthetic or the ascendancy of revived classical art forms and downfall of their folk counterparts that the cultural establishment of the time was engaged in, the *patua*s and the women embroiderers of Bengal found themselves directly and spontaneously responding to the new media, absorbing social changes, and commensurably recasting pictorial imagery. For them the transition from their inherited and, to a large extent, repetitive tradition, to absorption of new elements – both in terms of materials and

1–3
Advent of cinema in Calcutta, details from a storyteller's scroll
Bengal, mid-20th century
Pigment on paper
Crafts Museum, New Delhi
Photographs: J. Jain

techniques as well as exploration of new possibilities of expression – was smooth and natural. When in most parts of rural India comparatively closed and repetitive artistic conventions had brought about a certain degree of stagnancy and decadence in pictorial expression, for historical reasons in Bengal, by and large, there was more openness about the adoption and the articulation of a new media-based imagery. For the folk artists the absorption of modernity did not mean degeneration of tradition but its consolidation.

I shall use a few examples to illustrate how the rural Bengali artists responded to the new media and appropriated contemporary social events and imagery, side by side with their conventional art practice.

A Narrative Scroll from Medinipur – "After Independence"

This mid-20th-century scroll titled "After Independence" depicts, with a tinge of sarcasm, the family tensions, social conflicts, and agony that arose from the breakdown of existing moral values and economic structures, the effect of modernization around the time of India's independence. The scroll is a response to the so-called degenerative effect of cinema on the youth of the time. The

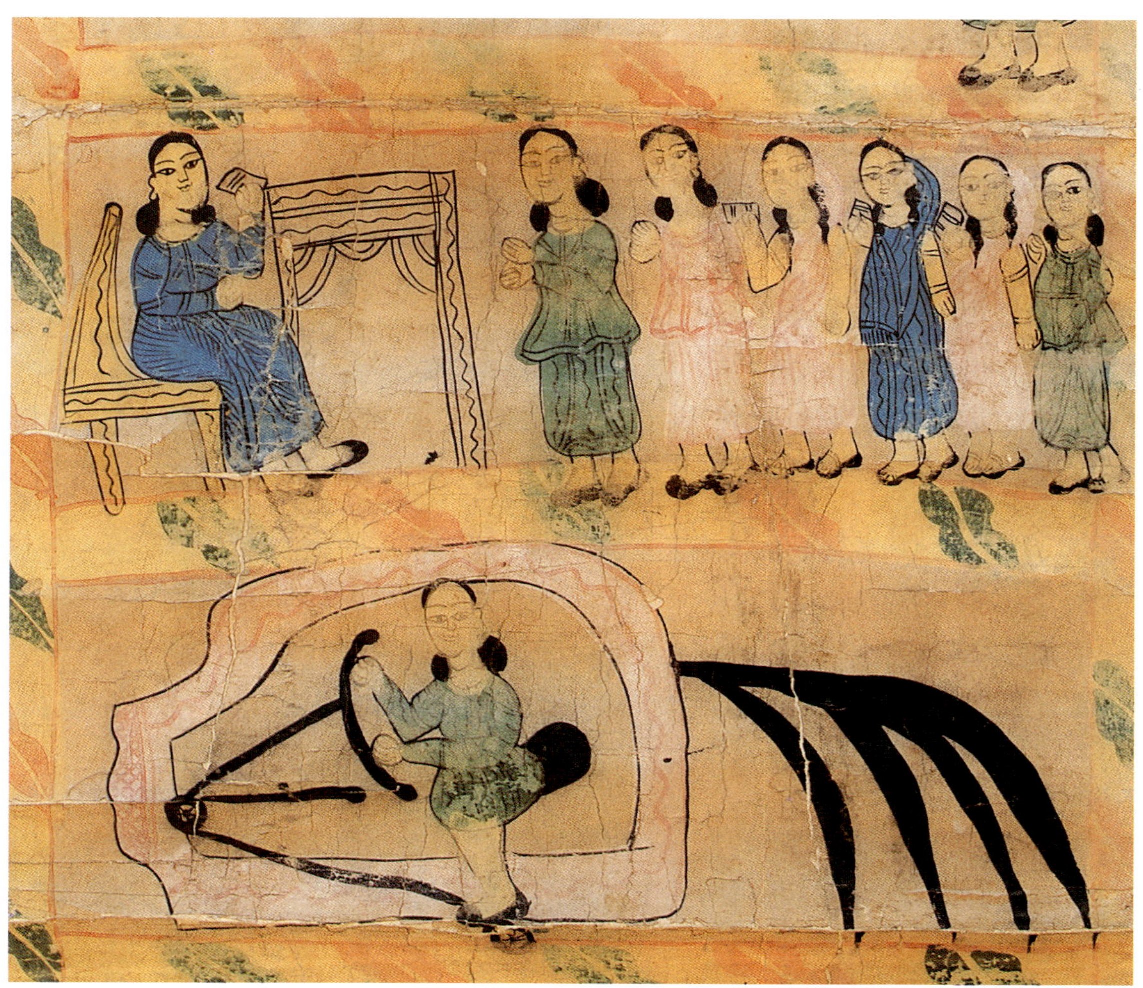

2

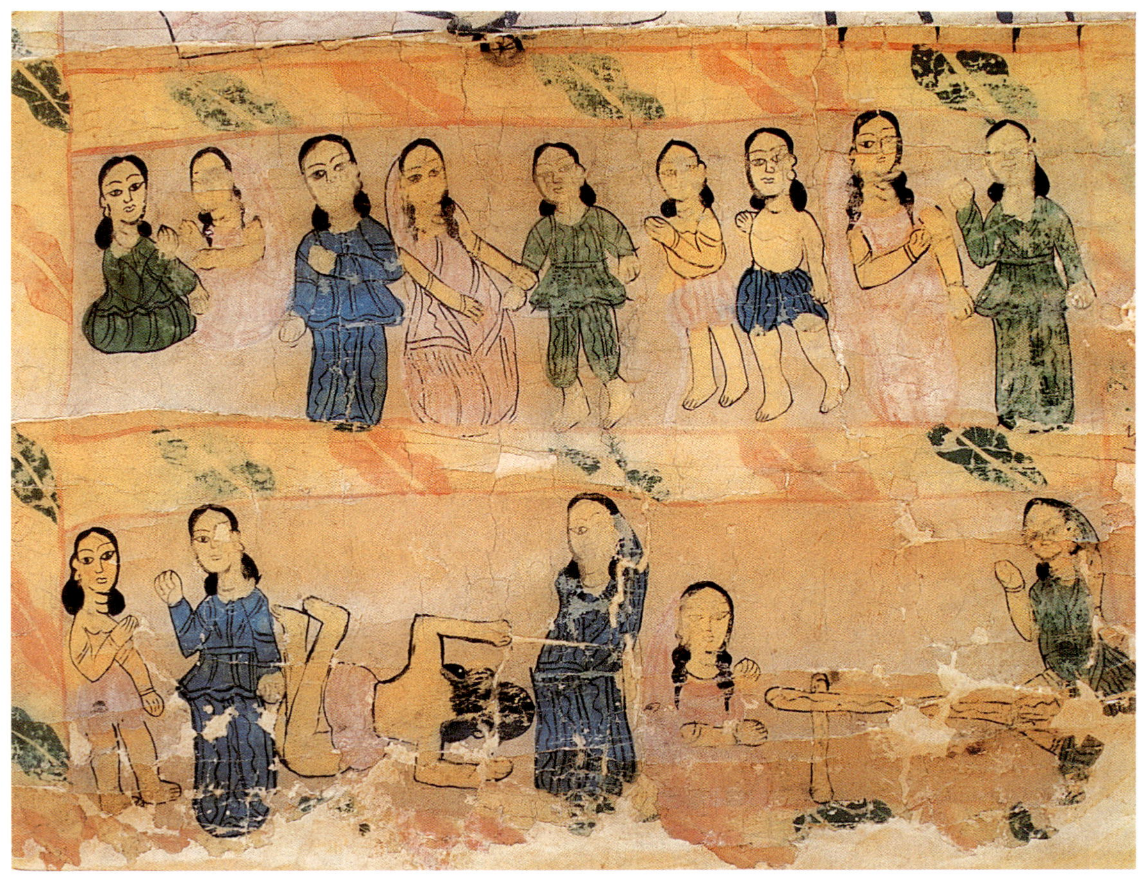

3

opening scene of the narrative depicts a young girl crying in the kitchen over her unfortunate economic circumstances, she does not have new clothes to wear. Below her is a queue of people waiting with ration cards to obtain their quota of rice. In contrast, young men and women wearing new and fancy clothes and shoes are shown going to a cinema hall. The next three panels are devoted to portraying people going to the cinema in motorcars, cycle rickshaws, and bullock carts. The old and physically handicapped too are shown rushing to see a movie (figure 1). The "bad" impact of cinema is represented by images of "modern" men and women standing in queue at a court with their applications for a court marriage, as a judge drives up to the court in a car (figure 2). In one panel a newly married "modern" couple is shown approaching their illiterate and uneducated parents and addressing them in English "Hallo dear", etc. The climactic scene shows the father-in-law falling at the daughter-in-law's feet sarcastically addressing her as "Mother Chandi", the destroyer of demons (figure 3). (These interpretations are based on the narrative songs of the *patua*.)

The scroll is in line with the Bengali *patua* tradition of responding in their art to contemporary social and religious scandals; satirizing politicians, the *bhadralok* class, the *ejuraj* (educated rajas), babus, and fashionable dandies, as also profusely depicted in Kalighat painting. It is an interesting phenomenon that when folk artists of India, even today, are busy mechanically churning out the umpteenth version of their past artistic conventions, their counterparts in late 19th- and early 20th-century Bengal had begun to respond to the contemporary social and political conflicts in their works. In terms of social satire and the mockery of half-baked Westernisms of the English educated youth and hypocritical upper classes, this scroll comes close to the caricatures of Gaganendranath Tagore who had engaged himself, in the first quarter of the 20th century, in producing three volumes of lithographs based on his bitterly sarcastic drawings exposing the banal Bengali upper classes. Gaganendranath's caricatures were in the well-established European tradition of cartooning, primarily meant to ridicule and amuse. In contrast, the *patua* scrolls of the kind described above had, in addition to lampooning, a dimension of human tragedy, helplessness, and agony, missing in Gaganendranath's work. Since the *patuas*, even while articulating new themes, did not change their medium/idiom from painting to cartooning, their work, while venturing into the changing contemporary realm, remained rooted in their conventional language of pictorial narration, having an established and well-articulated vocabulary with which their audiences had an emotional bond.

4–6
Indira Gandhi's murder,
details from a storyteller's scroll
Bengal, late 20th century
Pigment on paper
Collection: Indira Gandhi
Memorial Museum, New Delhi
Photographs: J. Jain

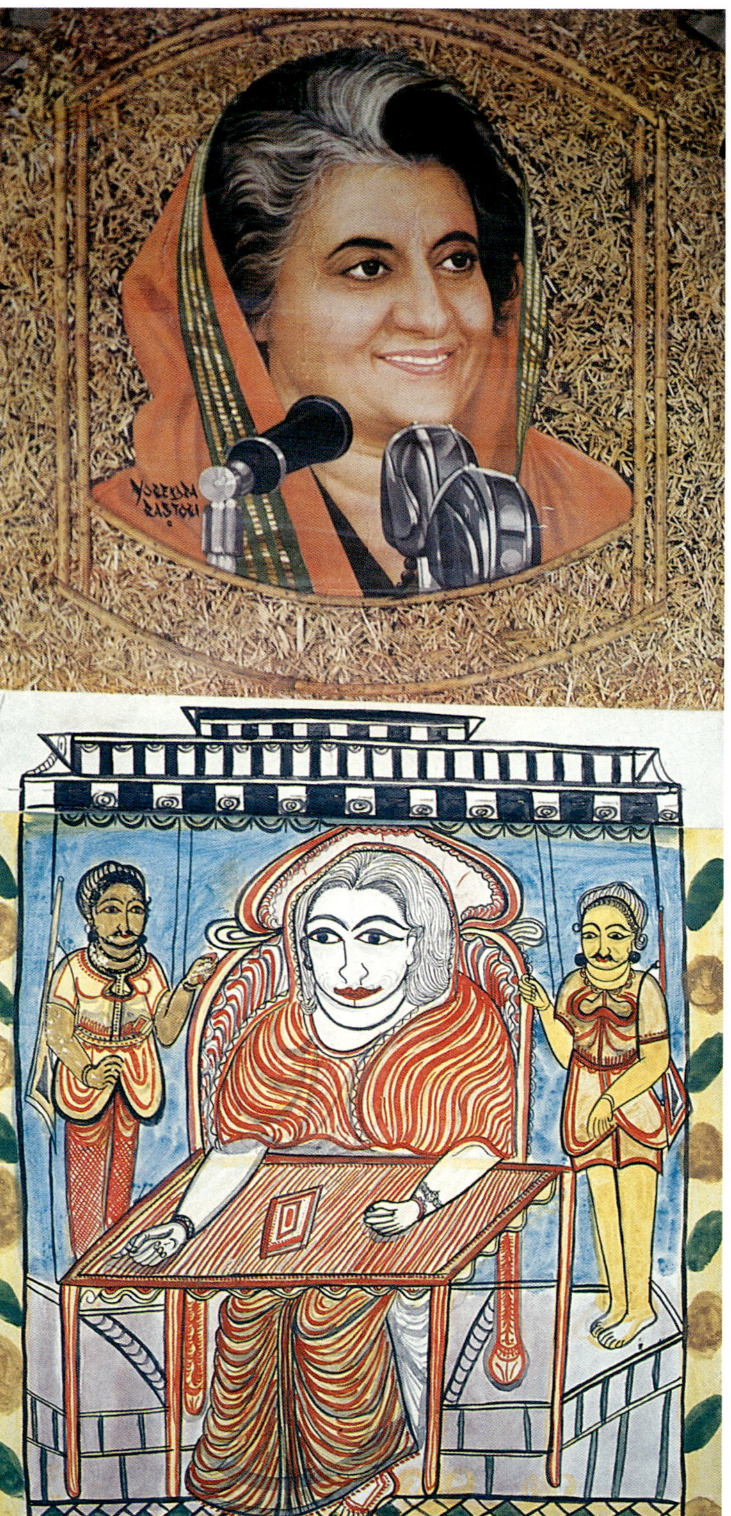

"Indira Gandhi Murder" – Another Scroll from Medinipur

Mythologizing reality, turning it into a fable or an allegory comes easily to the *patuas* of Bengal. Whether they pictorialize the mythological stories of Rama, Krishna, or the goddess Durga, or incidents from real life such as Elokeshi's murder (a scandalous event of 1873 in which Nabin Banerjee killed his wife Elokeshi for allegedly being involved in an adulterous relationship with a temple priest) or *narir hath driver khun* ("driver murdered by a woman", an incident of a newlywed woman stabbing a bus driver who attempted to rob her of her gold ornaments), they equally work with reductive imagery – two pillars indicating a building, a tree signifying a landscape, etc. This technique effectively transforms the locale from real to fictitious, from material to symbolic. In the portrayal of human characters in those scrolls, iconicity dominates – again a feature of mythologization. *Patuas* were used to portraying divine personages such as Rama, Lakshmana, Sita, or Durga in the image of ordinary people – Rama would be shown as a member of the *bhadralok* of Calcutta, wearing Mughal court costumes, and his palace would be one of the Victorian buildings of the city. Sita or Durga would be no different from middle-class Bengali brides. On the other hand, while narrativizing contemporary events from real life which reach them through the media, the *patuas* fall back upon the pre-existing model of depiction of mythological characters and locales and thereby transcend reality. The day-to-day images of contemporary life – cinema houses, cars and buses, palatial mansions of Calcutta, helicopters and aircrafts – are images from another world which come to *patuas* through the media: newspapers, photographs, cinema, and so on. They come to them already sensationalized, fantasized, and therefore mythologized. As they use a mythological locale and the iconography of Hindu deities to depict contemporary scandals, they once again mythologize "reality". The painted contemporary images thereby

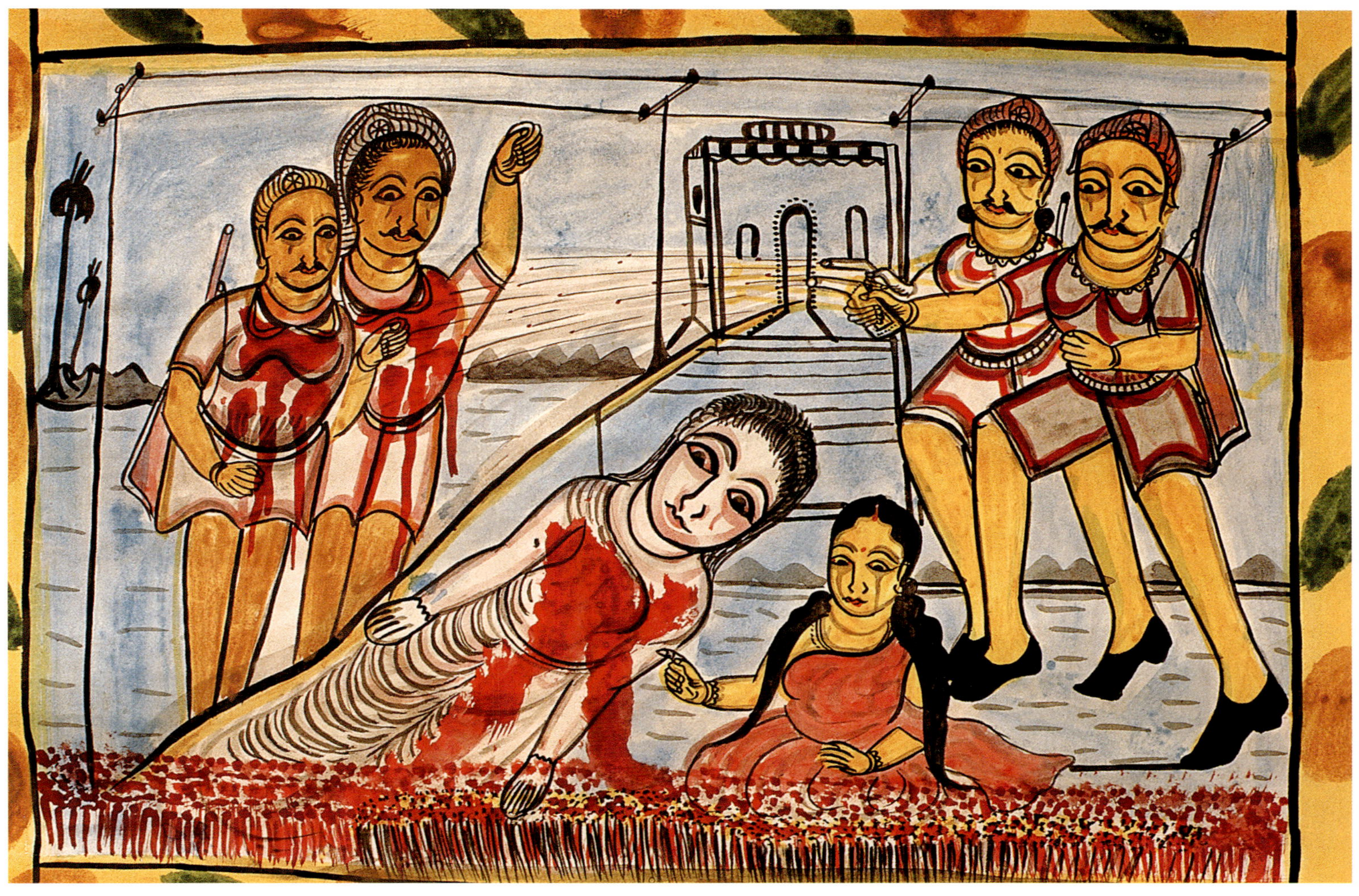

5

undergo an immediate metamorphosis to become legends. This essentially formal pictorial device of easy transformations mastered by the *patua*s also facilitated the conversion of national heroes into deities, a process that has gained popularity in the last fifteen years, especially with the wider outreach of the media in rural Bengal.

Against this background let us examine a *patua*'s scroll depicting the murder of Indira Gandhi. It was painted in 1989 by Bahar Chitrakar of Noya village in Medinipur district.

Just as any conventional scroll devoted to the goddess Sarasvati, Kali, Durga, or Manasa would start with a representation of the respective goddess invoked at the beginning of its narration, this scroll starts with a photographic portrait of Indira Gandhi taken from an election poster (figure 4). As Sarasvati would be depicted with the *vina*, her attribute, Indira Gandhi is shown with a microphone in front of her. The conventional representation of any of the goddesses in the opening panel would be in the form of a cultic image – frontal and facing the devotee. This cultic image for worship would be in sharp contrast to the rest of the scenes depicting the goddess in action in various participatory episodes. As the *patua* seeks to iconize Indira Gandhi and literally give her the position accorded to a deity in the scroll, he needs to find a device by which the icon can be marked off from her mortal life. The *patua* attains this crucial differentiation by using for her deified representation a photographic portrait placed in a frame within a frame, while in narrativizing her mortal life he paints various episodes with watercolour and brush. As the *patua* opens the scroll, he first displays the photographic portrait and invokes the "goddess" through laudatory verses, and then proceeds to narrate the episodes: Indira Gandhi seated in her office in Delhi, flanked by her guards (figure 4); a bus from Medinipur heading for Calcutta carrying villagers to her rally; two guards saluting her as she steps

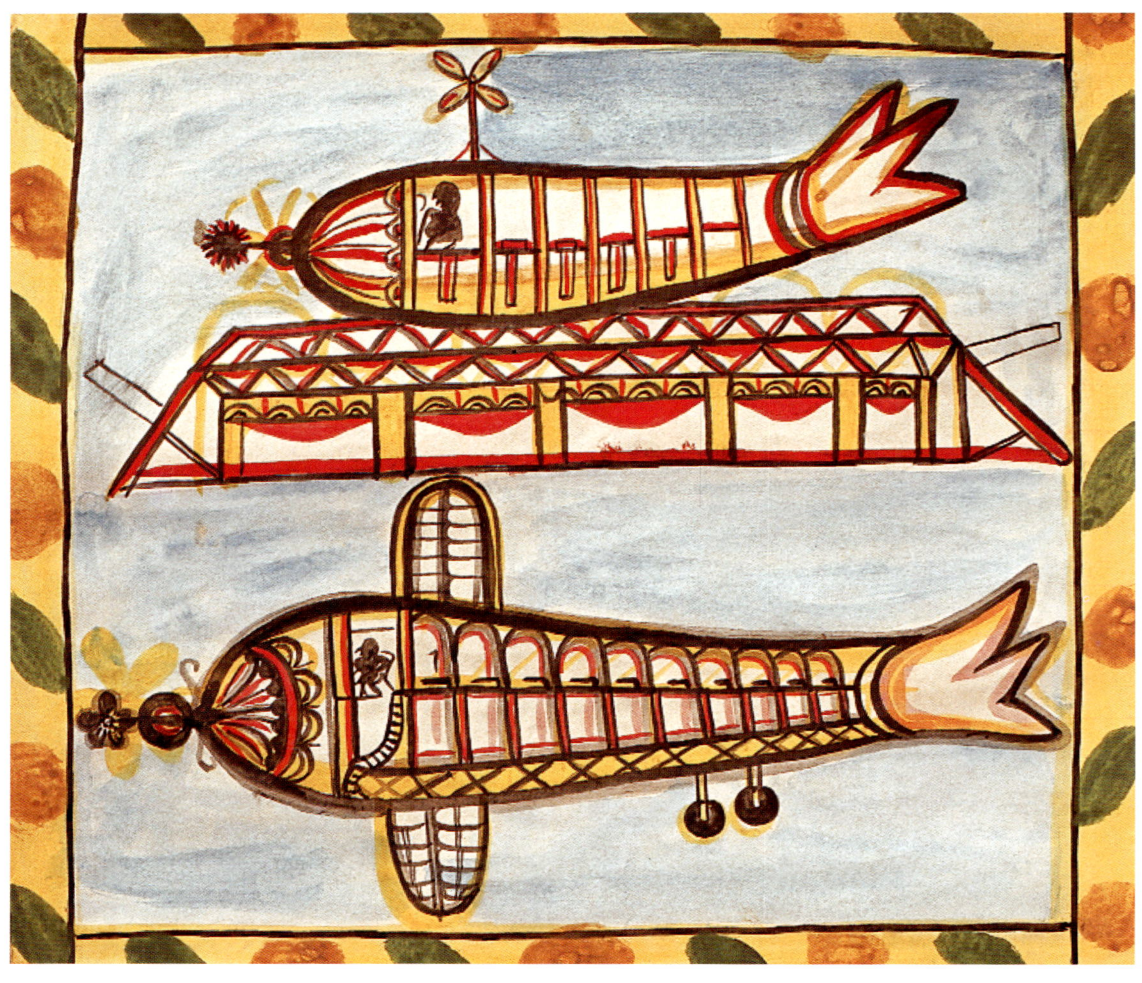
6

out; guards shooting her; Sonia Gandhi with the wounded Indira Gandhi (figure 5); Rajiv Gandhi addressing an election meeting in Medinipur; Indira Gandhi brought to hospital; Rajiv Gandhi piloting a "special helicopter" to Delhi (figure 6); Indira Gandhi's body lying in state for public homage; a Delhi jail where the guards are imprisoned; Indira Gandhi's body being brought to the crematorium accompanied by a helicopter overhead; her ashes being scattered over the Himalaya from an aircraft.

The choice of episodes and the moulding of characters by the *patua* are in line with the news and images broadcast to the nation by the media at the time of Indira Gandhi's death – both retain an equilibrium between myth and modernity. The images, as they appear in the scroll, create in the minds of the *patua*'s audience an imaginary faraway setting, as remote as the "land" of Rama or Durga.

Here, ironically the present, the modern, the real is translated into the past, the distant, and the mythic by conversion of images into metaphors. This attribute of the language of the *patua*'s art provides him with the facility to imbibe modern media-based images and enrich his orbit of expression. Indeed he was aware of the magical properties of the artist's power of attaining transformations – of one image into another, of time present into time past, of space profane into space sacred, and vice versa.

Kantha Embroidery: Albums of Popular Imagery

Kantha, a form of traditional embroidery done over layered rags with threads drawn from old sari borders, served as quilts and coverlets in rural Bengal for centuries. Unlike the embroideries of other regions of India, which remained repetitive and utility-based, *kantha*, in adopting new images of the age of mechanical reproduction, rose to the level of a "fine art".

The Bengal folk artist's fascination for new, mechanically reproduced imagery finds culmination in *kantha* embroidery. The women embroiderers, as nowhere else in India, lustily savoured the joy of consuming the popular, printed imagery of the time – whether from the colourful chromolithographs, oleographs, playing cards (figure 7), postcards, textbook illustrations, photographs, biscuit tins, or even product labels. They saw no inconsistency in juxtaposing the old images of fish, umbrellas, lotus flowers, horse and elephant riders, women engaged in daily chores, with those of forks and knives, aircrafts and railway trains, fashionable dandies and courtesans – all part of a continuously growing, changing, transforming reality called tradition. This openness to contemporary media-based imagery and the capacity to appropriate it in art practice lent a certain vigour and dynamism. The most distinguishing feature of this genre of Bengali folk art is that it served as a mirror of its own time – it did not repeat the past in one more hackneyed reproduction but forged a fresh new expression.

The *kantha*s rarely adopted a narrative mode. They concerned themselves with images, each having its own reality, each equal to the other in terms of pictorial value. Since each image was an

7
Detail from an embroidered *kantha*, using the imagery of imported European playing cards
Bengal, late 19th century
Cotton threads on quilted cotton ground
Crafts Museum, New Delhi
Photograph: J. Jain

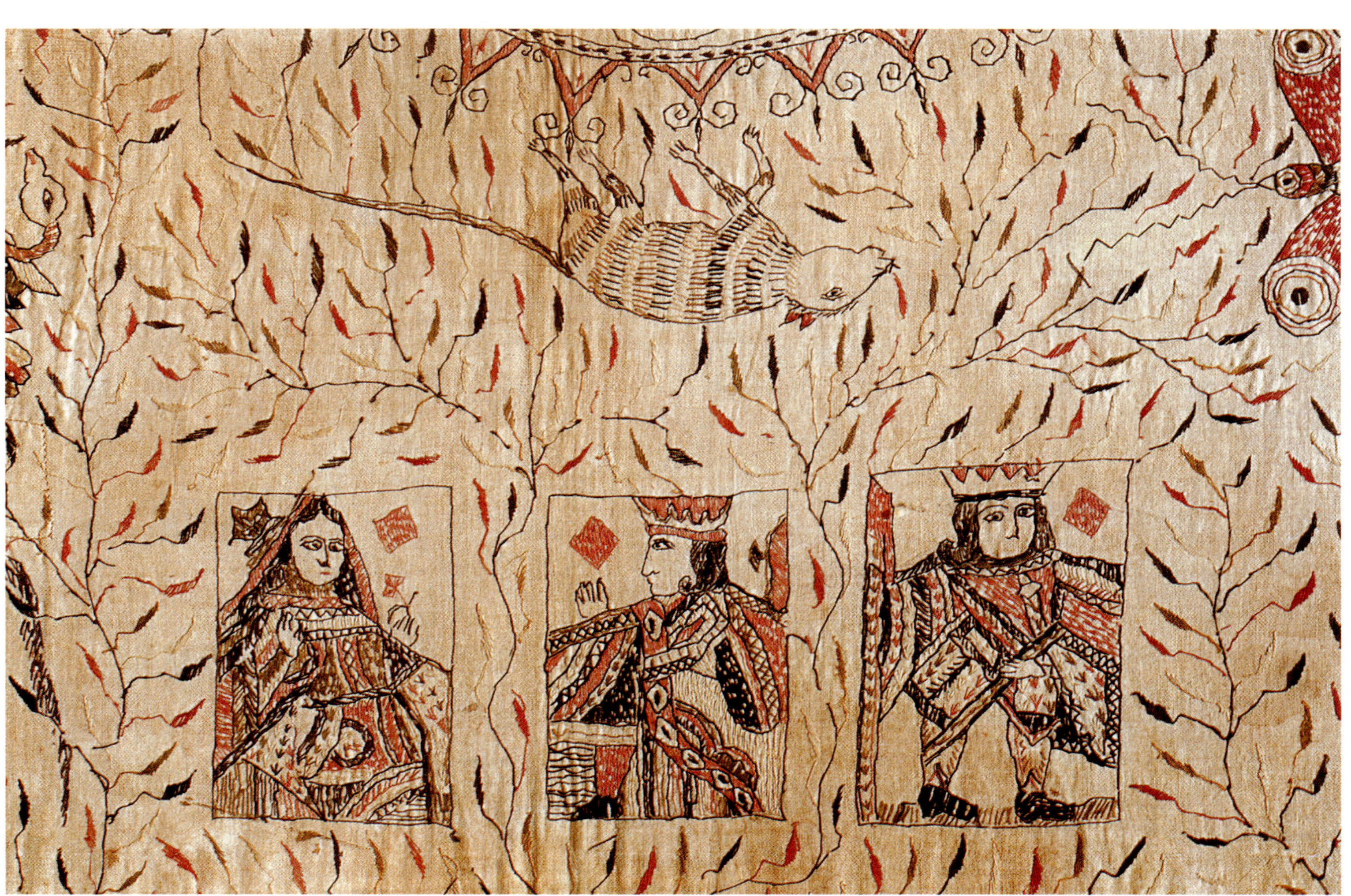

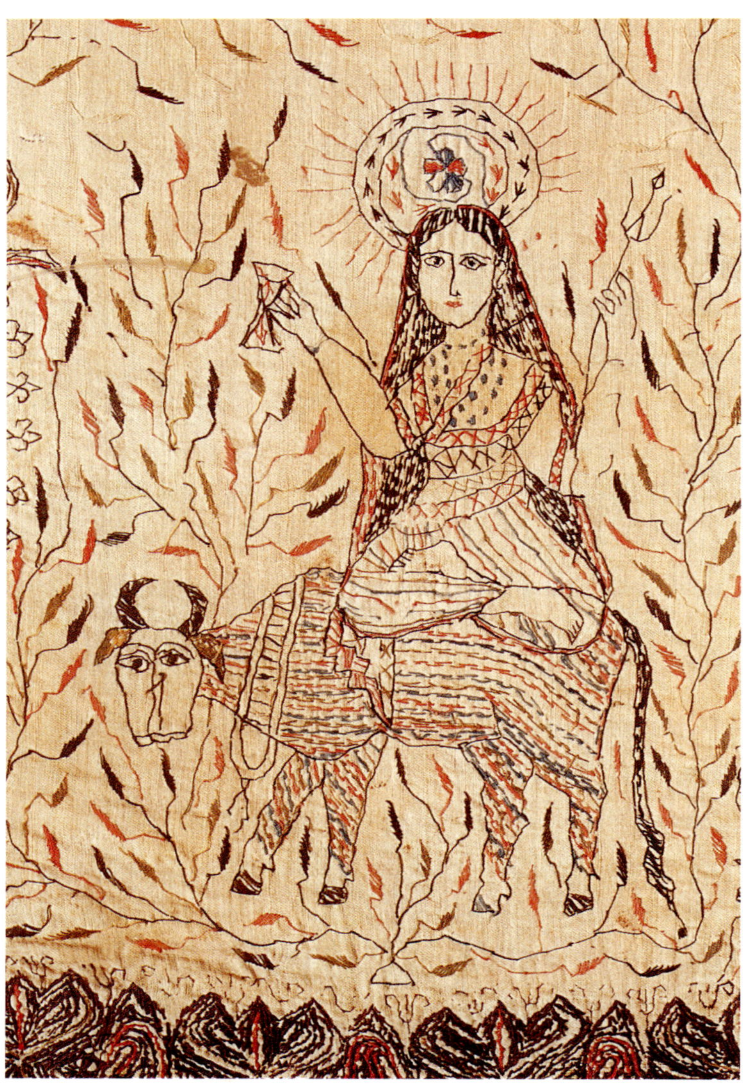

8
Detail from an embroidered *kantha*, depicting Shiva, carrying his *damaru* and riding Nandi, modelled on the popular prints of the Madonna, circulated in Calcutta by 19th-century Christian missionaries
Bengal, late 19th century
Cotton threads on quilted cotton ground
Crafts Museum, New Delhi
Photograph: J. Jain

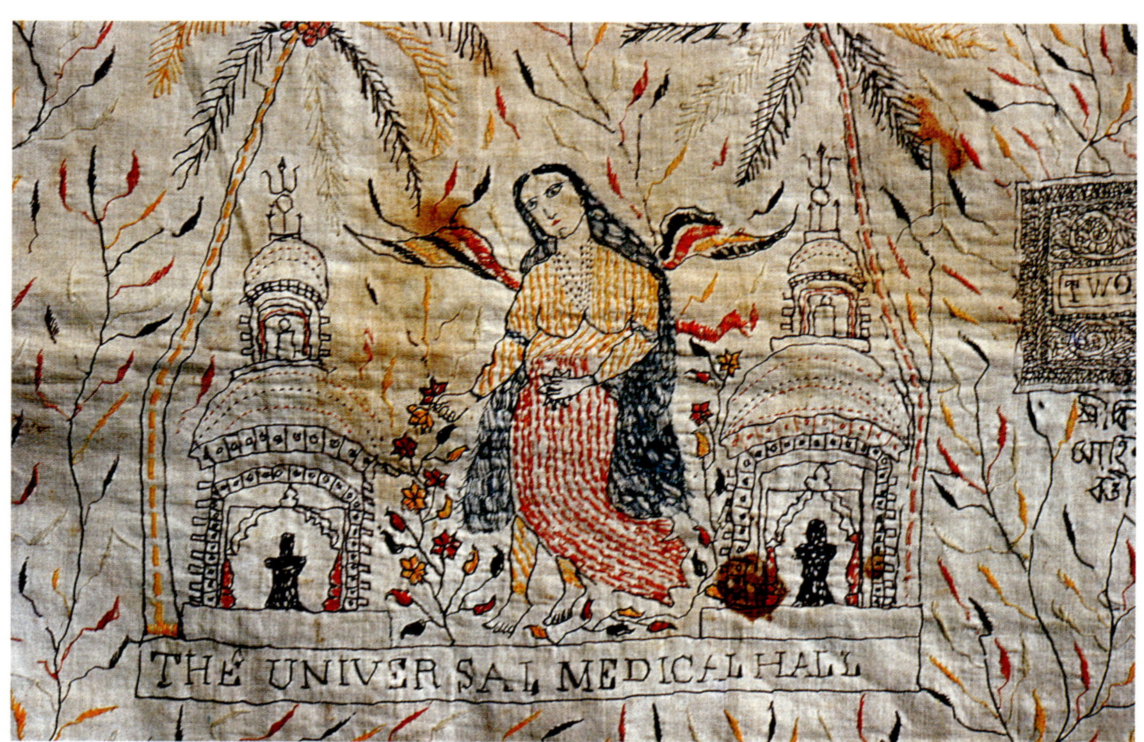

9
Detail from an embroidered *kantha*, depicting an angel descending into a garden between two Shiva temples inscribed as "The Universal Medical Hall". In this album of unrelated juxtaposition of images even a signboard fulfils the function of a visual image.
Bengal, late 19th century
Cotton threads on quilted cotton ground
Crafts Museum, New Delhi
Photograph: J. Jain

independent and complete entity in itself, and not an element of a narrative, it did not demand a context and therefore one image could exist next to the other, not necessarily sharing a common genealogy. Shorn of narrative function, each image stood for itself and by itself (figure 8). It is this nature of the pictorial form of *kantha* which allowed the simultaneous representation of modern images with conventional ones.

In this context, I would like to describe a few new images from *kantha*s which reflect the contemporary face of this traditional art form and once again demonstrate how Bengali folk artists remained open to change and thereby saved themselves from the position of cultural isolation and stagnation. If creative interpretation of the images of one's own time has anything to do with being "contemporary" and being "artists", this is evident in the work of the rural *kantha* embroiderers of the second half of the 19th century (figure 9).

Of Ravi Varma, Biscuit Tins, and Playing Cards

The new bazaar imagery reproduced on product labels, sold as oleographic and chromolithographic prints, and published in school textbooks was widely collected, framed, and even worshipped in homes at the turn of the century. The practice continues, replaced with calendars today. A huge number of religious pictures once used as labels on cloth bales exported to India from the textile mills of Manchester, Glasgow, and Birmingham, framed and stained with vermilion used in worship, have recently come onto the market. Popular imagery had charged the vision of the rural and bazaar artists of Bengal and had even entered the sacred space of Hindu worship, while both the art establishments – the British art schools and the indigenous resurgent art movements (one of the leading expressions of the latter being the Bengal School) – had kept away from it as it stood, in their minds, for a degeneration of the much coveted traditional aesthetic values, originality, authenticity (these enhanced the market value of Indian goods abroad), and corrosion of national identity (this in the sphere of art stood for rediscovery and revival of the "glorious" ancient tradition). It was only in

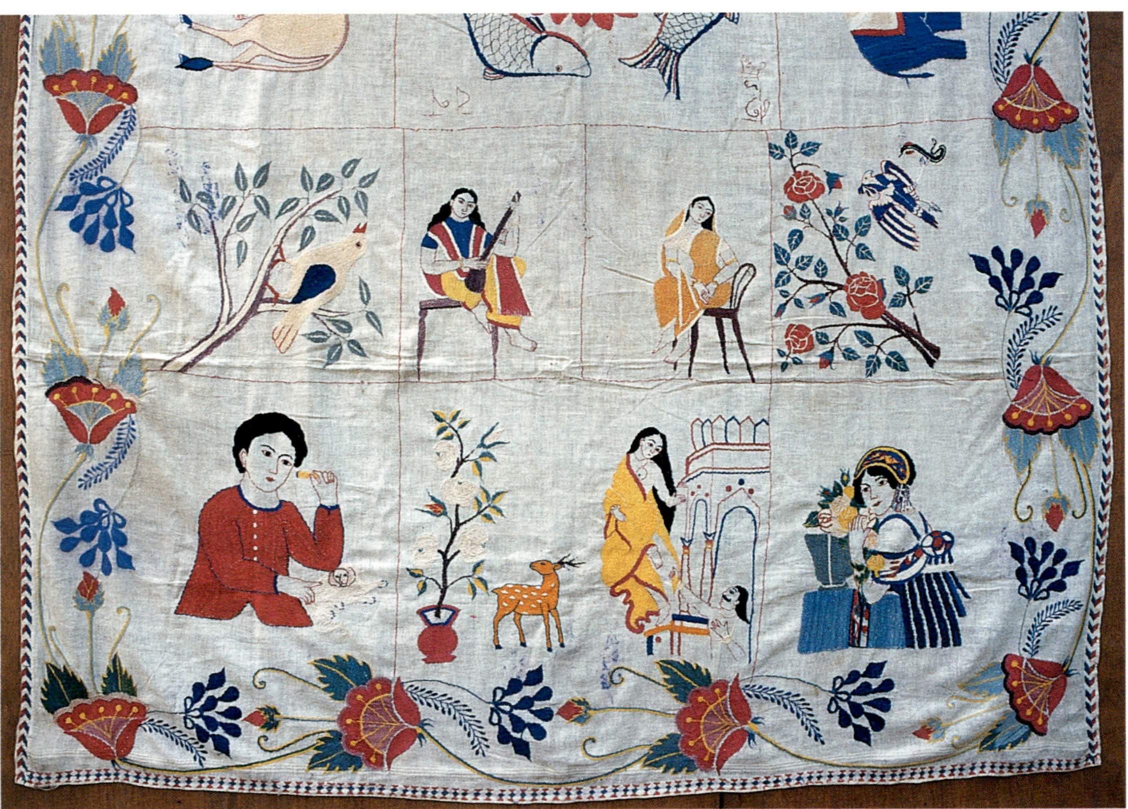

10
Detail from an embroidered *kantha*, with a unique jumble of images from Kalighat paintings, Ravi Varma's prints, as well as British textbooks and biscuit tins
Bengal, late 20th century
Cotton threads on quilted cotton ground
Collection: Jutta Jain-Neubauer
Photograph: J. Jain

the last quarter of the 20th century that modern art establishment artists of India began to respond to the bazaar aesthetics under the shadow of influences from the West – Robert Rauschenberg, Andy Warhol, and more recently Francesco Clemente.

The *kantha* embroiderers, the storyteller's scroll painters, as well as the bazaar artists were not only enchanted by the new visual experience provided by the glitzy images of the popular street culture of the time, full of transcultural quotes, but were open enough to bring them within the sphere of their art practice so as to widen their repertory of images and therefore the language of expression (figure 10).

As they juxtaposed their familiar motifs of lotus and fish medallion, peacock on a tree, woman milking a cow, an elephant or a horse rider, with new images of European playing cards, woman seated on a Victorian chair posing as if playing a sitar (sourced from photographic pictures), Ravi Varma's heroines (sourced from oleographs and postcards) (figure 11), Jesus and his lamb (sourced from "Happy Easter" cards), a European milkmaid holding freshly cut flowers (figure 12) and ears of wheat

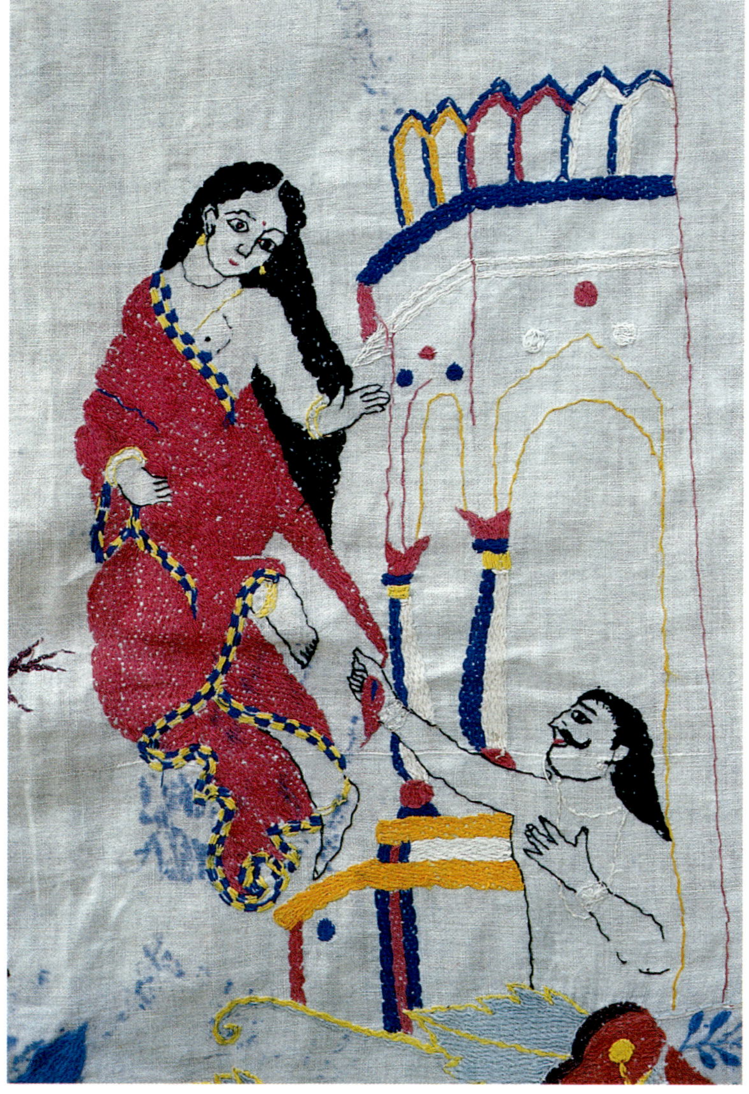

11
Detail from an embroidered *kantha*, depicting Urvashi, the nymph, deserting Pururavas, the king, derived from a Ravi Varma painting reproduced on postcards at the turn of the 19th century
Bengal, late 19th century
Cotton threads on quilted cotton ground
Collection: Jutta Jain-Neubauer
Photograph: J. Jain

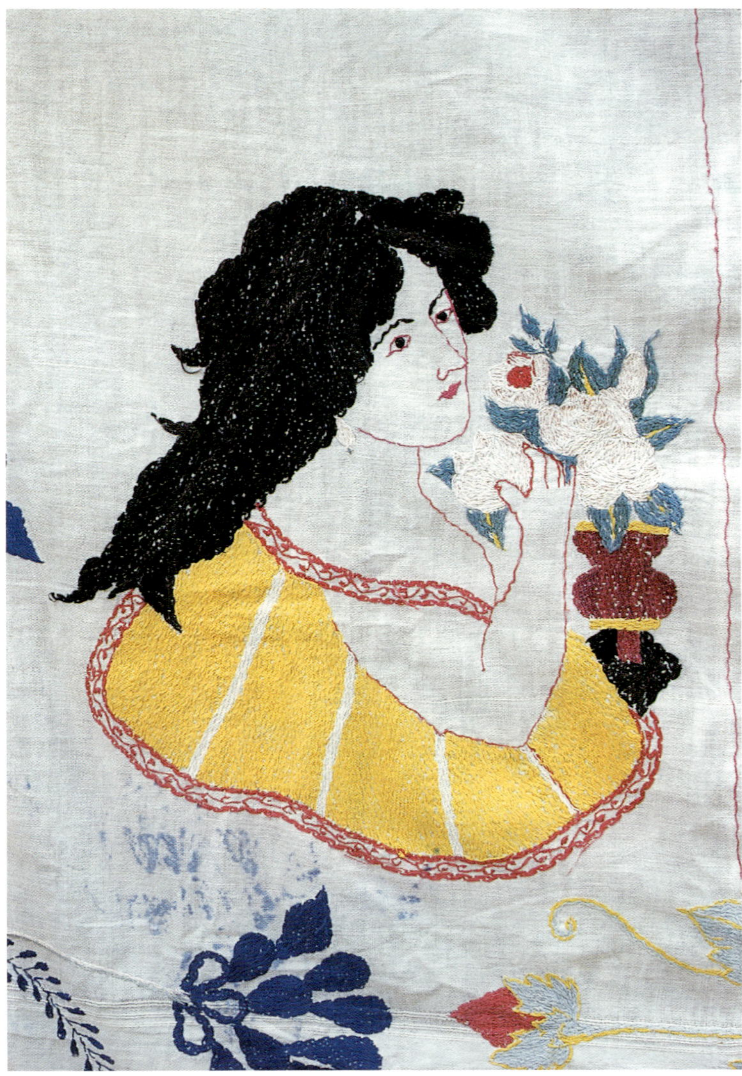

12
Detail from an embroidered *kantha*. British biscuit tins often showed images of farmer girls and milkmaids. One of these has inspired this *kantha*.
Bengal, late 19th century
Cotton threads on quilted cotton ground
Collection: Jutta Jain-Neubauer
Photograph: J. Jain

(sourced from British biscuit tins), Shiva cast in the image of a Madonna (sourced from Christian missionaries' house altar pictures), and a European boy with his pet dog, holding a whistle (sourced from British school textbooks), the *kantha* embroiderers reschematized tradition and modernity without fussing over a hierarchical order.

As the principles of Western art history began to set aesthetic criteria for indigenous cultural objects, irrespective of their inherent utilitarian objectives, through the new art establishments of the late 19th and early 20th centuries, comprising art schools, galleries, art criticism, and the market, the ethnographic object began to be aestheticized as "art". The makers of the cultural objects of everyday life – the artisans – were completely oblivious of the phenomenon of transfiguration of their smoking pipes, cultic images, and pots and pans into "art objects" brought about by the universal art establishment of the period. The artisans had no voice in the discourse that defined their creations; their space could always be invaded by establishment artists at will but they had no access to the formal art world which had assumed authority over setting aesthetic criteria for their expressions. The late Khatri Mammad Siddiq, a master handblock printer from Kutch, Gujarat once narrated to me how an American called "Roshandaan" had come to his workshop and made patterns on pieces of cloth with bicycle tyres dipped in a dye solution and how his rich hosts from Ahmadabad had asked him to put his signature on each of these pieces. Siddiq took pride in the fact that his own unique designs, colours, and neat printing served as *his* signature and his village clients all over Kutch recognized his fine work and appreciated it, and therefore could never understand why there was a need for "Roshandaan Sahib" to actually write his name on his "cycle-tyre prints". Siddiq's "Roshandaan Sahib" was the celebrated American artist Robert Rauschenberg who had done some experimental cloth printing in the early 1970s at the Kutch craftsman's workshop. The implications of the incident go far beyond the issue of style, but this discussion may be reserved for a future occasion.

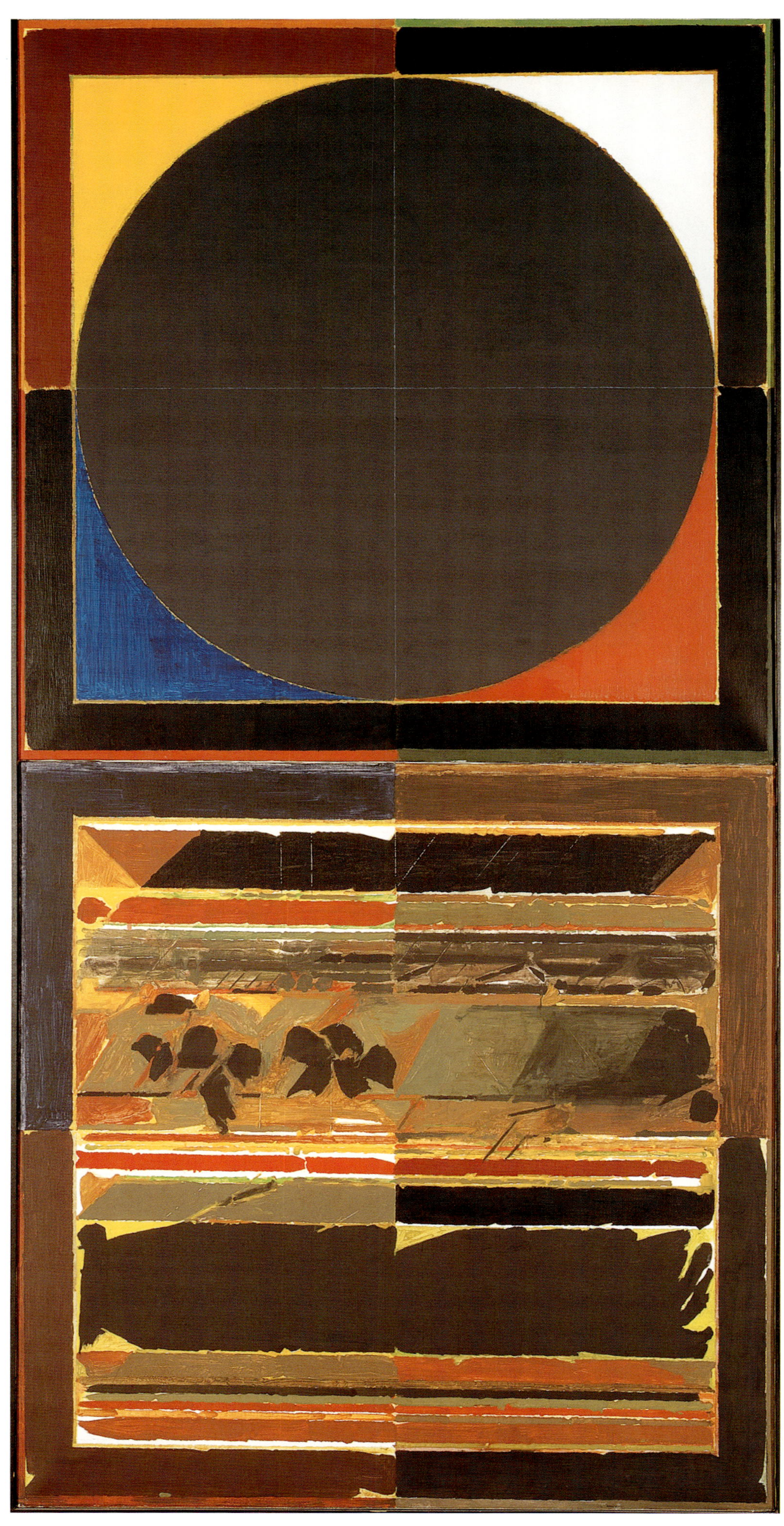

1
S.H. Raza
"Bindu la Terre", 1983
Signed and dated on back
Oil on canvas;
diptych: 159.4 x 80 cm
Herwitz Collection, Peabody
Essex Museum

Susan S. Bean

now, then, beyond

time in india's contemporary art

Conceptualizing time – its flow, cycles, and ages; origins, eternity; the future, the present moment – has been a central philosophical and theological matter for millennia. Concepts of time are a perennial focus of South Asian thought, deriving from a rich variety of sources – among them Hindu, Buddhist, Islamic, Christian, and more recently from modern science. In the Indian visual arts, representations of time and eternity are ubiquitous, for example in *kalachakra*s at Hindu temples, monumental tombs of Muslim saints and rulers, sculptures of Nataraja, and portrayals of seasons and musical modes in miniature painting.[1]

From the beginning of Indian art history in the 19th century, scholars have recognized the significance of concepts of time beyond the disciplinary concern with the temporal sequence of styles and schools. In 1947 pioneer art historian A.K. Coomaraswamy published a small book, *Time and Eternity,* in which he proposed that in the great religions – Buddhism, Hinduism, Islam, and Christianity – eternity resides in the present moment.[2] Though he drew no direct connection to his art-historical studies, the paramount place that time and eternity held in his thought is clearly articulated.

The enduring significance of time in the intellectual discourse of contemporary India, including the visual arts, is amply demonstrated by the 1996 volume published by Kapila Vatsyayan from an international conference held at the Indira Gandhi National Centre for the Arts in New Delhi. It encompasses a broad range of contributions on philosophy, theology, science, religion, and the arts.[3]

Time is uniquely positioned in contemporary art practice in India and elsewhere. Contemporary art is the only art designated indexically, by its inextricable connection to the ever shifting moment of its production. It is quintessentially a product of Now.[4] As a consequence contemporary art must always be on the move, always changing, innovating, differentiating. This is the basic modality of its production and in India differentiates it dramatically from most art of the past and traditional arts of the present which, whether religious or secular, were expected to remain close to their antecedents.

Almost paradoxically most contemporary art, though defined by the moment of its production, is created to transcend it, to defy the passage of time, to last for decades beyond the time of its creation, and to be renewed in encounters with a succession of viewers. Indeed the success of a work is often gauged by how well known it has become, by increased viewership, and in the marketplace by its rising value. A painting can reap no greater honour than to be recognized as a master work decades or centuries after its production. The work of some performance and installation artists is aimed precisely to upset and undermine these relationships by creating works that are inherently ephemeral.

While the time-situatedness of contemporary art applies to work created anywhere in the world, the temporal aspect of contemporary art in India is unusually rich because of the complexity and sophistication of co-present philosophical, theological, and scientific concepts. Time can be cyclical or linear, mythic or quotidian; eternity may be beyond or in the present moment; memory can bring the past into the present and the future can be anticipated and captured.

S.H. Raza, in his "Bindu" series, adroitly integrates concepts of time and creation with the aesthetics of modernism. In these compositions Raza works with a subject that is simultaneously eternal and cyclical, the source and end of all, immensely energetic and profoundly still, the *bindu*, "the seed-bearing potential of all life".[5] At the same time, the *bindu* is an abstract geometric form, a circle. Through this *bindu*/circle Raza explores an Indian cosmology of creation – being and becoming – and the core concerns of modernist painting: form and colour. In the diptych "Bindu la Terre", the upper section is a black *bindu*, the absence of all, the potential for everything, surrounded by the primary colours red, blue, and yellow, with all-encompassing white opposite (figure 1). The *bindu* is positioned over the lower section of the diptych, as a black sun over a landscape consisting of sharp contrasts of light and dark. Raza has given to modernism's preoccupation with colour and form a particular Indian content. For Raza the *bindu* offers "a visible form containing all the essential requirements of line, tone, colour, texture, and space".[6]

Both of these terrains, the cosmological and the aesthetic, transcend time, but the painting is also meant to have a heightened presence in the moment of viewing. It posits an interactive role for the viewer, an opportunity to experience creation and absorption and to sense the timeless in the present moment, perhaps paralleling the artist's own experience in the act of painting – preoccupied with colour and form, yet connecting with the ontogenic potential, and, quite possibly, a sense of creating the source of creation. The works of Raza from his "Bindu" series privilege the viewer and the artist by offering an immediate experience of the transcendent.

In his drive to create an Indian contemporary art, M.F. Husain has become a master of myth, not only portraying deities and episodes from the Mahabharata and Ramayana, but in projecting historical figures into the transcendent realm of the mythic. His "Gandhi", for example, shows his subject larger than life, wearing his signature loincloth and holding his staff, but with

2
M.F. Husain
"Gandhiji", 1972
Signed and dated lower right
Oil on canvas; 255.3 x 113 cm
Herwitz Collection, Peabody
Essex Museum

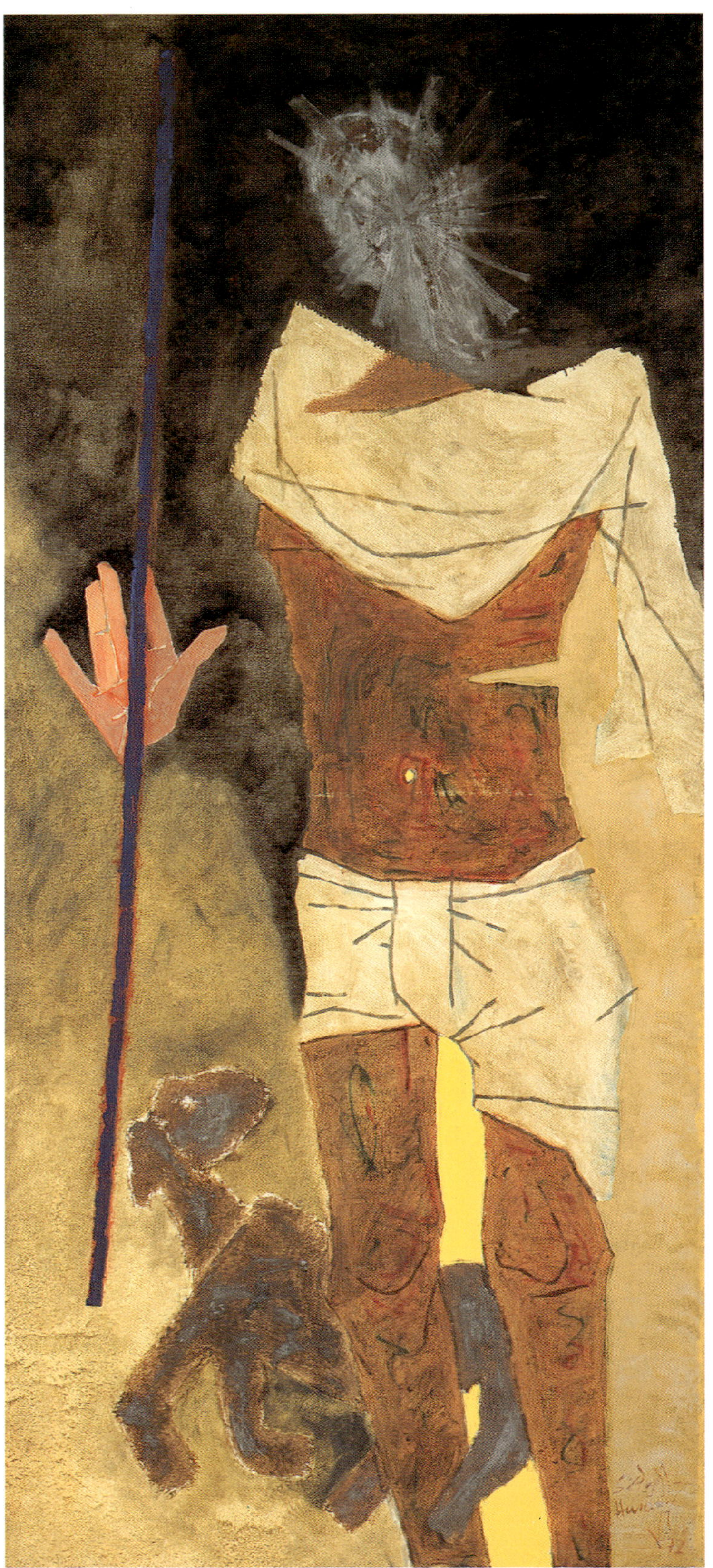

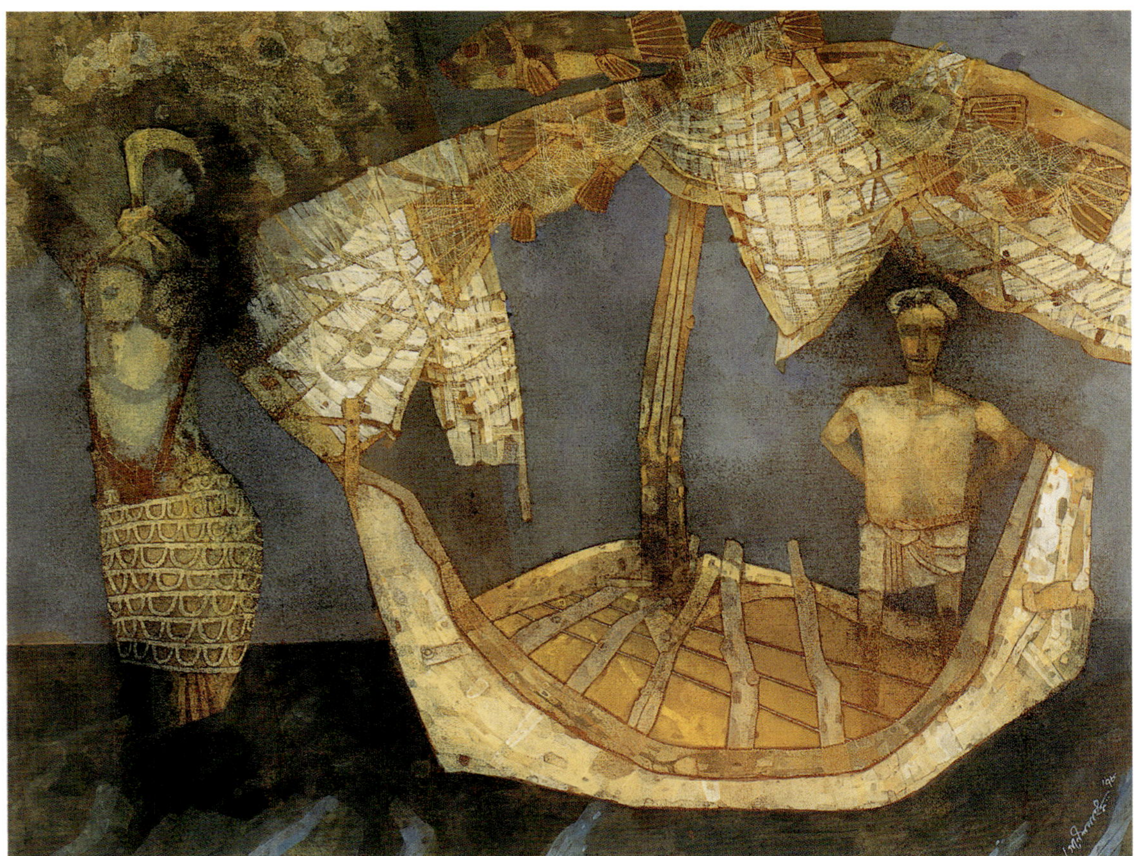

3
Ganesh Pyne
"The Net", 1978
Signed
Paint on canvas; 61.6 x 68.6 cm
Herwitz Collection, Peabody Essex Museum

a featureless haloed visage that conveys no individual identity. In this painting we are looking at a person, a saint, a demigod, who has surpassed history, whose significance is timeless (figure 2). A goat huddles at his feet – the leader with his flock; at the same time suggesting the Judeo-Christian-Islamic lamb of sacrifice and redemption which also appears in Husain's "Cyclonic Silence", where the artist focuses on a single victim, larger than life and without individuality, powerfully depicting the anguish of death and the promise of salvation.[7] His "Mother Teresa" series similarly uses her distinctive habit and her hands to effect a transformation of the historical to the mythic, the mortal to the eternal.

In contrast, Ganesh Pyne creates works that are profoundly local and interior, sometimes drawn from historical events, religious lore, or folktales. These are transformed and re-envisioned in his own idiom, which remains never quite fully accessible, retaining an aura of mystery. Whereas Husain and Raza's subjects and images are widely known, Pyne's work seems to belong to an interior universe, a zone apart from the shared realms of history, cosmology, and myth. In "The Net" a fisherman finds not only a net full of fish but a magical being – part woman, part fish, with a hook in place of a head – emerging from the water, like a mermaid or goddess (figure 3). The fantastic atmosphere is enhanced by the sparing use of colour – basically blues and browns, by the strongly articulated textures, and by the pervasive darkness. The visual allure of Pyne's image draws viewers to penetrate his private realm of time and space, a foray that correspondingly calls up viewers' own imaginaries to supply interpretations. Timeless zones are cosmological, aesthetic, and mythic; they can be private too.

In "Town" and "Over Bridge" Sudhir Patwardhan represents quotidian time, capturing moments of ongoing transactions, as if these were a single frame in a film. Actors are caught and revealed carrying on their lives (figures 4 and 5). Without being naturalistic, his portrayals are realistic; the viewer is clearly directed to see the scene as real, as something that has or could have happened, a moment rescued from the ordinary passage of time, re-presented on canvas. The two paintings share this quality but diverge in other ways. "Town" is a calm, affectionate, almost loving depiction by an observer. Both the artist and the viewer are outsiders to the scene and see from a distance people stopped in the midst of going about their daily tasks. In the foreground a builder consults with his client on the construction of a house. Nearby two labourers go on with their work; another, a woman, takes a break. In the background the life of the town is momentarily halted and we see a man carrying his child on a bicycle, a dog, people walking in the streets, a man asleep in the back of a lorry.

"Over Bridge" has a very different emotional tone – urgent and mysterious. The central figure on the bridge appears distraught. One of the two men walking with his arm around the other looks back with deep concern. In the background a town sprawls over a hillside; its people caught on canvas in the midst of going about their routines. On the bridge something disturbing has transpired, maybe Sudhir Patwardhan knows what it is, but maybe he doesn't either; viewers are simply left to wonder. Is it fear that the distraught man might jump? Has bad news passed between them? The man looking back is distracted from the comradeship of his companion, who is himself oblivious to the

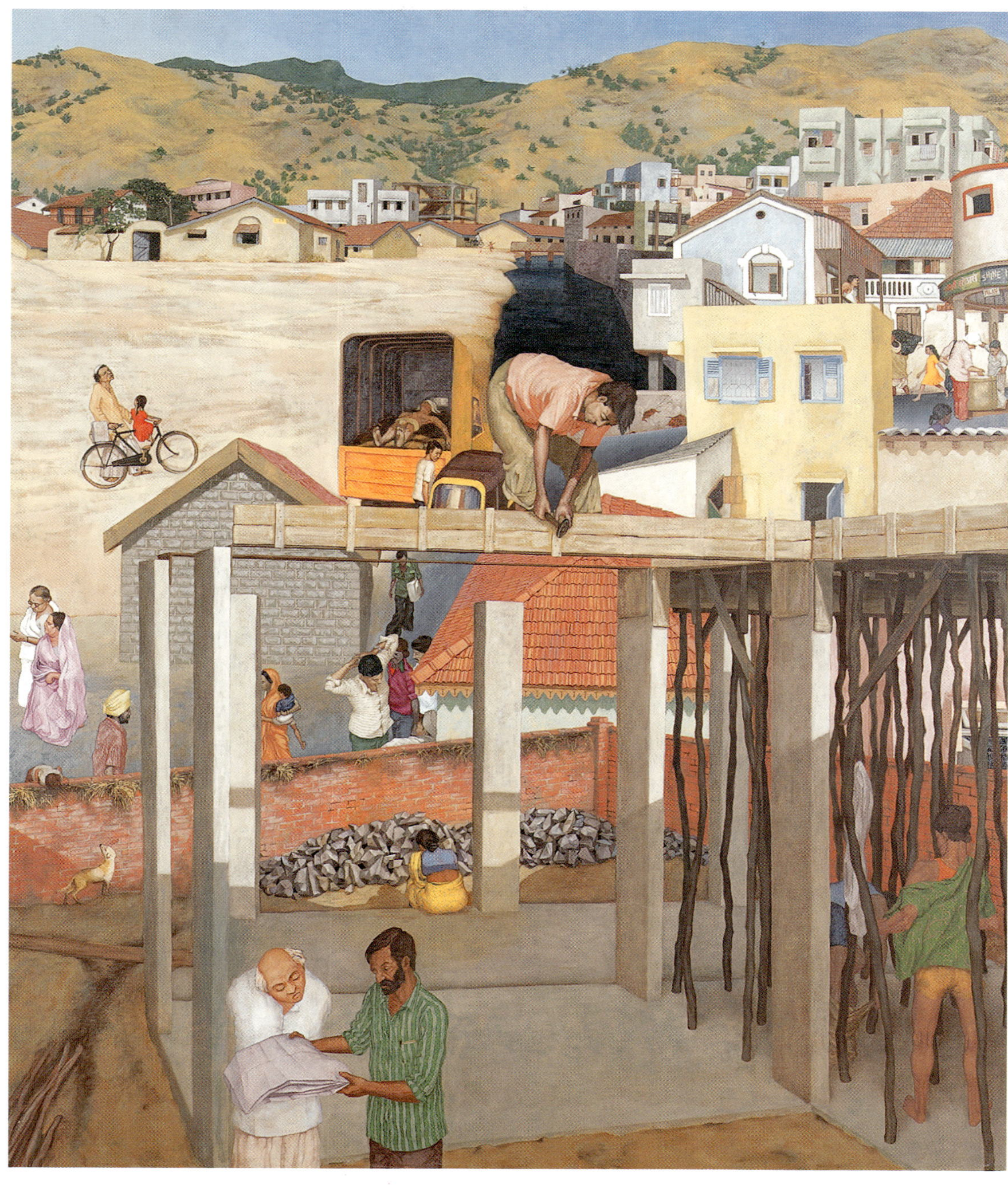

4
Sudhir Patwardhan
"Town", 1984
Signed
Oil on canvas; 182.4 x 153 cm
Herwitz Collection, Peabody Essex Museum

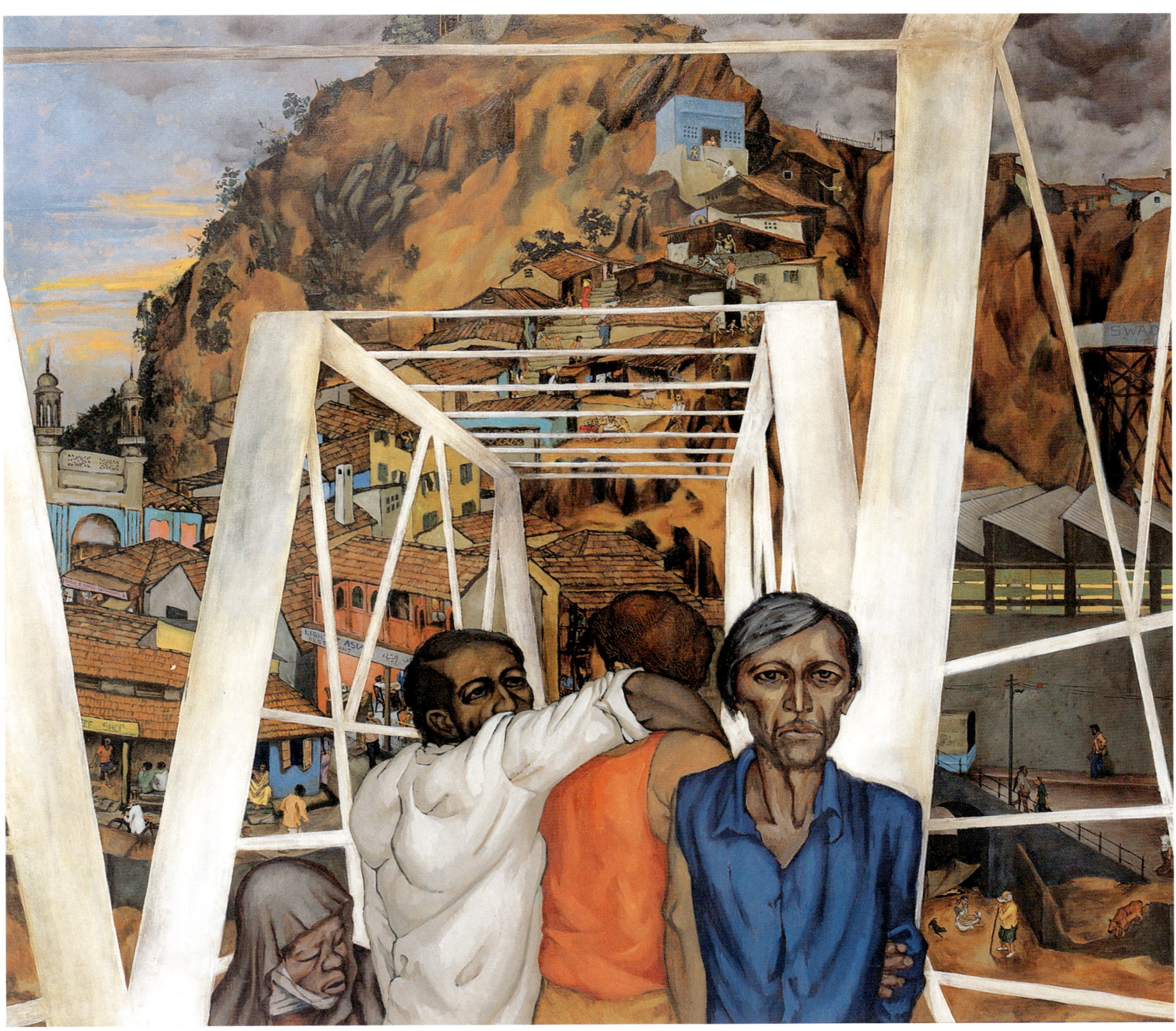

5
Sudhir Patwardhan
"Over Bridge", 1981
Signed
Oil on canvas; 125.7 x 140.9 cm
Herwitz Collection, Peabody Essex Museum

encounter. A fleeting, dangerous moment in strangers' lives is revealed, leaving us in the moment of viewing to feel our own anxieties and vague forebodings. Patwardhan's paintings delve into the ongoing procession of daily life, like photographs capturing moments on canvas, making these happenings transcend their occurrence, memorializing them to be revisited and reconsidered.

Gieve Patel's "Two Men with Handcart", similarly brings the viewer to a scene that has been extracted from the flow of life (figure 6). Both the artist and the viewer are outsiders, distant observers of an interaction whose substance they cannot know. Two men stand beside a handcart talking, perhaps resting from hauling a heavy load. Behind them is the wall of a dilapidated, humble, brick, tile-roofed building. Beyond in the distance loom the skyscrapers of a modern city. The scene is flattened giving primacy to the canvas, deploying buildings as abstract shapes. Colour, the play of light and shadow, and the textures of architectural surfaces are as visually prominent as the narrative itself. The men and their handcart are dwarfed by the metropolis around them. Though the viewer never loses the impression of looking at an encounter in progress – labourers engaged in conversation – the manner of its painting makes the scene an abstraction and renders the atmosphere stronger

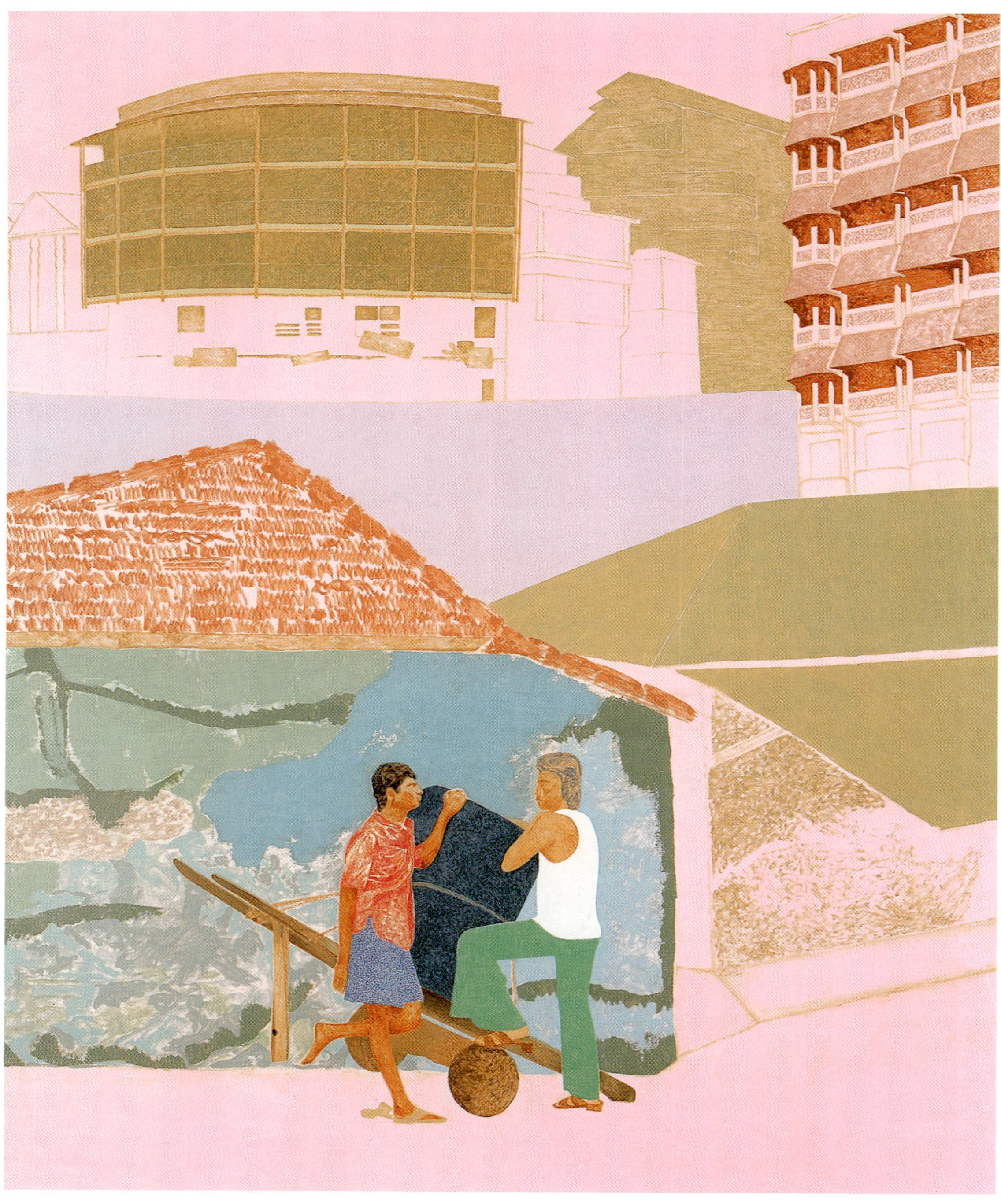

6
Gieve Patel
"Two Men with Handcart", 1979
Signed
Oil on canvas; 176.5 x 144.8 cm
Herwitz Collection, Peabody Essex Museum

than the event unfolding. The labourers and their handcart, juxtaposed with the high-rise buildings of a modern city, fix on the paradoxical condition of life in urban India – the simultaneity of simple and sophisticated technologies, the co-presence of the past in the present.

Laxma Goud, too, paints everyday scenes; his are peopled with strong village men and women, often with Goud's ubiquitous goats. While these works may represent a moment extracted from the flow, they are not strongly narrative, and read not as freeze-frames from an encounter, but as nostalgic scenes of village life (figure 7). The nostalgia is that of a city dweller for the ancestral place left behind (a locale of great ambivalence for many urbanites in India), but it is also a temporal nostalgia, a romantic longing, for a bucolic simplicity and purity that exists no more, if it ever really did. Such images are only one kind of engagement with time in Goud's work which is remarkably varied and playful in its approaches. He has also experimented, for example, with cyclical time in a series of far more edgy works. Adapting the modern guise of recycling, he constructs reassembled people – stitched, clamped, and pinned together from previously extant elements (figure 8).

7
Laxma Goud
Untitled, 1983
Signed, lower right
Etching and aquatint on paper; 68.6 x 52.1 cm
Herwitz Collection, Peabody Essex Museum

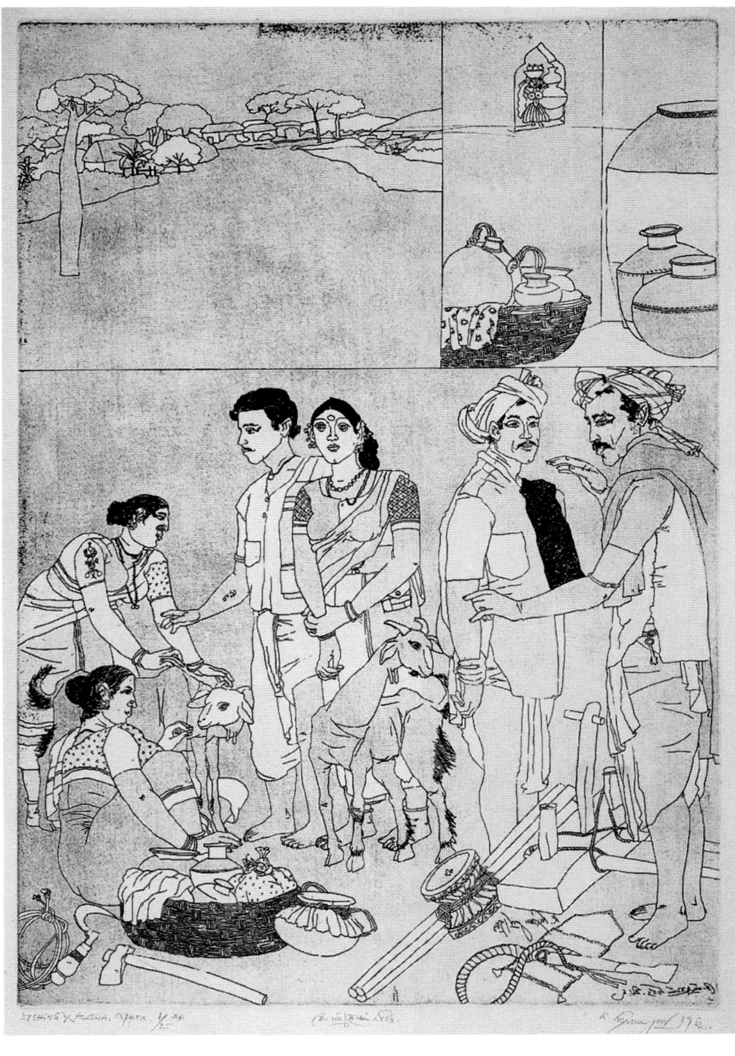

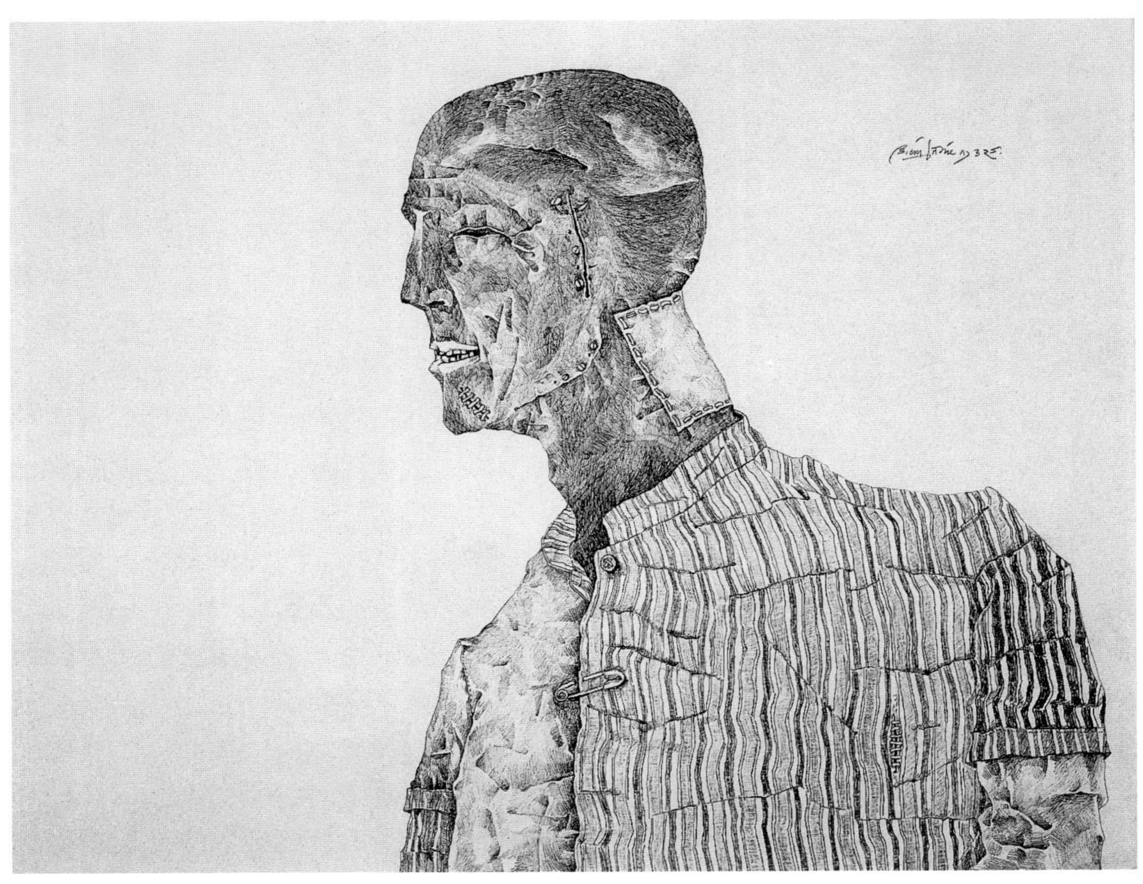

8
Laxma Goud
Untitled, 1978–80
Signed and dated, upper right
Pencil and coloured pencil on paper; 27.9 x 35.6 cm
Herwitz Collection, Peabody Essex Museum

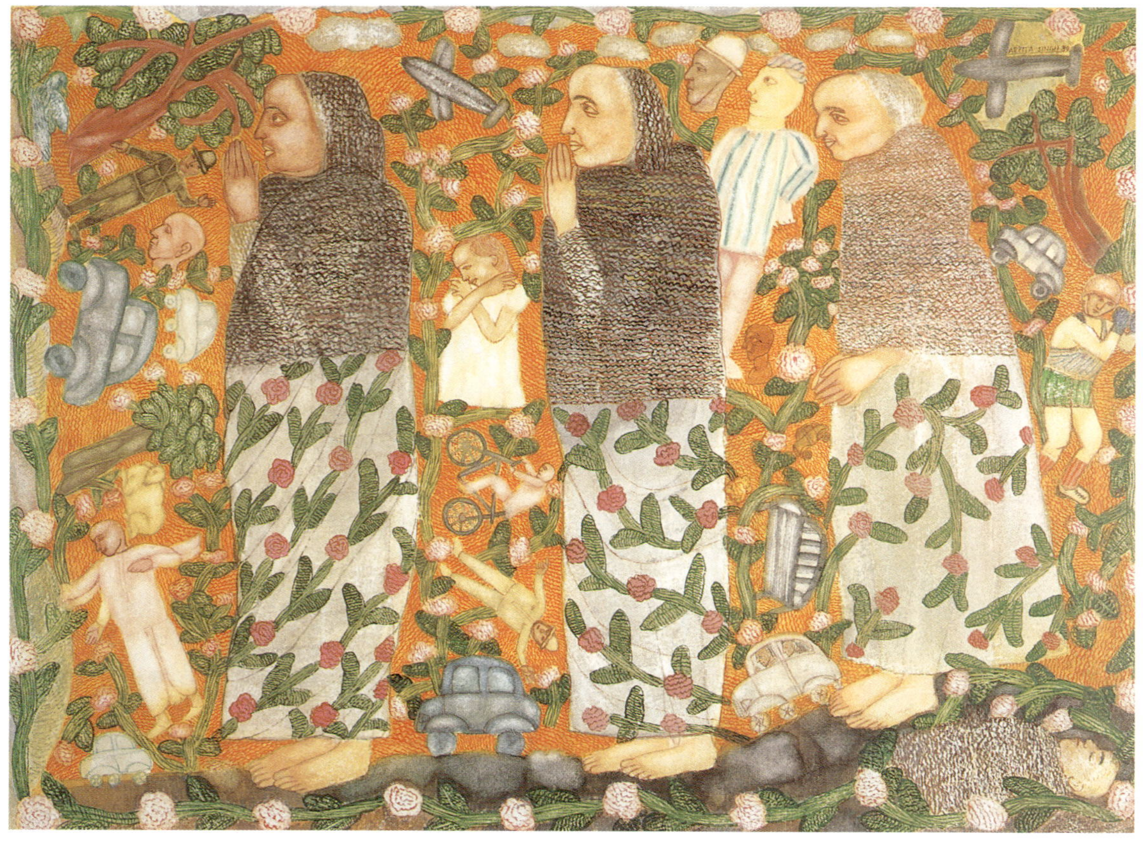

9
Arpita Singh
"The Worshippers", 1989
Signed
Watercolour on paper;
48.3 x 35.6 cm
Herwitz Collection, Peabody Essex Museum

The subjects in many of Arpita Singh's paintings are plucked from different time zones. She uses pictorial space as a region where disparate things, separated in time and space can be made co-present. The perimeters of the pictures are often delineated and decorated with flowers in a folkloric way, reminiscent of Bengal scroll paintings, while flowers, birds, people, vehicles, guns recur, recombined in ways that recall the embroidered quilts (*kantha*) of Bengal. In "The Worshippers" these strategies are combined to enhance the three women in the foreground, the worshippers, who are praying, probably to assure the wellbeing of their family (figure 9). In the background, scattered among the flowers are bicycles, automobiles, aircraft, a boxer, men, children, dead bodies, an angel. If the women are the strong, still centre of family and intimacy, the planes and autos are the comings and goings, the inevitability and implicit danger of separation and reunion, and the inescapability of death. Arpita Singh makes the past and the faraway co-present, in the anticipation of separation, by travel or death. Writing this article just weeks after the September 11, 2001 assault on the World Trade Centre in New York City in which commercial aircraft were used as deadly missiles, some of Arpita Singh's paintings have a new immediacy, a prescient reflection of intimate worlds in danger, a sense of inescapable menace. Each new viewing brings fresh eyes and different contexts with which a painting is seen and creates new meanings.

The special status of the moment of viewing has been known and privileged in India for centuries. Artists at Rajput courts, for example, painting *nayika*s in postures of waiting and longing, conveyed not just their desire for union, for wholeness, with the beloved, with god; they also captured time standing still. In anticipating, yearning, time is slowed to halting and the present moment is powerfully extended. When the viewer in the act of viewing encounters a painting whose subject is herself (or himself) deeply experiencing the present moment, the painting and the viewing experience are augmented reflexively. The potency of bringing together the moment of viewing with the depiction of a strongly heightened present – waiting, longing, anticipating, yearning – is a source of the enduring popularity of this subject. Contemporary artists treat it in fresh ways.

In "Waiting for His Beloved", Jogen Chowdhury's subject holds a flower, an explicit reference to court painting. But, the lover is a paunchy, dhoti-clad, middle-aged man, looking old-fashioned in his Congressman's cap (and opening the possibility for political readings) (figure 10). Time stands still as he holds his pitiful little flower yearning for the appearance of his love. Even the most ridiculous of us long for love; we viewers long with him, for him, and for ourselves in an eternity of the present moment. Laxma Goud's untitled watercolour shows a woman seated at home gazing into the distance (figure 11). She has paused in the midst of some work, perhaps cleaning the pot she holds in her hands. She sits, maybe she is waiting, for a child, husband, lover, sister, perhaps

10
Jogen Chowdhury
"Waiting for His Beloved", 1979
Signed
Crayon and ink on paper;
55.2 x 55.2 cm
Herwitz Collection, Peabody Essex Museum

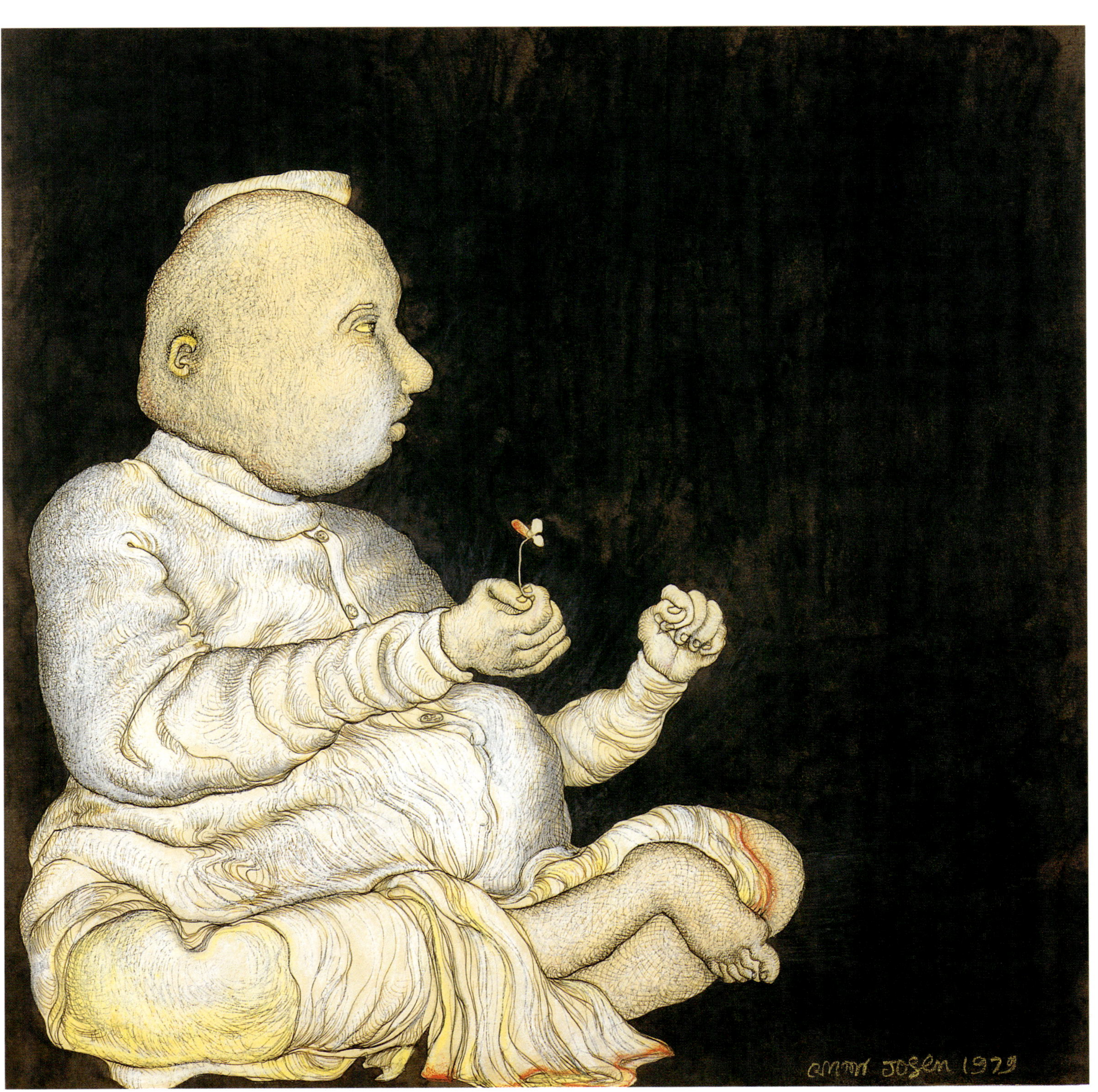

she is lost in reverie. Only the expanse of the moment is clear, the slowing of time.

The solitary woman in Gieve Patel's painting is bathed in the golden light of morning, encircled by the shapes and textures of the buildings around her (figure 12). She waits, perhaps for other members of her family, certainly for the other guests to fill the empty chairs and for some event to begin. No facial expression or gesture guides us to her feelings. Perhaps she is lost in thought, in her memories, barely thinking of the others who will surely soon arrive. The stillness of the scene, its luminosity, heightens the sense of the enduring moment.

In his depiction of a seated artisan with his tools nearby, and a steaming pot on a small fire, Ganesh Pyne achieves a parallel intensification of a moment. The artisan has stopped his work, propped his chin on his hand, and is gazing to the side, possibly in the expectation of someone's arrival, or just resting, perhaps daydreaming (figure 13). The scene, as in the related works by Jogen Chowdhury, Gieve Patel, and Laxma Goud, conveys a halt in the flow of quotidian time, a deep experience of Now. Each of

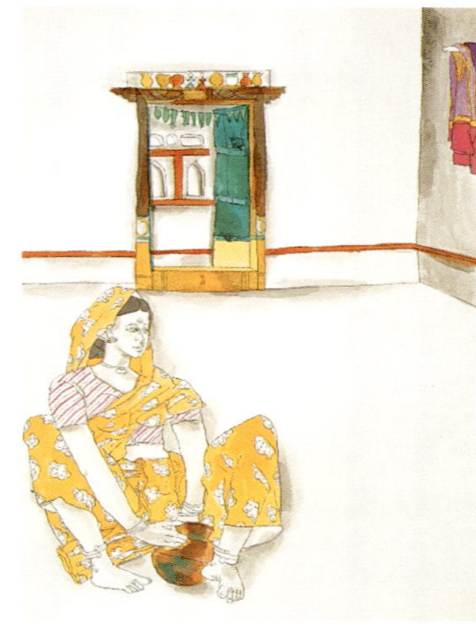

11
Laxma Goud
Untitled, not dated
Not signed
Watercolour and ink on paper;
38.1 x 27.9 cm
Herwitz Collection, Peabody
Essex Museum

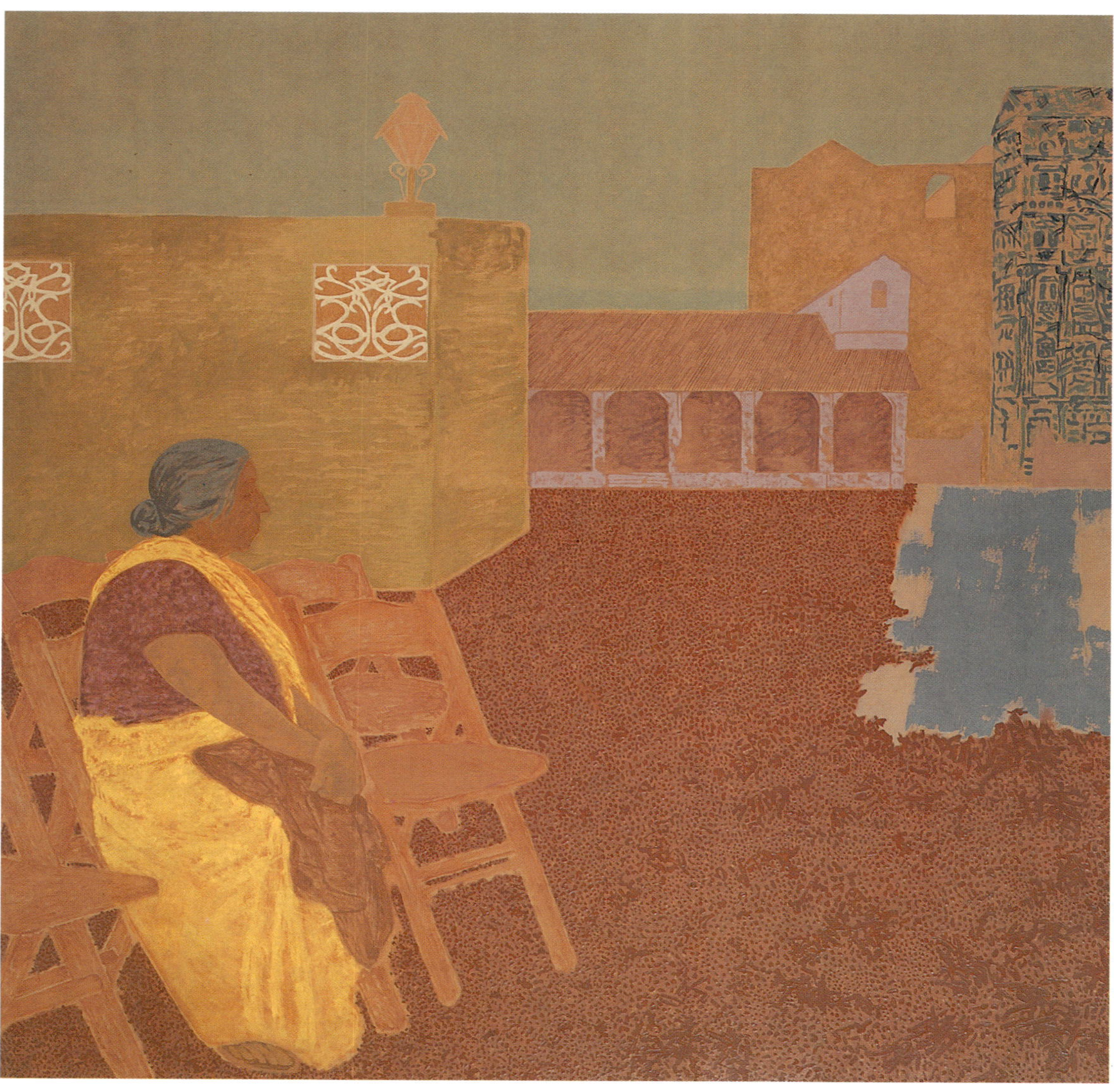

12
Gieve Patel
"Early Guest", 1981
Signed
Paint on canvas;
136.5 x 136.9 cm
Herwitz Collection, Peabody
Essex Museum

these paintings portrays a moment in which the passage of time is suspended by an experience of waiting, anticipating, reverie. The paintings effect the primacy of the present moment.

Time has a special place in contemporary art with its ever-changing claims to timeliness. In India where concepts of time have been lively topics for millennia, it is not surprising that contemporary art practice deploys especially rich and various approaches. The temporal nuances that artists give to their subjects are intricate and varied. Time is linear, cyclical, fast, slow, or standing still; it is a moment in the past, a memory (the past in the present), or a prescience (the future in the present); it is quotidian or transcendent, as in myth, fantasy, or nostalgia; or it reaches beyond to timeless eternities. The time dimension in India's contemporary art is fertile territory for extended consideration and especially for amplifying the dialogue between works and their viewers.

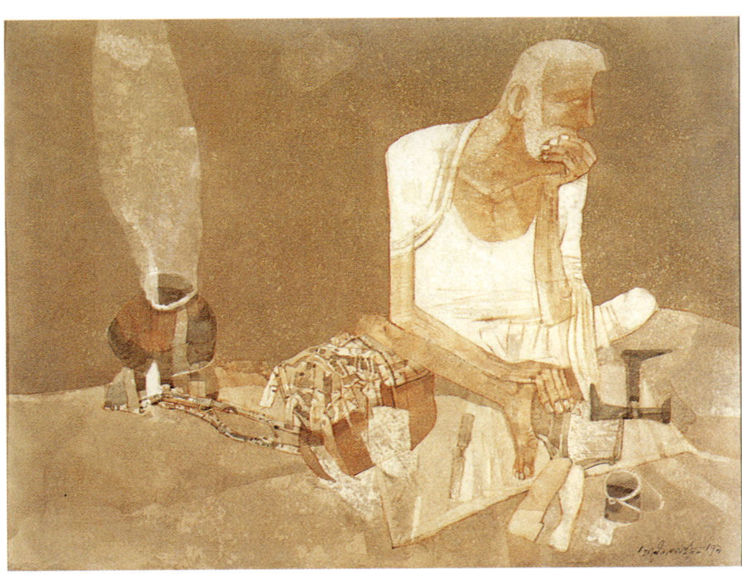

13
Ganesh Pyne
Untitled, 1979
Signed
Watercolour and ink on paper;
26.7 x 34.3 cm
Herwitz Collection, Peabody Essex Museum

NOTES

1. The discussion that follows is an extension of the catalogue essay written for the 1999 exhibition *Timeless Visions: Contemporary Art of India from the Chester and Davida Herwitz Collection* at the Peabody Essex Museum, Salem, Massachusetts. The exhibition's 53 works were selected from a collection, which at the time comprised more than 4,000 items, to focus on timeless, transcendent themes, hoping that such universal issues as the nature of masculinity and femininity, of divinity and creation, of colour and form, would make the works more accessible to a new audience. An invitation from Yashodhara Dalmia, guest editor of this issue of *Marg* encouraging me to take this exploration further was a welcome opportunity. Some of the works I consider were shown in *Timeless Visions;* all are from the Herwitz Collection, the core of which, roughly 900 works, was gifted to the Peabody Essex Museum in 2000.

2. A.K. Coomaraswamy, *Time and Eternity*, Ascona, Switzerland, Artibus Asiae, 1947.

3. Kapila Vatsyayan, ed., *Concepts of Time, Ancient and Modern*, New Delhi, Indira Gandhi National Centre for the Arts, 1996.

4. Perhaps this was once the case with modern art in the West, but no longer, as the scope of the modern has come to be anchored to the century ending in the 1970s.

5. Quoted in Geeti Sen, *Raza*, New Delhi, Lalit Kala Akademi, 1990.

6. Ibid.

7. See Susan Bean, *Timeless Visions: Contemporary Art of India from the Chester and Davida Herwitz Collection,* Salem, MA, Peabody Essex Museum, 1999, p. 43.

1
Anita Dube
"Silence (Blood Wedding)", 1997
Bone, lace, velvet, beads, glass, thread
A thirteen-piece sculpture installation at Sakshi Gallery, Mumbai

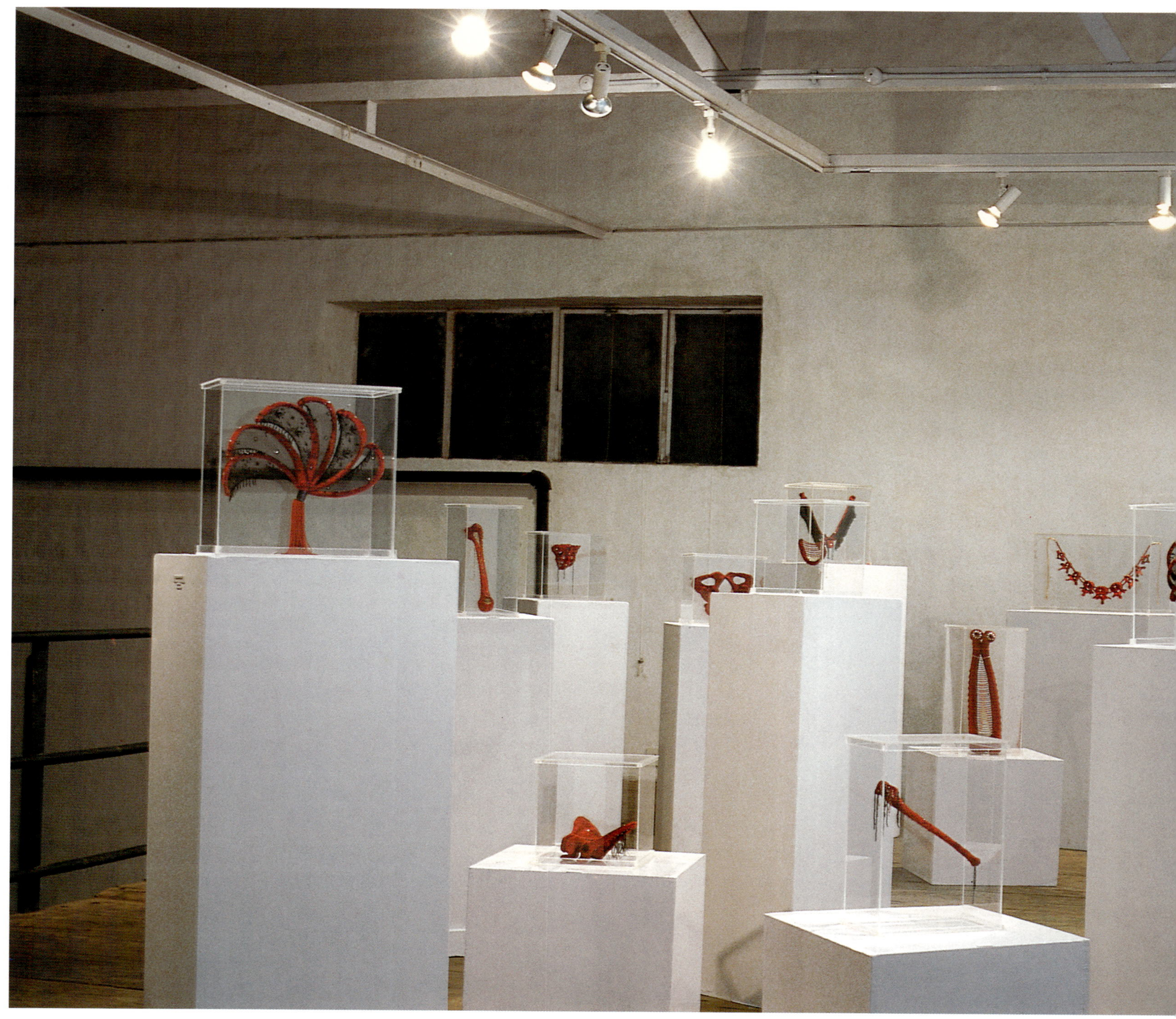

Gayatri Sinha

feminism and women artists in india

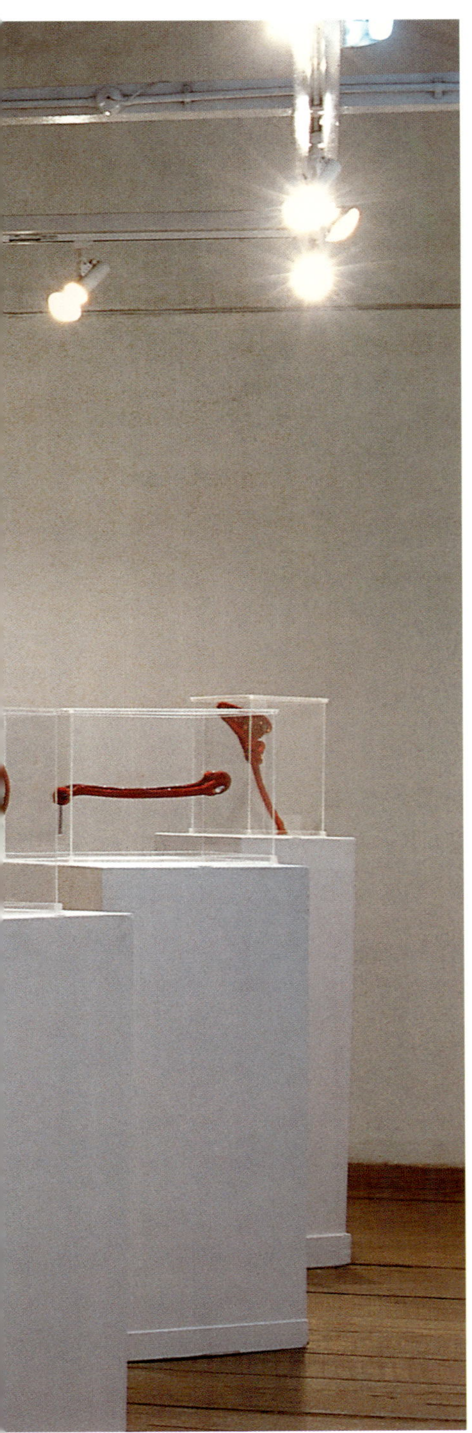

Women's participation and engagement in art became suddenly conspicuous during the decade of feminism, the 1970s. But even as women rode the crest of visibility in art, their work did not echo prevailing feminist polemic. In the intervening three decades, in an ironic inversion, even as feminism in India gasps and flounders for new directions, women's art seems to acquire a sinew of intention and expression.

An interconnection between the work of the artists under consideration in this article is their treatment of the feminine form, its selection as a site for resolution, cathexis, and debate. As a formal entity that locates borders and defines boundaries, the feminine body is rendered a zone of contest and celebration.

The Body and Its Parts: Anita Dube, Sheba Chhachhi

In an area of still nascent debates, the body and the objectification of its parts has become an urgent concern. Anita Dube and Sheba Chhachhi (both born in 1958) have in strikingly different ways developed an aesthetic argument around body parts. In the words of Anita Dube, "My work is essentially a part of my subjectivity that can be transferred and connected through time, across structures. It records my mind-body continuum, like a sieve of physis...." Dube's strategy in recent times has been to dismantle and reconstruct parts of the human frame, thus validating each body part. In "Silence (Blood Wedding)" (1997), an assemblage of thirteen sculptural pieces, she pushes the idea of beauty to contain the macabre (figure 1).

In this work, a human skeleton is taken apart, and the bones exquisitely stitched in red velvet, decorated with sequins and displayed in transparent cases. In this way Dube acknowledges the twin inheritance from her parents: her father, a medical doctor, her mother's skill in craft traditions. Precious, bejewelled in appearance, macabre in the retrieval and the fetishization of the skeleton (particularly in the Hindu context of disposal through burning and the "uncleanness" of bones), the sculpture thrives on the exquisite tension between eros and thanatos. Like Julia Kristeva, to whom she refers, Dube constructs a language that embodies the contradiction of life and death, being and non-being, good and evil. In the bejewelled beauty of the object, the contrary realization of hair, torn flesh, or exposed flesh on bones is contained.

In the fragmented body picked clean, the idea of the feminine sensuous nestling up to the deathly draws upon these dualities. A student of history and art criticism (M.S. University, Baroda), she worked on the theme of "desire-fear" in a sculpture bearing the same title (1992). Dube pushes this idea further in her work "From the Theatre of Sade" in which different forms are encased in black velvet. Inspired by the Marquis de Sade and the thin line between pain and pleasure, of sexual collaboration and dominance, the work treats the feminine form obliquely. Velvet, with its irresistible tactility and its invitation to touch and stroke, becomes in her hands a symbol of duality, a palimpsest on which are inscribed the subtle gradations of emotion, from fear to desire. Dube also herein successfully develops the theme of the glib, smooth packaging of violence.

It is also important to realize Dube's fine craftsmanship in which the handiwork of cutting, stitching, and embroidering – all aspects receding in art practice – are privileged. In another more direct work Dube created a wall sculpture of the iconic eye ("Intimations of Mortality", 1997). The kind of eye that is embellished in temple deities, the *chakshudaan*, that invests "life" in the deity, here becomes an organic entity. The eye mounted on the wall like a swarm of bees urges the question of the gaze and its peculiarly intimate transaction. What immediately comes to mind is the kind of transaction sanctioned through the gaze in formal worship, as in say the *Devi Kavach* (*Durga Saptashati*) in which praise of the goddess is rewarded by protection, through the icon's all-seeing eye. Even as Dube's installation "profanes" the religious associations of the iconic eye, the formal aspect of the sculpture explores the possibilities of negative wall space, particularly the meeting of the walls at three points. Dube returns to the iconic eye in her work "River/ Disease" (2000).

In Sheba Chhachhi who also objectifies the female form, the issues are sharply etched in feminist politics and sexuality. Through the 1980s Chhachhi worked with Lifetools, a design unit, and recorded the burgeoning feminist movement. As the stereotype of the engaged feminist became more entrenched Chhachhi turned to photography, sculpture, and installation. Through the '90s Chhachhi's work has moved with a bipolar intensity, in her freewheeling use of materials and focus on feminist concerns. In her installation she questions the tyranny of the linear narrative to collapse historical representations of women.

From her photo archive of women activists Chhachhi worked towards creating imagined or constructed histories. In the photo installation "Seven Lives and a Dream" (1997) Chhachhi worked with seven activists to construct through a photo narrative their sources of pleasure and fulfilment. In several cases for the women,

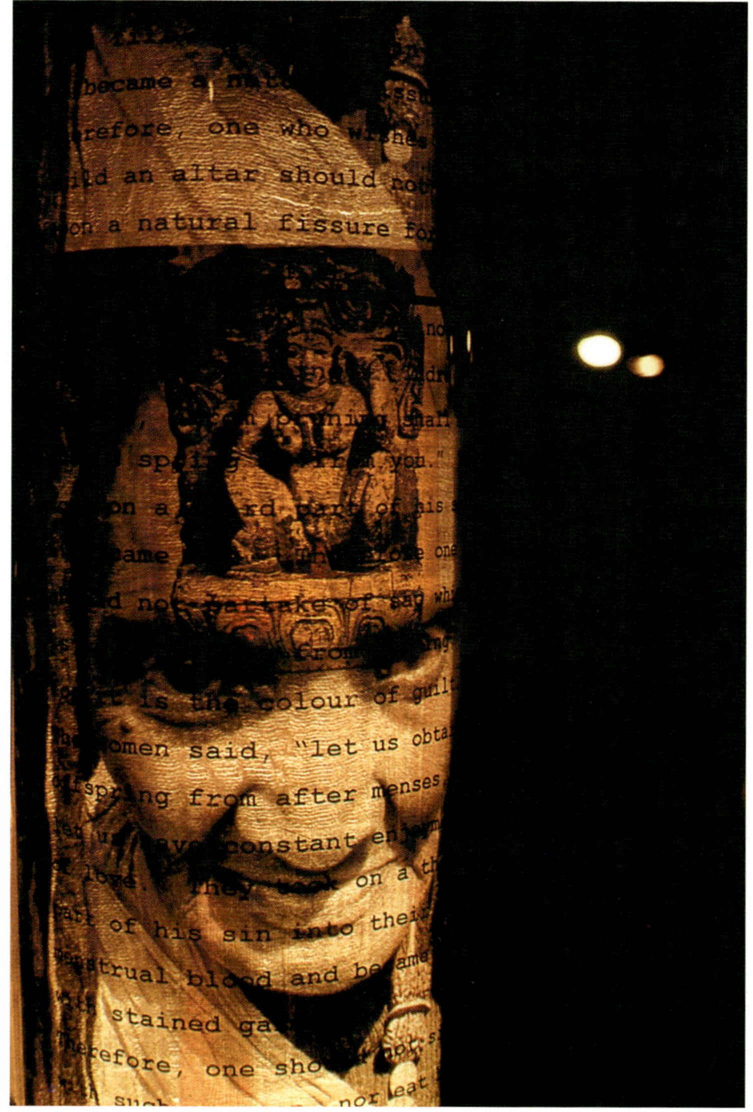

2
Sheba Chhachhi
"Raktpushp I" (detail), 1997
Polycarbon sheet,
black and white photos (bromides
and film positives), text on
acrylic, red cord, miscellaneous
objects, light

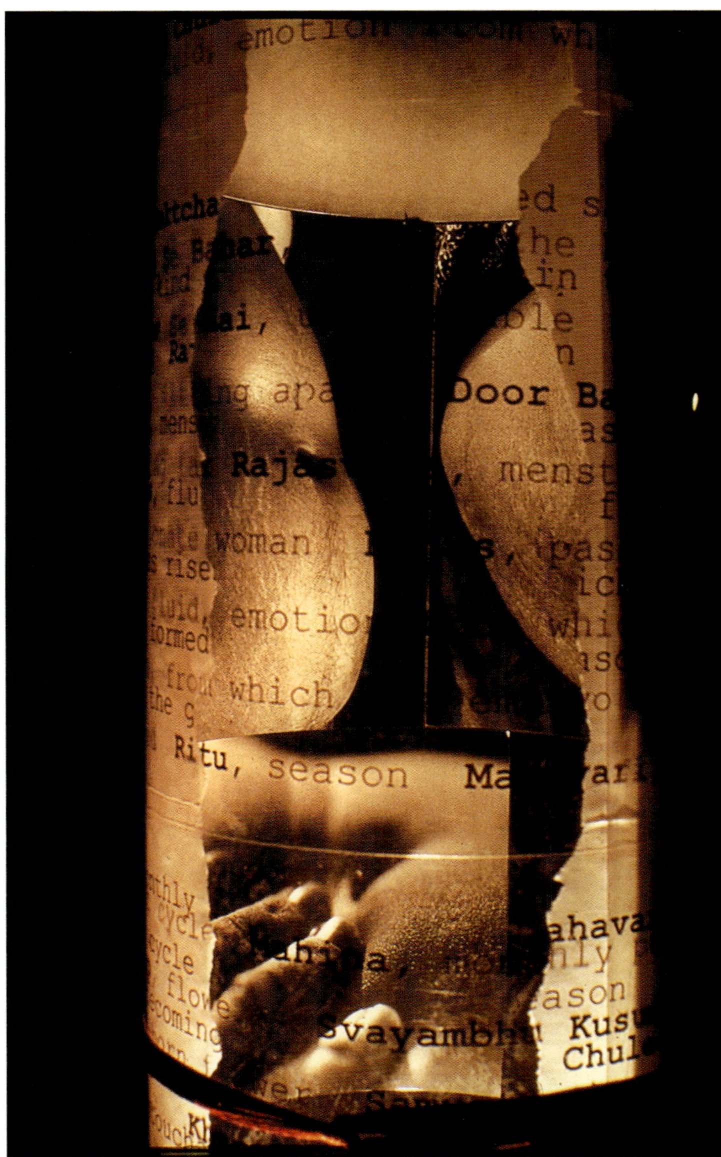

3
Sheba Chhachhi
"Raktpushp I" (detail), 1997

pleasure or the "dream" lay in redressal in law or even in markers of middle class desires, like stainless steel utensils.

In sharp contrast was Chhachhi's highly romanticized installation on the Hindi film tragic heroine, Meena Kumari, titled "A Box of Shards" (1994). The viewer was guided through a black satin labyrinthine passage, strewn with shards of smashed glass, with large images of Meena Kumari, hauntingly beautiful in the film *Pakeezah* (1972), and then finally led up to multiple toy televisions creating visual distortions of love scenes from her films. Meena Kumari in her screen roles played the perfect woman – the virginal *bhabhi*, the good *bahu*, the idealized *pativrata* – in sharp contrast to the reality of her tragic life – her lovers, her alcoholism, the bloated body still playing the young debutante or fledgling hospital nurse. Here Chhachhi foregrounds the famous tragedienne, and the coming together of the screen persona with the woman/poet to critique the idealization of the beautiful feminine as victim:

> Meena Kumari the star
> from four to forty, ninety-one movies, ninety-one roles
> Sighing crying dying
> for love

In later works, Chhachhi returns again and again to the body as a site for multiple debates. Her preferred method is to inscribe text on transparent surfaces, to allow a work to be read or constructed through layers of text that evoke suggestion and memory. In the installations the layering allows for reading into attitudes surrounding women's health as well as women in the margins of society. Thus in "Wild Mothers Part I and II" (1993 and 1994) she draws a connection between women ascetics through history, and provokes questions around their representation, the power and sexuality inherent in their poetry, the modernity and individualism of their positions. Through a provocative conjunction of text, image, and vaginal sculptural forms, she also challenges the notion of asceticism as divested of sexuality. "Raktpushp I" (1997) which evolves images of vaginal icons is constructed through images and text that question the Indian and the post-colonial treatment of menstruation in India (figures 2 and 3).

Chhachhi clearly takes huge risks in that she gives feminist polemics a formal language in art. She works around classic feminist issues of social justice, women's health, and sexuality, and what she describes as "women on the fringes". Like Dube however she sidesteps or ignores overt interpersonal relational questions, which become critical in the larger picture drawn by other women artists.

Body – Procreative, Retributive: Arpita Singh, Navjot Altaf

In Arpita Singh (b. 1937) the treatment of the feminine ranges from the overwhelmingly protective to an arch mockery. Arpita as an artist tantalizes because her tools are instruments of subversion and disguise. In her hands a favoured genre of the 1980s was the portrait-like figure, which attained a mysterious alchemy of the real and the fantastical. In the paintings of this period there are several figures, usually women, in recognizable portrait stance, as in her paintings of Ayesha Kidwai, a friend of her daughter's. Ayesha and her family, through family bereavements, weddings, communal clashes, become a part of the narrative of Arpita's paintings (figure 4) . Comparisons between her choice of elements and miniature painting and the Nathdvara school have been made. However in Arpita Singh the elements themselves transgress bonds of the safe, the normal. Thus flowers extend from a decorative device on the borders across the canvas, like potentially threatening

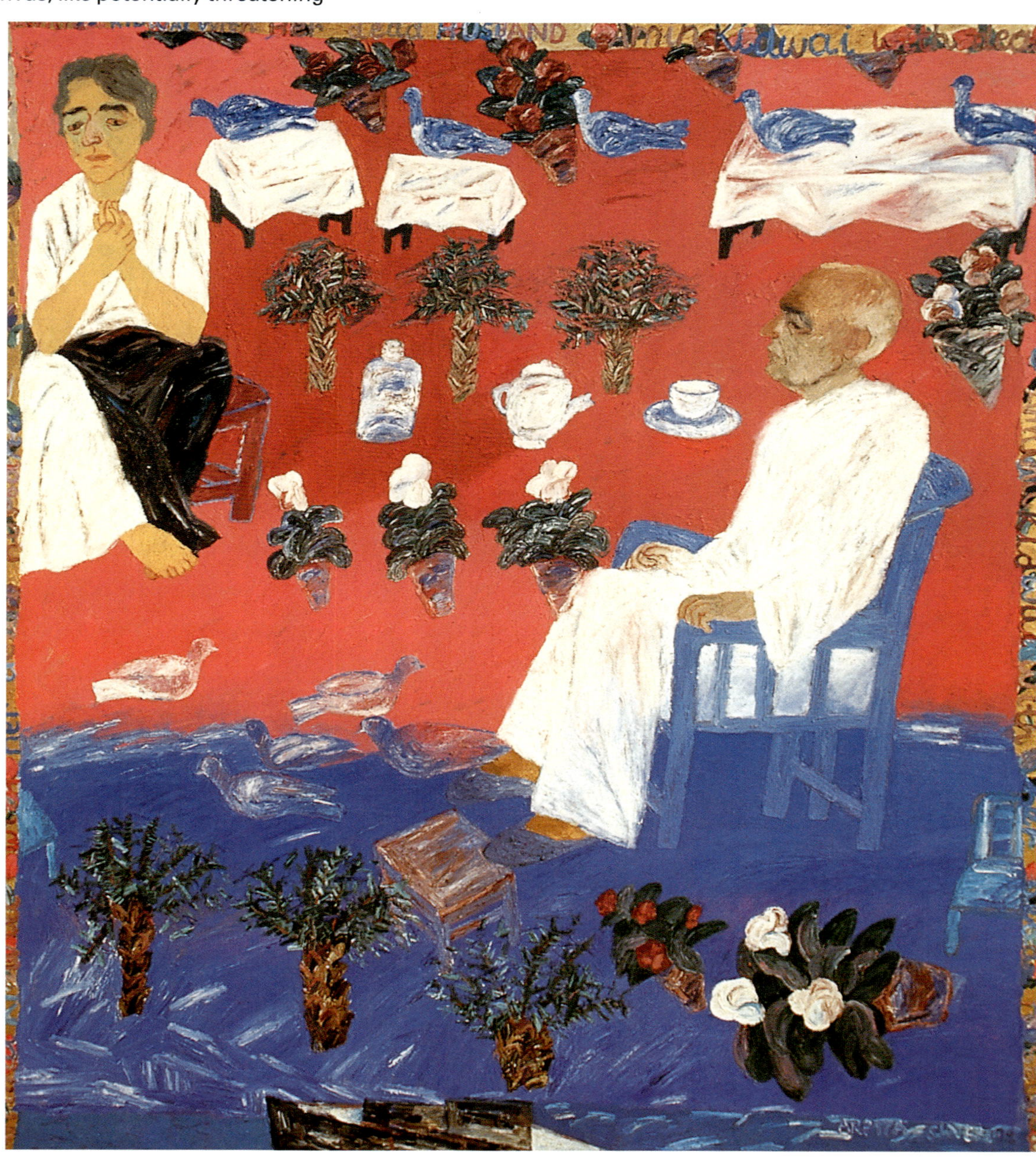

4
Arpita Singh
"Munna Kidwai and her Dead Husband", 1992
Oil and acrylic on canvas;
173 x 157 cm
Collection: Dr Mahesh Chandra

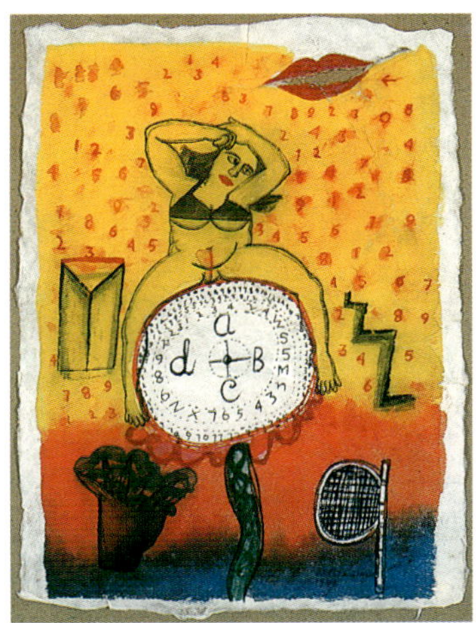

5
Arpita Singh
"Feminine Fable", 1996
Watercolour on handmade paper;
29 x 21 cm

hornets over the central figure. In the series of paintings on the Kidwai family, guns, armed men, corpses all enter the frame, and are caught up in a weblike spread of foliage. This involves, in the Freudian sense, transference from the figure to the decorative patterning in the frame. If an analogy with the Indian *rasa* theory may be drawn, then the *sthayi bhava* (fixed emotion) of the central figures does not change but the *vibhava*s (fluid elements) that heighten our perception of the enactment are fully exploited. It is in the tension between the apparent calm and normalcy of the central figures and the chaos of minor narratives all around them that Arpita Singh becomes a sharp commentator on the urban Indian miasma.

Singh has also evolved images that challenge conventional representations of women in art (figure 5). The fact that she uses devices from miniature painting but subverts the notion of the *nayika* (heroine) makes her images doubly ironic. In "Child Bride" (1985) the open hair and awkward nude stance compel the viewer to engage almost with a sense of voyeuristic shame in the young girl's vulnerability. Singh largely bypasses issues of sexuality surrounding the young woman to dwell on the middle-aged nude who becomes participant and spectator in her own exposition. "Figures around the Table" (1993) is a telling example, and it serves in sharp reversal of the erotic titillation of say Manet's "Picnic in the Garden". The erotic tension in Manet's work hinges on the contrast between the nude woman and the fully clothed men. In Singh, the same elements of the meal and the fully clothed men are employed. However, with her head shaven, the pendulous breasted nude figure – denied the marks of feminine beauty – sharply contradicts and exposes the expectation of titillation.

Where Singh does use the nude with an overt optimism is in the role of the procreative. Several images of mother cradling daughter evoke the picture of monumental strength reminiscent of Paula Modersohn-Becker's maternal figure. The essential image is of the earth mother, pushing powerfully to the edges of the frame, cradling an infant, or a miniaturized woman. Singh emphasizes that knowledge, indeed life, transmits from mother to daughter; as such she exalts this relationship in her paintings of her daughter, her mother, their extreme vulnerability and heightened perception of threat. "My Mother" (1993), of an elderly woman stepping out with her shopping bag on a street of chaos and carnage is the apotheosis of the artist's inherent sympathy and fear.

From the affirmation and anxiety of this period Arpita Singh enters a phase of a wry randy inversion of the idea of feminine beauty. Typically in her series of oil paintings and watercolours of the 1980s, sits a Lakshmi trope on a lotus emerging from a pond. This image comes obliquely from the large number of calendar Devis of Indian popular art. (Singh has worked on variations of this theme as in "Devi in the Marketplace", or a revolver-wielding "Durga".) Middle-aged, prominently red-lipped, wearing the kind of bra strung out for sale in New Delhi's Lajpat Nagar, the figure gains the ultimate subversion – by forcing the question of beauty and desire, she turns the viewer's gaze upon itself. The lotus, which opens up into a clock – or the calendar, a device that she has used frequently – signifies the feminine biological clock. The tenderness of middle-aged desire in her earlier series of paintings has been replaced by a tart cynicism, an in-your-face inversion of lust. There is also a realization that the cynicism of these pictures comes in the wake of exhausted earnestness, and marks thereby the loss of hope and optimism.

In Navjot (b. 1949) the issue of women is an extension of her work as a political activist. From the urban context of middle-class Mumbai to tribal Bastar (in Chhatisgarh), she uses an archetypal feminine, to posit concerns of womanhood and self expression. The introspection of the series of paintings, "Me Myself" (1978), and the three series of 1986–87 titled "Confrontations", "Process of

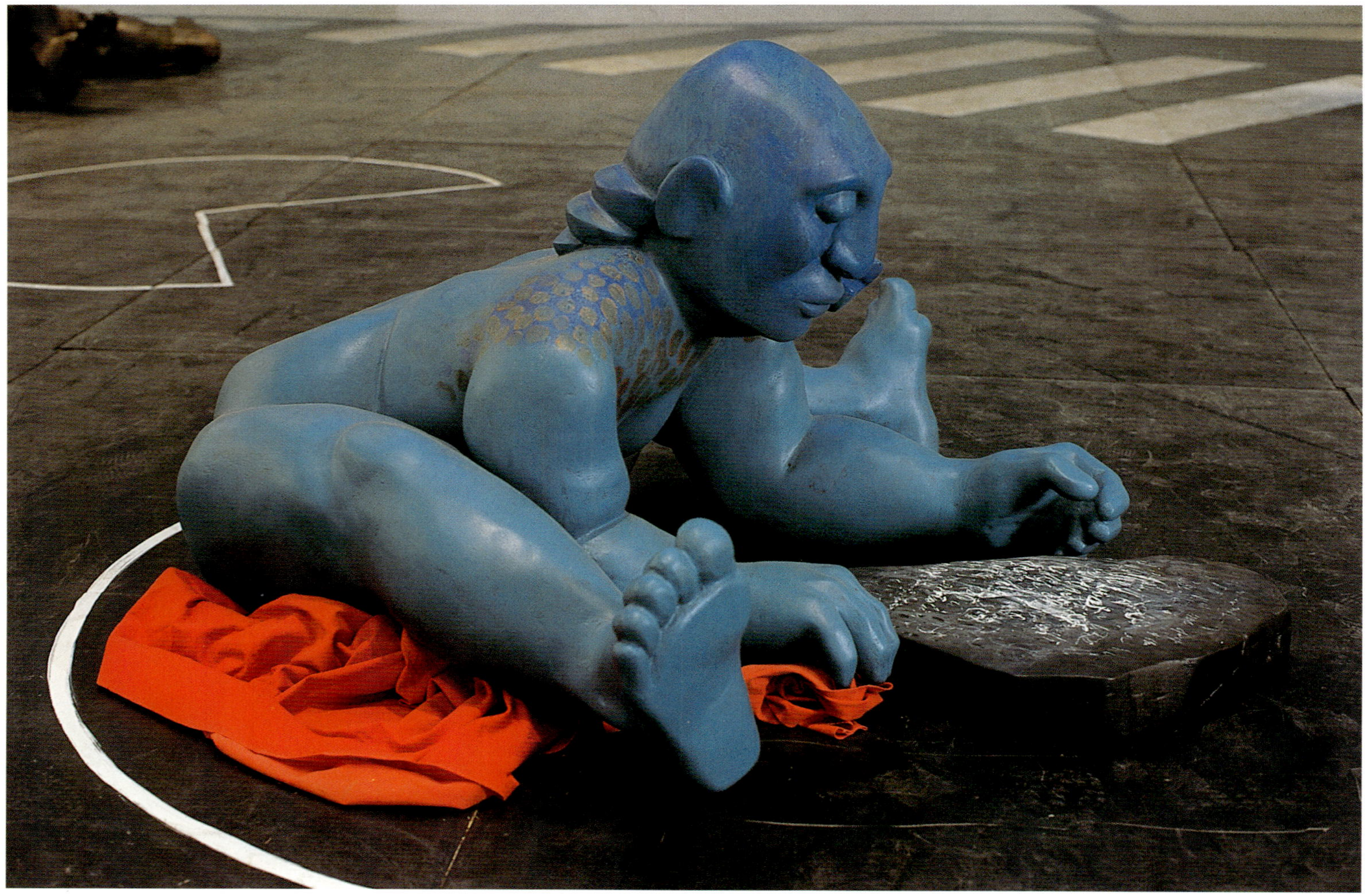

6
Navjot Altaf
"Yes, I Want to Read", 1995
Painted wood sculpture in
the "Images Redrawn" series

Self-Analysis", and "Actress" centred her concern on the psychological state of the female subject. In the last decade the engagement with a heroic feminism (rather than a feminist heroism) has lent her work its urgent monumentality, and power of graphic statement (figure 6).

Navjot's engagement with tribal art, specifically wooden sculpture, is ideal for the kind of archetype she creates in "Palani's Daughters", or "I have No Fate Lines – Thank God". Palani, a village woman who murdered her seventh infant daughter since she could not bear the burden of any more daughters, is the inspiration behind this powerful piece. Like Arpita Singh, Nilima Sheikh, and Arpana Caur, Navjot emphasizes the regenerative aspect of femininity, by making Palani's daughters like vaginas/seeds, spilled on the floor. More recently, working with craftspersons in Kondagaon, Bastar district, she has strived to imbue her "sculptures with an iconic power as they interrogate the existing power structure". Effectively, she seizes the place of the tragic-heroic in her sculptures as in the large multimedia installation "Modes of Parallel Practice: Ways of World Making".[1] In these Navjot dignifies the earthiness of the female form, drawing on the concept of Maulimata, a *virangana* (a woman who takes recourse to militancy for a good cause) of the area, who defended her people and is immortalized on elaborately carved wooden poles. Like Aditi, the primal mother, her open-legged, fecund body stance reveals her strong procreative ability. In "Whitening the White of the White" she exalts the dignity of labour, reflecting on the kinship not only of women but also of kinds of art practice, of an unbroken interface between art/craft, rural/urban, and high/low art.

The Body as Polemic: Nalini Malani, Rummana Hussain

Nalini Malani (b. 1946) positions herself consciously as a Third World artist, even as she challenges structures of race, gender, and class. As she states, "The skin is our boundary, it doesn't allow people to flow into each other." The woman's point of view is foregrounded – subjective, yet potential zone of contest, even as she argues for a recognition of ourselves as "bisexual human beings", whose concerns perhaps transcend gender.

Malani's work has progressed from painting on different surfaces to multidimensional video installation and performance as in "Medeaprojekt" with the actor Alaknanda Samarth,[2] to collaborations for stage performance as with director Anuradha Kapur in Bertolt Brecht's *The Job*. She has also expanded the possibility of the painted surface, as in her work in a cargo container in Denmark (she painted inside the container). Through the 1970s Malani's woman-centred focus has grown in a funnel-like progression, from a darker labyrinthine subjectivity to issues of global and particularly Third World concern. Any retrospective of Nalini Malani would in fact trace a genealogy of the feminine, of her frequent recourse to literature or theatre or history to create the (feminine) character as an allegory of our times, to interrogate existing patterns of patriarchy.

7
Nalini Malani
From the "Mutant" series, 1998

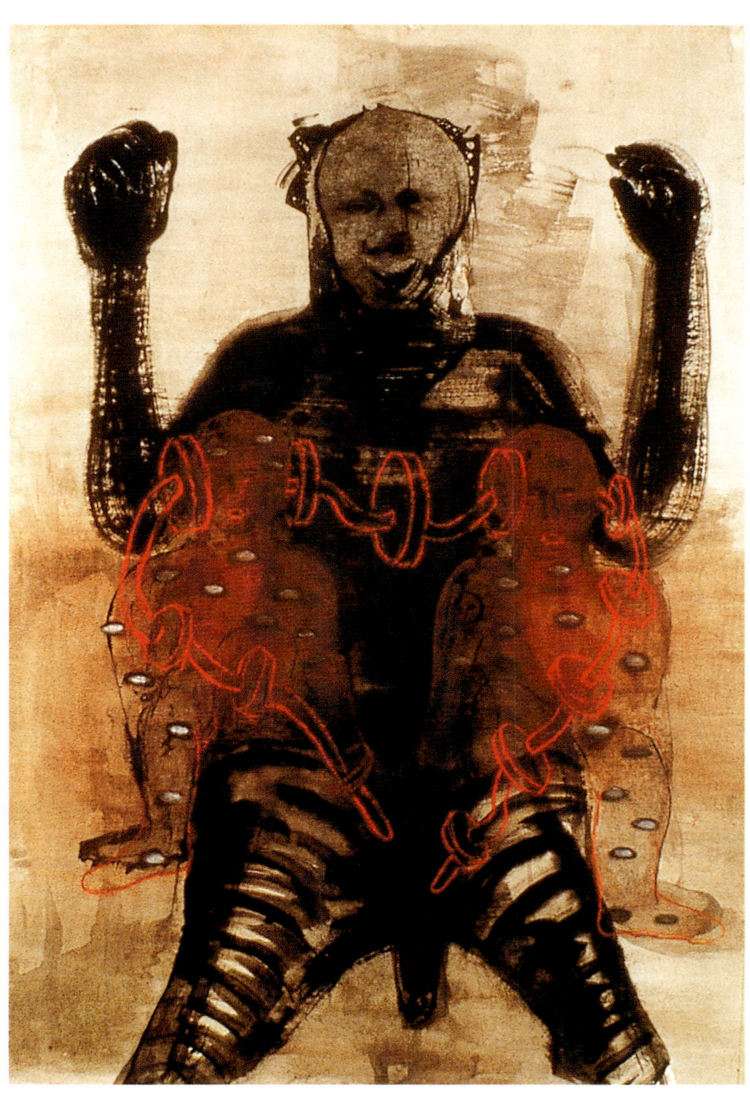

Malani's two paintings "Homage to Artemesia" and "Rethinking Raja Ravi Varma" establish her claim to the twin artistic lineage of the Indian-Asian tradition on the one hand and classic-modern European on the other. Within this frame, she has continually presented the figure under physical-sexual-psychological duress. This twin inheritance affords her a rich fount of stylistic possibilities. Thus in her painted books *The Degas Suite* she "enters" the tantalizing zone of the Parisian brothel, to build narratives of conjecture and suggestion around the lives of its inmates. What she achieves here, in the palimpsest or overlay of form within form and form over form, is repeated in her small works on paper of the late 1990s, in which the eye moves from one female body to another, in attitudes of embrace, closure, a gestalt of support.

Malani's political concerns have been expressed through distinct phases in her work: *Medeaprojekt* (1993), based on the play by Heiner Mueller proffered in Malani's work a fresh reading of the relationship between the colonizer and the colonized, in Jason's sexually exploitative relation with Medea through which the larger questions of gender and economic exploitation, notions of strength and weakness are mediated. From "Lohar Chawl", her series of hieroglyph-like figures that labour anonymously on the streets of Bombay, to her painting of nuked mutants – rendered grotesque by exposure to environmental poisons – Malani demonstrates her place as a concerned world citizen (figure 7).

In short, she develops a language in art that will straddle social change, history, myth, the subjective and the general, sexuality; or the gamut of human experience in social exegesis.[3] Malani's work, especially her theatre-based projects have the dramatic, climactic quality of a hundred violins balanced by the contrapuntal individualism of a soloist – her protagonist. In this sense, she is closer to the spirit of drama, of a montage of effects, especially a central figure before a background of historical or social complexity. That the figures as painted on a surface are rendered with a certain translucence allows layers within layers of statement/narrative to be collapsed in a single frame. Malani also uses the language of paint to integrate and define her choices. As she said in an interview, "In my work I will pull in Benodebehari Mukherjee – Sia Kalam and Kalighat and just in the line of it will be its history."[4]

What is significant in her work is that over the years the actors and their concerns have changed: the individual in her private identity (see her paintings of women, "Sleeping Figure I to IV" of the 1970s) has become the individual in a global conflict of interests. Malani, through a defined discourse in fact locates her artistic self firmly within the realm of the social/political; individual anxieties tick only beneath the surface of an articulated ideology. Within this layering and overlap Malani, with an unusual beauty, still asserts the heroism of the human being.

In Rummana Hussain (1953–99) gender justice and the post-colonial woman in a patriarchal majoritarian society is the primary concern. Rummana as an artist made a radical shift from fairly conventional painting, after the demolition of the Babri Masjid in December 1992. Thereafter, her areas of concern were the location of the individual in an uncertain, politically volatile environment. From 1993 to her death in 1999, Rummana produced a small but highly significant body of work, in which the leitmotif is the female body seen against architectural forms that symbolize both the construction and the violent dismantling of cultural values. In the installation "Fragments/Multiples" (1994) the dome/breast images of organ mutilation and destruction are developed simultaneously. That monuments such as this, a national inheritance, are no more

8
Rummana Hussain
"Home/Nation", detail, 1996
Multimedia photo-text
installation at Gallery Chemould,
Mumbai

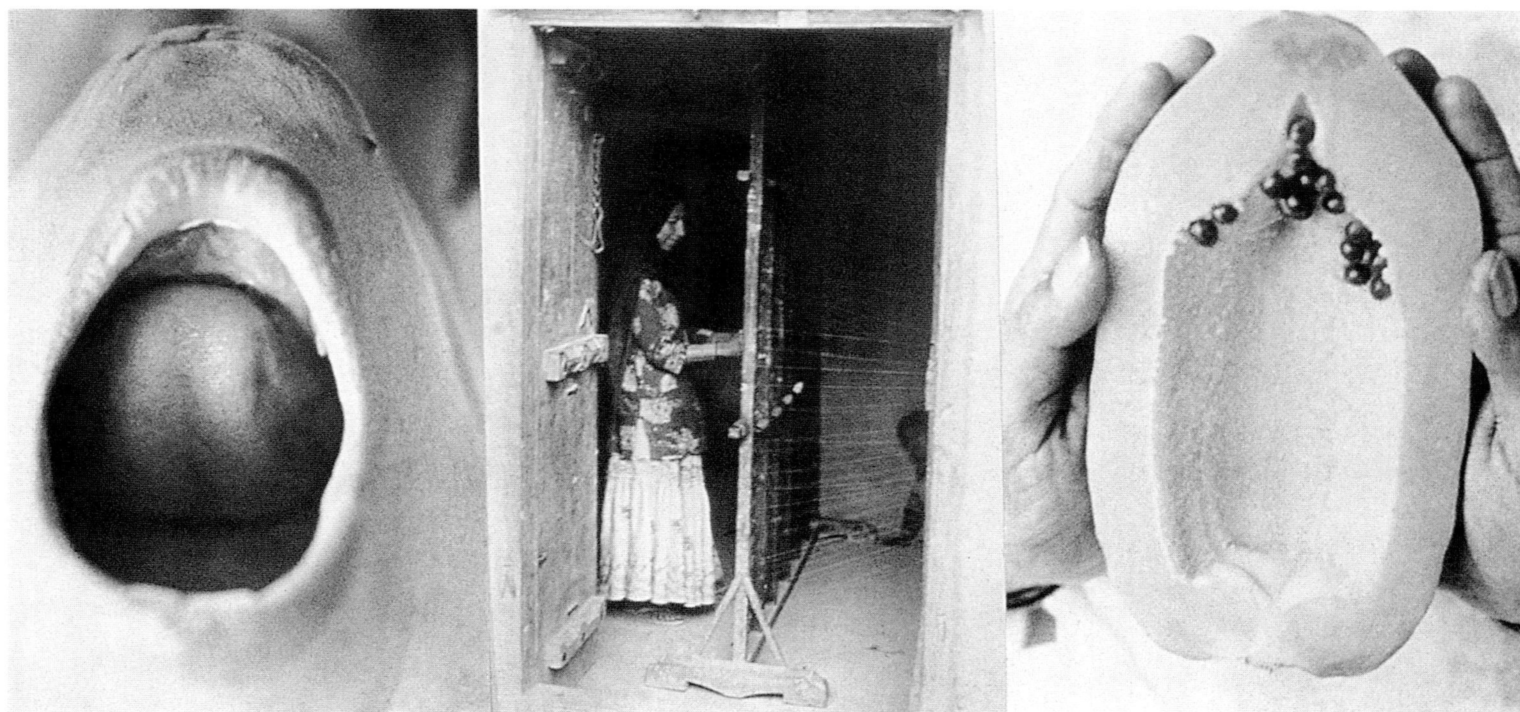

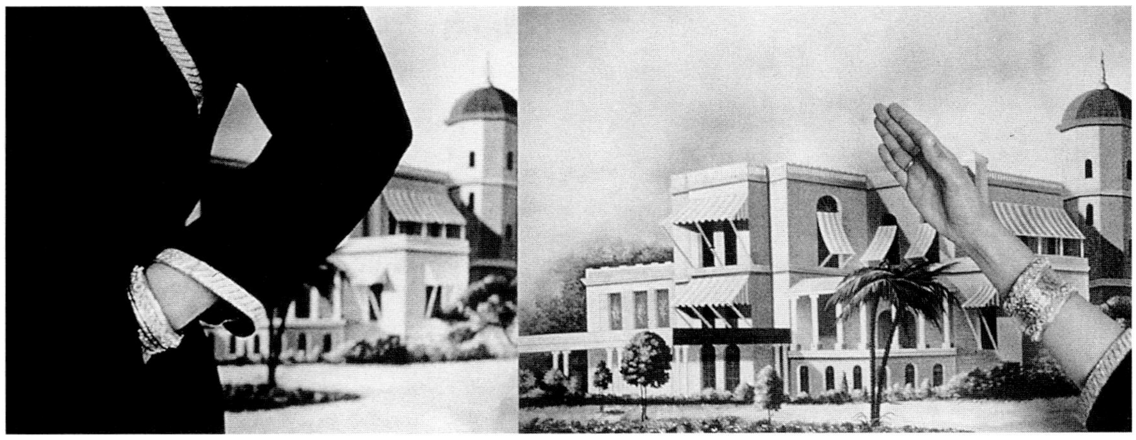

9
Rummana Hussain
"The Tomb of Begum Hazrat Mahal", detail, 1997
Multimedia photo-text installation in the exhibition "Telling Times" curated by Jane Connaity and Rama Bhushan, Bath; New Delhi, 1997.

secure than the woman in India, that violation/betrayal can be enacted at the level of the state, is enunciated.[5]

In her installation "Home/Nation" (1996) the possibility of peaceful coexistence between Hindus and Muslims is poignantly captured by images of mosques flanked by temples in Ayodhya, emblematic of India's culturally complex history. These images were juxtaposed with photographs documenting the daily enactment of female chores – grinding, cutting, washing, etc. An important aspect here is that Rummana allies not with women made visible through feminist activism (as in Sheba Chhachhi), but in the anonymous figure, with quotidian concerns, the kind of women that may have lived in the interiors of the fort of Golconda, or within the Imambaras and palaces of Lucknow performing the same unsung chores as her 20th-century counterpart (figure 8). The feminine presence humanizes a space or structure. Further, the monument's parts are corelated with body parts, to extend the idea of decay or violation; in arch/mouth opened in a silent scream, the violence is suggested rather than enacted. In this work she also used a number of objects to collapse stereotypical and popular images of women, to posit present pleasure with the ever present sense of decay. A quote from Abdul Halim Sharar who describes how Wajid Ali Shah liked his *paris* or the women of the harem to dress their hair is reproduced, embellished with a lock of hair. She also uses images of reproductive organs, gloves, earbuds, thimbles, buttons, and photographs of herself with her young daughter to drive home the idea of feminine vulnerability. In her work "Tomb of Begum Hazrat Mahal" (1997) (figure 9) the notion of feminine resistance to modes of dominance is articulated.

Rummana's courage lay in examining her own condition, of confronting terminal illness within the context of India's social polity. In the performance "Living on the Margins" (NCPA Mumbai) she drew a parallel between a cut papaya, her mouth open in a silent scream (as in "Home/Nation"), and a breast prosthesis which she removed and laid out for public view. The clarity with which Rummana cut through polemic to tie individual destiny with the nation – as exemplified in her own body – gave her work its directness and power.

Body as Poetic Metaphor – Arpana Caur, Rekha Rodwittiya, Nilima Sheikh, Anju Dodiya

Arpita Singh's positioning of the aging woman in Indian art may be only vaguely self-referential. In Arpana Caur (b. 1954) and Rekha Rodwittiya (b. 1958), the enactment of the feminine presence is direct and engaged. In their work, the identification of "issues", both personal and social, become a source of dramatic encounter and enactment. In Rekha Rodwittiya, the feminine self is usually caught up in confrontations that challenge her to effect change and resolution both within herself and in her environment. The essential difference between her work and Arpana's is that Rodwittiya emphatically plays out the nature of the struggle/confrontation, while Arpana seeks solution and closure, usually through a metaphysical argument.

In Rodwittiya's paintings of the 1980s, sexuality, its exploitation and abuse become a metaphor for the state of women. The woman foregrounded on her canvas becomes an emblem of resistance even as chimneys spewing smoke, turbid waters, claustrophobic skyscrapers make up a congestive environment. Rodwittiya who acknowledges Western influences of Chirico or Goya – and whose work recalls the dramatic juxtapositions of Max Beckman – writes of "bleeding, an emotive quality so that it re-echoes through the painting or drawing".[6] What, in Rodwittiya, constitutes this highly emotive charge is that questions of childhood and memory, sexuality and desire, are played out. Shivaji Pannikar argues that Rodwittiya's personal and generalized feminist concerns do not essentially draw out of a Marxist paradigm.[7] Instead they draw from her state of "rootlessness" as much as her sensitivity to the emotional and physical violence of urban India.

In Rodwittiya the difficult transition from being to becoming, the evolution from one to another state – be it the chrysalis-like emergence from childhood, the state of motherhood and nurture, or the assumption of the artistic persona – and the dilemma of creative choices is powerfully recorded. Even as Rodwittiya works through emblem and metaphor, she steps outside narrative to universalize the image of the feminine self. It is the power which she vests in her women which saves them from the fate of victims, and instead forces a direct engagement with their concerns. In recent years, the fury and passion of her work has stilled somewhat. The figure is delineated with the fluid calm of the yogic body – even the symbols of violence are used with an ironic, heightened calm. The extreme medical and sexual violence to the female body is contained in the work, "Scissor, Gun, Knife, Cunt" (1995) (figure 10) and the objectification and wilful use of body parts is neatly, even dispassionately, framed in "Mappings – Body Imprints" (1997) (figure 11).

In Arpana Caur, a palimpsest of symbolism overlays virtually all her images. The feminine as archetype represents the forces of nature, death and regeneration, toil and the implosions of social violence that threaten a fragile social order. In this, Arpana accords woman the highest position even as she depicts her as economic and social victim. Arpana has reacted with urgency to issues that identify woman as victim (figure 12).

10
Rekha Rodwittiya
"Scissor, Gun, Knife, Cunt", 1995
Watercolour and acrylic on paper

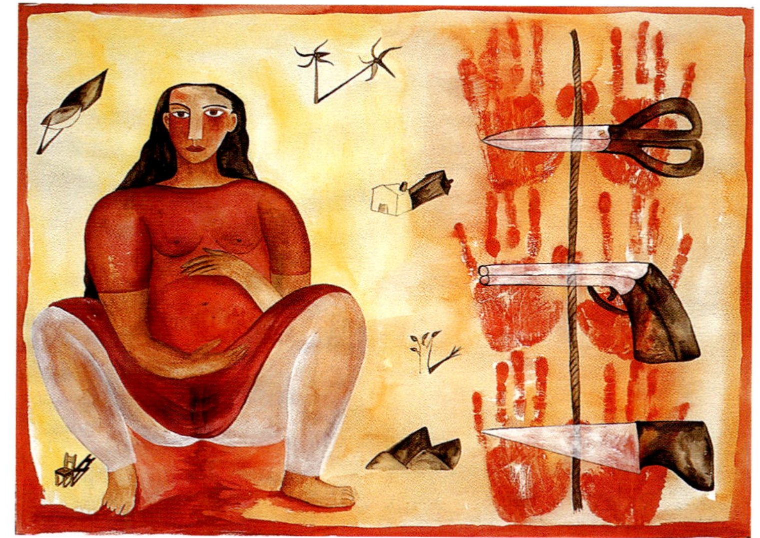

11
Rekha Rodwittiya
"Mappings – Body Imprints"
(assemblage of 16 works), 1997
Watercolour and acrylic on paper;
41 x 31 cm each

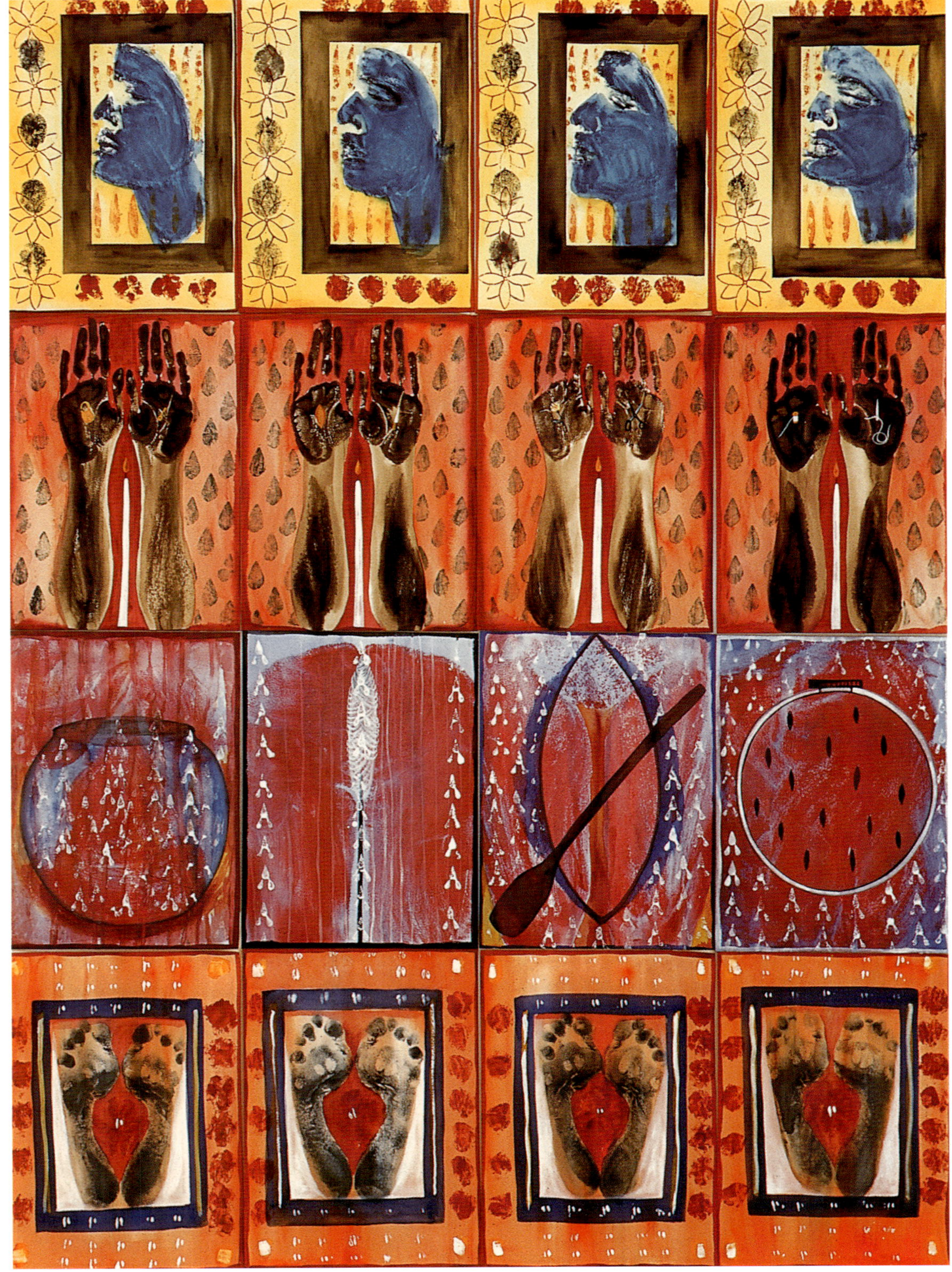

The widows of a mining disaster in Chasnala, the rape of Maya Tyagi, the overnight massacre of 3,000 Sikhs in Delhi in the wake of Indira Gandhi's assassination, the homeless abject state of Hindu widows who congregate to await the arrival of Lord Krishna in the holy city of Vrindavan – these are some of her subjects through the 1980s. The feminine as emblematic in Arpana pursues the dictates of style: the full-bodied figures trapped in the claustrophobic DDA flats in Delhi ("Women in Interiors", 1974–75), have gradually given way to figures occasionally delineated only in outline. Equally, Arpana has gradually moved from the subject of the oppressive city – of claustrophobia, women labouring on building sites, exploitative and damaging personal relationships – to a longing for an idealized calm. Increasingly, all sensuous pleasure is seemingly sacrificed as the feminine

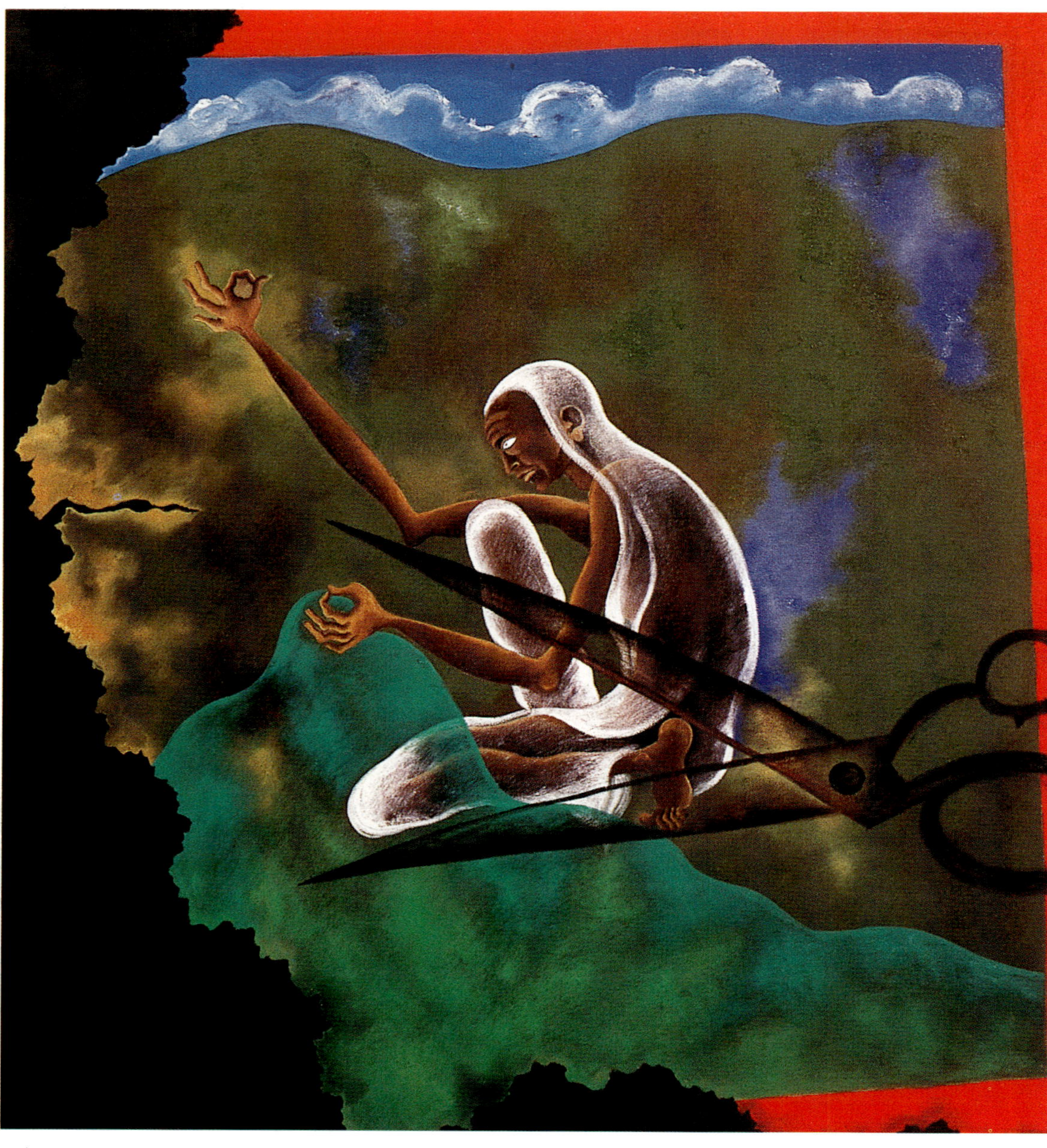

12
Arpana Caur
"Threat", 1994
Oil on canvas; 180 x 150 cm
Collection: Academy of Fine Arts and Literature, New Delhi

figure seeks resolution in a oneness with nature. She herself becomes emblematic of regenerative forces.

Like other women artists, Nilima Sheikh (b. 1945) directly addresses issues of life, death, and separation. But in the fluency of her forms, the language of poetry and metaphor, she introduces a sense of acceptance, even healing. Perhaps no painter has worked on the numerous aspects of femininity as has Nilima. However, the issues of birth and death, love, separation, and reconciliation – informed by the Hindu aesthetic of *viraha* and *sambhoga* – gain in Nilima's hands a transformative quality. She invests her figures with a great tenderness; miniaturized, within an awesome landscape, they have a tentative quality. Almost completely linear, they blend and merge without conscious oddity or psychological delineation. With a lingering romanticism, Nilima restores the human figure, in all its frail transient beauty, to dignity and wholeness, according it a pristine position even as she evolves a language of emotional fulfilment, loss, and longing.

Especially in her feminine figures, Nilima imbues an endurance and resistance. Like her friend and fellow traveller Arpita Singh, she is among the few in her generation of Indian painters to sensitively consider the familial issue particularly the mother-daughter relationship. In a series of small paintings titled "Maternity" and "Post Partum", she creates serial images of the mother assisted by two women

13
Nilima Sheikh
"Maternity 1", 1997
Gum tempera on paper

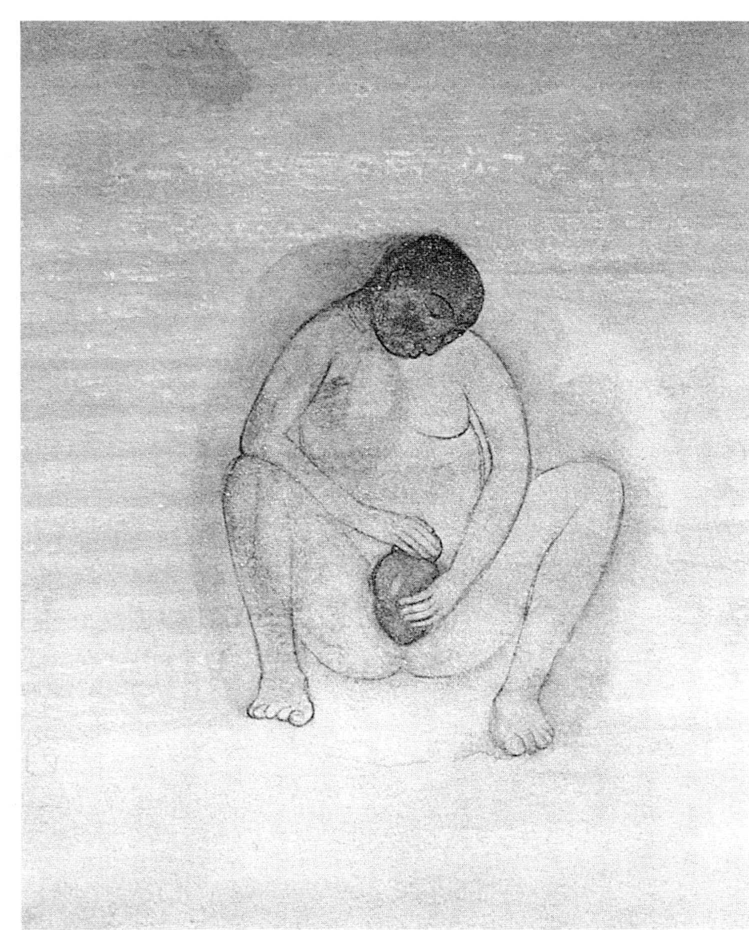

14
Nilima Sheikh
"Maternity 2", 1997
Gum tempera on paper

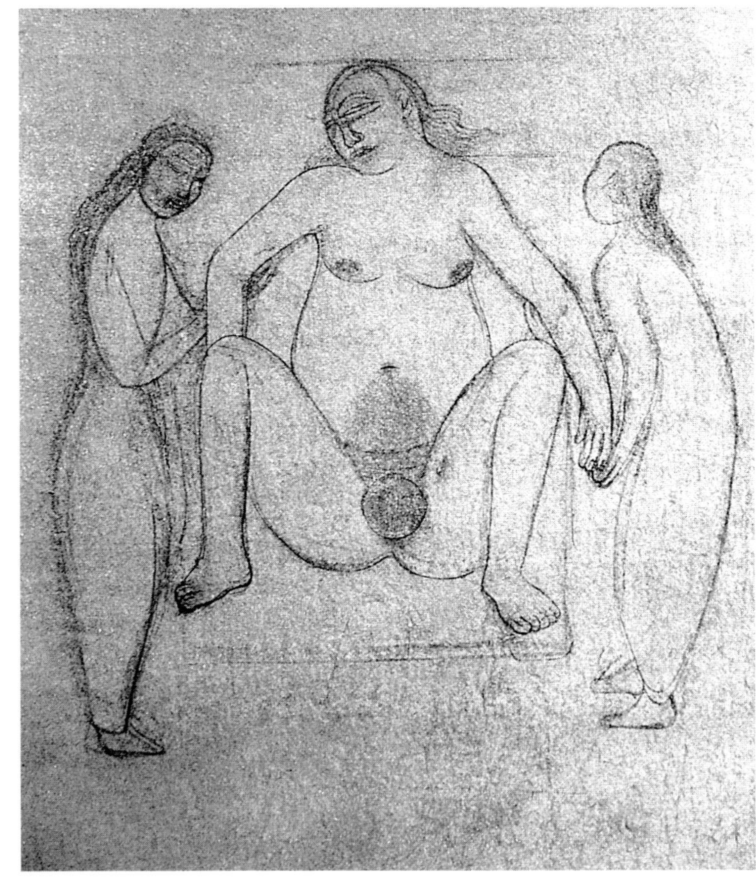

15
Nilima Sheikh
"Maternity 4", 1997
Gum tempera on paper

as the child emerges from her womb, and then the rapt, complete images of feeding and nurture (figures 13–15). That Nilima invests these with the stylized beauty of a Mughal or Pahari miniature affirms the transformative quality of her art and vision. The nascent awareness of the larger world through the eyes of a young girl ("Samira in Dalhousie", 1976), and the death of Nilima's mother depicted gently tending her garden, are in this strain of the use of nature as metaphor. More recently she has done a series of paintings on Mahadevi Akka, the Virashaiva poet who forsook a life of luxury to pursue the path of bhakti. Akka, nude but for her long hair, becomes emblematic of resistance even in the face of stubborn patriarchal structures. Even as Akka embodies an ascetic resistance, she personifies love for her Chennamallikarjuna, the Lord "white as jasmine". In this median of desire and renunciation that embodies the bhakti spirit, Nilima Sheikh finds a natural apotheosis.

In Anju Dodiya (b. 1964), the real confrontations are vigorously enacted in a theatre of the self. Dodiya's inward conflicts and concerns, particularly those that emanate from her art practice, are mirrored in a series of dramatic images (figures 16 and 17). The artist and her doppelganger engage with each other like Echo and Narcissus in highly charged debate, as if to represent polarities

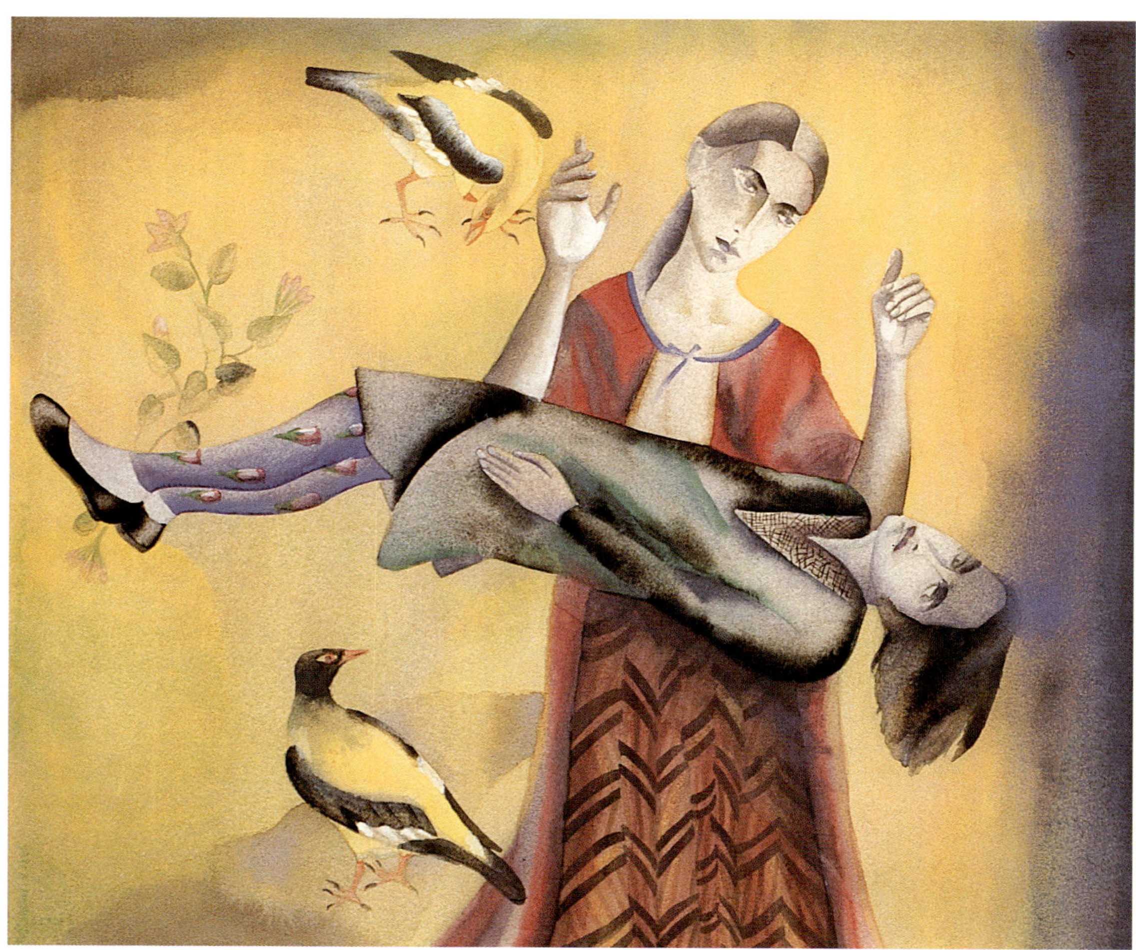

16
Anju Dodiya
"Two Orioles", 1996
Watercolour; 47.5 x 55 cm

17
Anju Dodiya
"Convoy", 2001
Watercolour and charcoal on paper; 175 x 112.5 cm

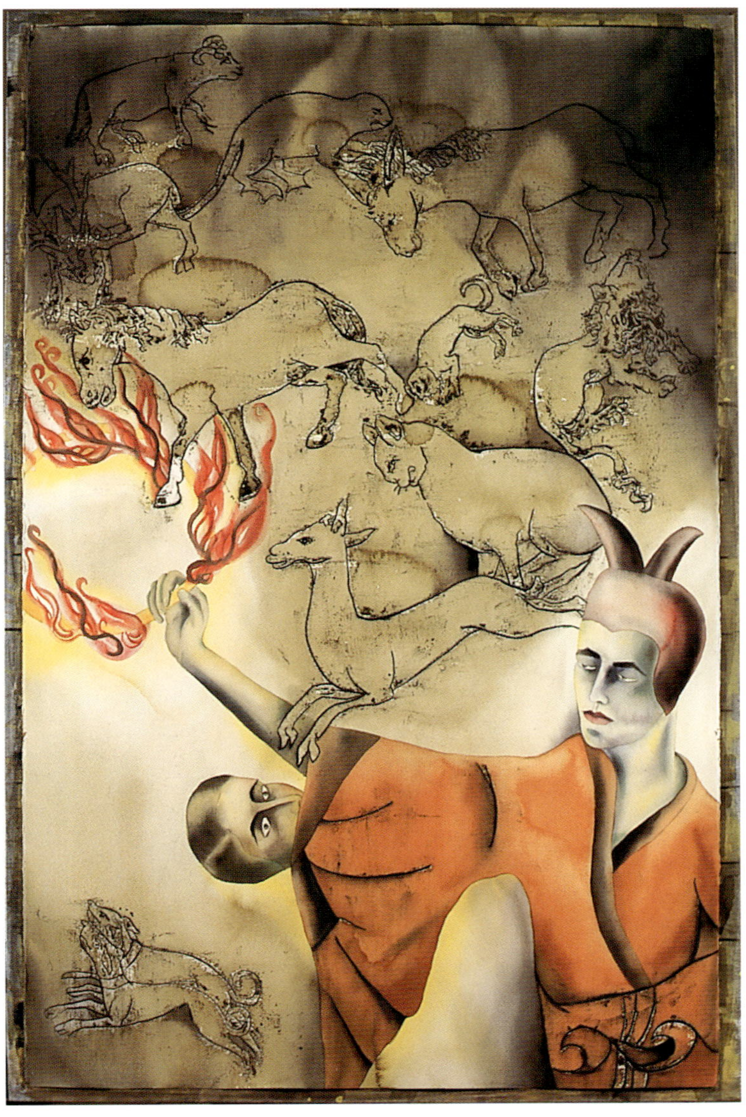

of thought. Anju is a fabulist, she is also her own subject, engaged in the special constructs of fantasy; to confront the very real issues of self and self-perception. Clearly such painting is an art of great vulnerability. The scene of confrontation is usually the studio, and the creative act with its tension and dilemma affords sharp even violent parody. She is the Sumo wrestler entering the ring of her studio ("Entering the Ring", 1998), or the artist ironically presented as vendor of wares in "Studio Guests" (1998), or even the terror of the empty canvas in "Fear of Fog" (1998). It is appropriate to close with Anju Dodiya because she returns the creative impetus to painting; she restores and recharges the potential of the painted frame even as she vests the form with a wholesomeness.

In conclusion, most of the artists under consideration may not subscribe to a feminist polemic. Yet they have in a period of nearly three decades pushed for an examination of the feminine as a complex site in the public and private spheres. In the process they have created a vigorous body of work that draws for a common ground not on the mediations of style or ideology but on a searching, moving scrutiny of gender difference.

NOTES

1. *Modes of Parallel Practice: Ways of World Making*, catalogue, Sakshi Gallery, 1998–99.
2. Nalini Malani, *Medeaprojekt*, edited by Kamala Kapoor and Amita Desai, Mumbai, Max Mueller Bhavan, 1997.
3. "Johan Pijnappel interviews Nalini Malani" in *BEAM*, vol. 18, January 1999.
4. Nalini Malani, interview with Shanta Gokhale.
5. Ashish. Rajadhyaksha, *Rummana Hussain: Fragments/Multiples*, Bombay, Jehangir Art Gallery, 1994.
6. Art Heritage catalogue.
7. Shivaji Pannikar, *Rekha Rodwittiya: Of Feminist Concerns and Beyond*, Calcutta, A Seagull Exhibition, 1992.

FURTHER READING

Geeti Sen, *Image and Imagination*, Ahmedabad, Mapin, 1998.

Gayatri Sinha, ed., *Expressions and Evocations: Contemporary Women Artists of India*, Mumbai, Marg Publications, 1996.

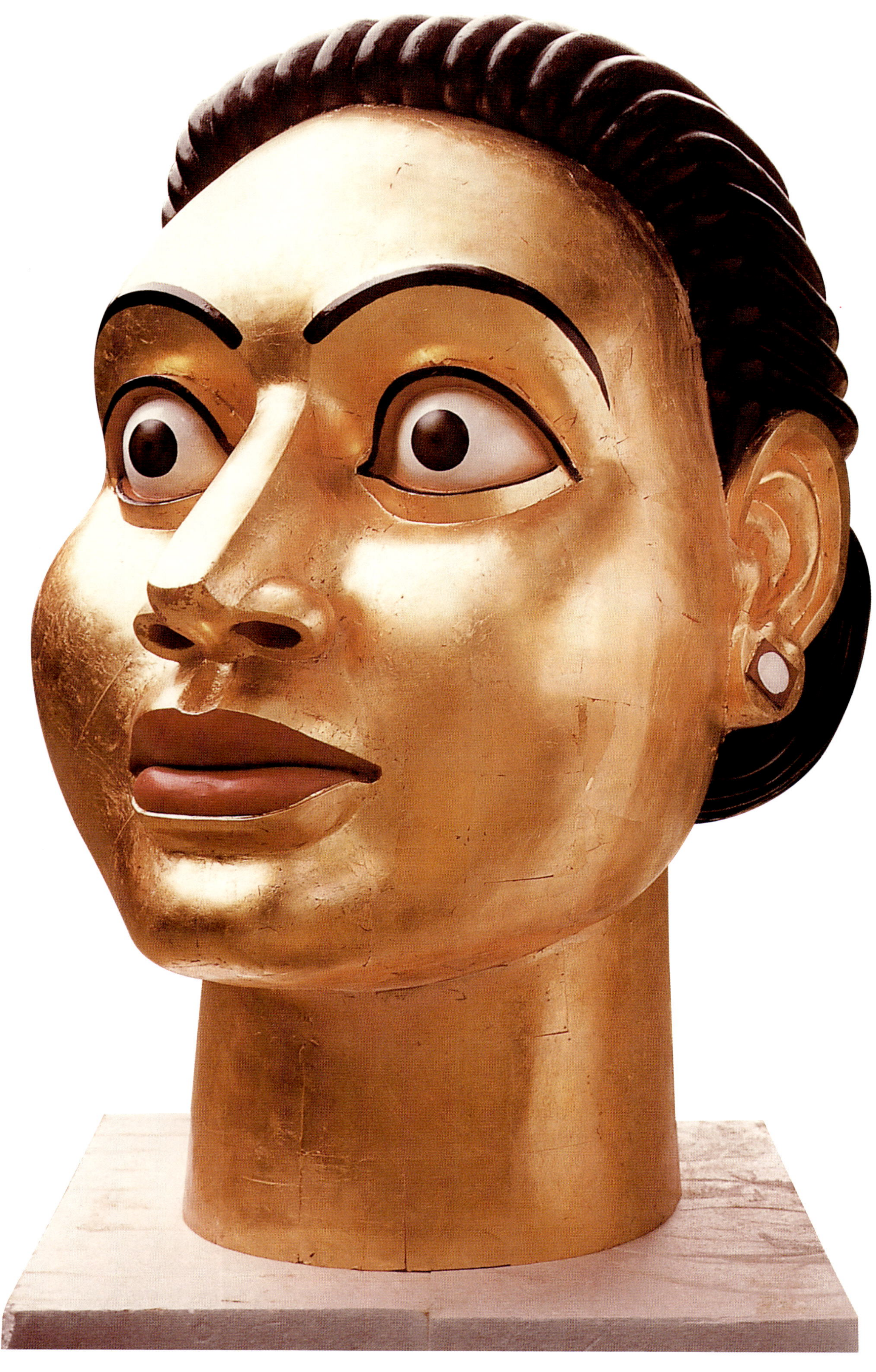

Yashodhara Dalmia

the paradigms for post-modern art in india

It could be said that modernism in Indian art is barely half a century old, as it was only by the 1950s that it began to manifest itself in a powerful manner. A concerted attempt at nationalism from Ravi Varma to Abanindranath Tagore was to leave its imprint on art and forge a unity among several diverse styles at the start of the 20th century. By the late '40s, immanent energies in modernism began to gather force and led to practices which broke the shackles of academic art. These were harnessed initially to the aspirations of a newly independent nation in its quest for selfhood. Even at that stage, modern art in India was imbued with notions of identity and its strivings were always informed with devolving contours. Thus the modernist mode in India, never free from the historical destiny of the people, was to find its self-expression consistently blended with political and social aspirations.

It has often been contended that art in India is both hybrid and imitative. That would be a contradiction in terms, for modernism as it took root in the West had avowed its affiliation to universalism and internationalism. Then again when artists like Picasso borrowed from African sculpture or Matisse from Persian miniatures it was to lead to "high modernism". In a similar vein the borrowing of Picasso's inventions by Ramkinkar Baij or F.N. Souza were considered derivative art. The implicit hierarchical notions contained in such labelling were only to come to light later.

The formation of the Progressive Artists Group in 1947 acted as a watershed in that a definitive move towards modernism was to be made by artists henceforth. The Group – which consisted of F.N. Souza, M.F. Husain, S.H. Raza, K.H. Ara, H.A. Gade, and S.K. Bakre – opposed both the revivalistic tendencies of the Bengal School as well as the academism of the British-situated art colleges and forged a link with the historical reality of the present. They were to construct their forms from the medley of schools that existed in the India of their time as well as international modes. While taking hybrid realities into account, however, their allegiance was to plastic values in art and in that they were unabashedly modernist.

It was only by the 1990s that artists began making works which went beyond the frame of the painting and extended into real space incorporating actual, everyday lives. The gallery began to be substituted by public space, and site-specific works which aimed to marginalize commodification began to rear their heads. As with modernism, the impetus for this came from the international arena as also from circumstances within, where the need to register reality in all its shifting hybrid forms

1
G. Ravinder Reddy
"Head of a Woman", 1990
Polyester resin fibreglass;
59 x 43 x 66 cm

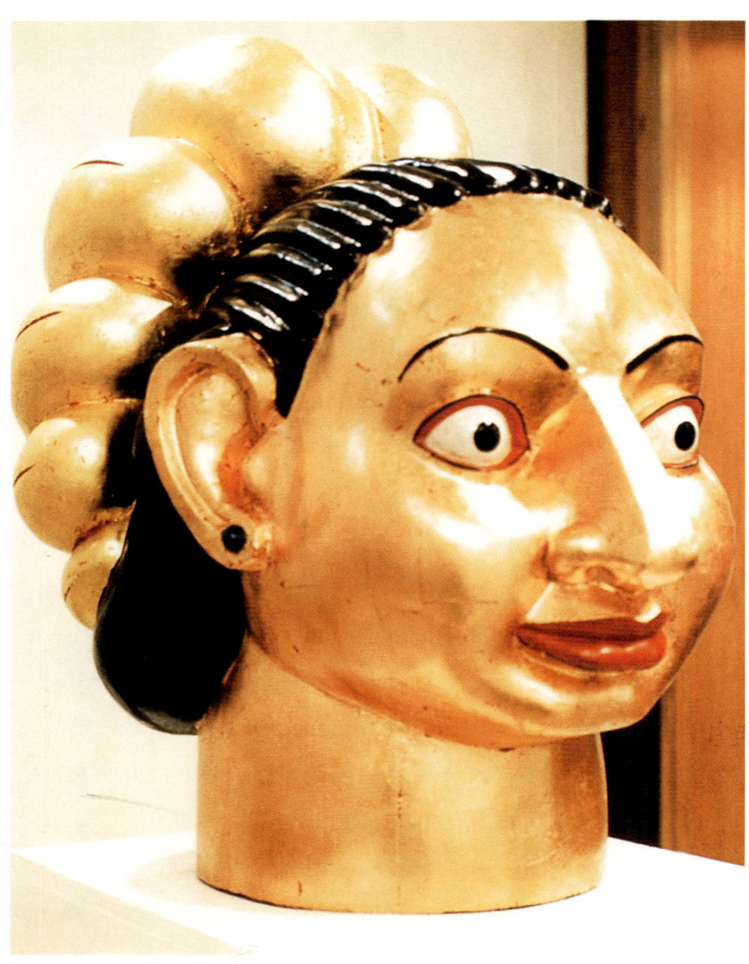

2
G. Ravinder Reddy
"Woman with Flowers", 1990
Gilded polyester resin fibreglass;
59 x 43 x 66 cm

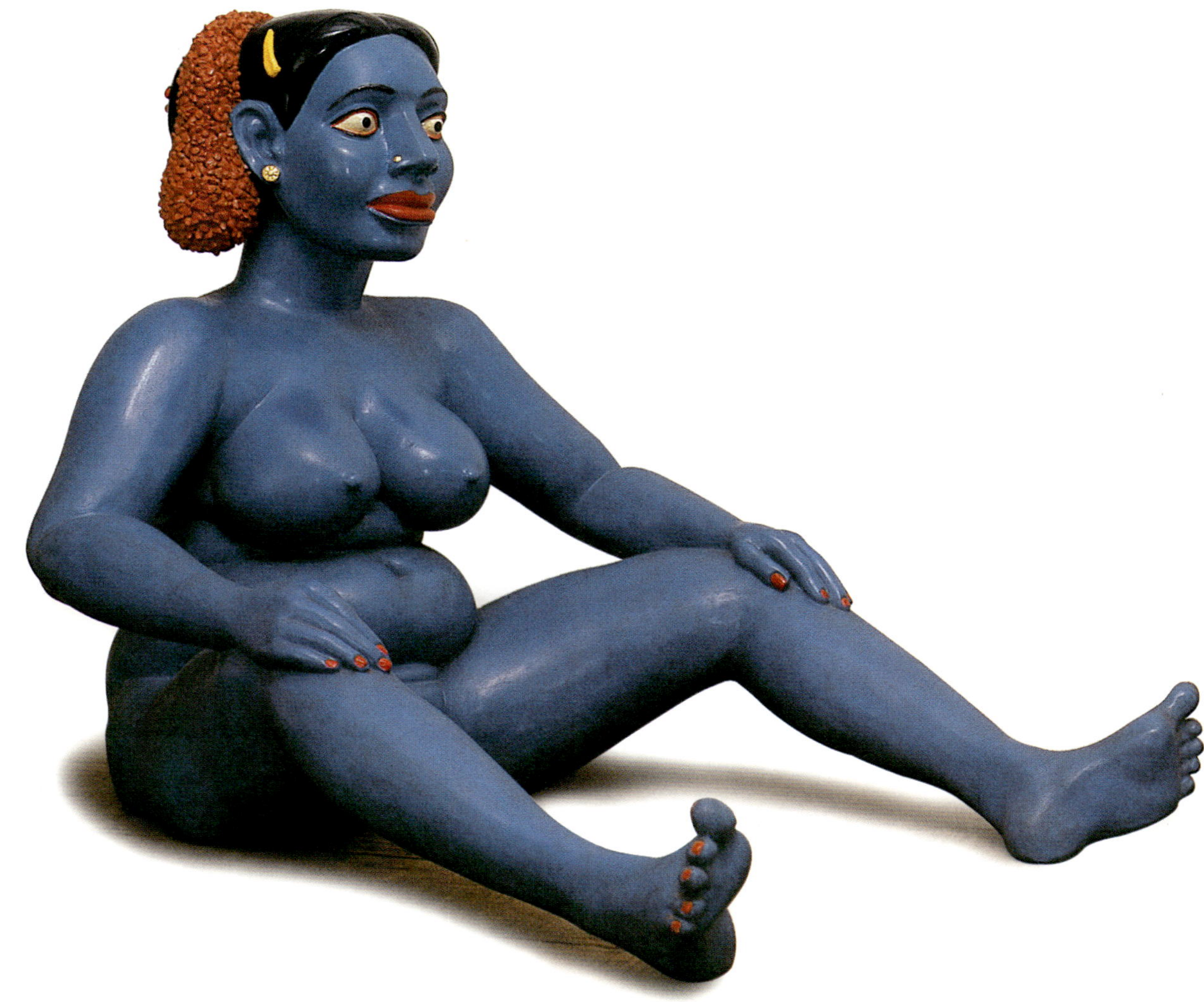

3
G. Ravinder Reddy
"Sitting Woman", 1995
Polyester resin fibreglass;
104 x 90 x 87 cm

became compelling. By the mid-'90s a number of young artists had begun to make installations and site-specific art objects even as others continued to work in the conventional mediums of painting, sculpture, and print-making. Before discussing the implications of these, however, we need to reflect on some of the debates that have arisen around the new modes in the past decade.

By its very nature multiculturalism and the emerging cross-fertilization in art breeds hybridity where the contours of identity are blurred. This has led to the belief that a kind of globalism in art is taking place which will result in an unhealthy homogenization. Often voiced by the Left, this argument by itself is untenable since historical processes have shown that appropriation implies a passivity on the part of the "victim" which is by its nature non-existent. As Partha Mitter observes, "For example, Edward Said, in his classic study, *Orientalism*, chooses Marx's famous statement, 'the orientals cannot represent themselves; they must be represented' to show how a certain body of knowledge about the orient was pressed into the service of colonial ideology. An unintended effect of such a postmortem has been to perpetuate the very stereotype of the passive oriental which his own work set out to challenge. Both orientalists and their critics, who are diametrically opposed to each other, essentially treat the history of the colonisers rather than the colonised."[1] The colonized are not after all mute but have active responses which can transform the nature of knowledge.

It is felt that just as the underlying nexus behind modernism was white, male, and colonial, similarly multiculturalism is an aspect of global imperialism that transnational corporations find convenient to espouse. But if internationalism spells out the last phase of imperialism, surely the best way to counter it is to appropriate the means to our end rather than reject multiculturalism? Would we have denied modernism or its parallel activity in culture simply because of its colonial origins? In blurring our identity, as some of the examples below will show, we have actually facilitated our own vocabulary and dynamicized it by incorporating new perceptions.

It is at the same time worth considering whether, in espousing the cause of pluralism, we are becoming a showcase for the West, a kind of ethnic museum. The carnivalesque aspect of multiculturalism cannot be denied and needs to be scrutinized. As the art historian Geeta Kapur pointed out at the "Traditions/Tensions" seminar held at the Asia Society in New York in 1996: "A continued insistence on eclecticism and its conversion to various ideologies of hybridity within the postmodern can serve to elide the diachronic edge of cultural phenomena and thus ease the edge of historical choice."[2] Kapur validates a space which is a "real battle ground for cultural difference"[3] where as against hybrid solutions there is a dialectical synthesis. In so doing we do not have to serve causes, subaltern or any other, but heighten our own perception of multiplicities. In heightening polarities without homogenizing we would sharpen and arouse sensibilities. We would then be offering a critique of the globalized, transcultural notions of the Third World served up to us and also harbour no other interests but our own. I propose now to discuss the works of three artists who exercise their choices as well as create distinctive modes of visualization.

Contemporary Iconism

In a hybrid climate, the sculptures of Ravinder Reddy invite attention because of their presence. While their abundant sensuality alters notions of post-modernism, their brassiness creates a diachronic edge to art as spectacle. Reddy's lifesized female heads from the '80s, made in terracotta and polyester resin fibreglass, were reminiscent of his earlier biomorphic works with their humps and curves. These large heads which he coated with thick car-paint, which retained a neutrality, were essentially urban

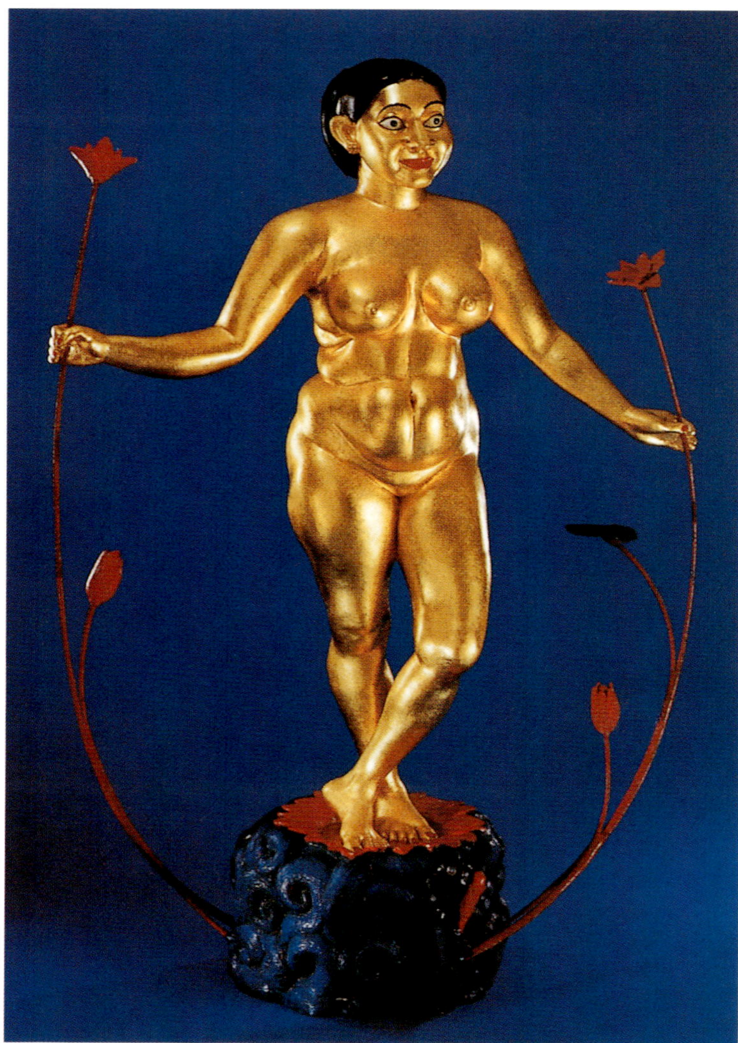

4
G. Ravinder Reddy
"Woman with Lotus Flowers",
1998
Synthetic polymer paint and goldleaf on polyester resin fibreglass; 212 x 148 x 63 cm
Kenneth and Yasuko Myer Collection of Contemporary Asian Art

types with their brightly painted mouths and "modern" coiffure secured by plastic bands (figure 1). Some of the heads were painted in gold with streaks of the underlying red showing here and there, re-creating the brilliance of idols in Nepal, Thailand, or Japanese Buddhist temples (figure 2). Their iconicity was emphasized by their wide enamelled eyes which are often attached to the Hindu cultic images at Nathdvara or Mathura. As the art historian Ajay Sinha points out, "In spite of the maximum alertness in their expression, these heads are dispassionate and impersonal, as if they were embodiments of some mysterious, mythical life, or perhaps venerated objects."[4] The later heads became qualified by details from the streets of his native Andhra leading to greater annunciation. Thus in "Krishnaveni" (1996–97) the high arch of her eyebrow and hair lead on to a luxurious braid which seems to reach out to the sky. "Woman from Kapulpadu" (1996–97) has a shell-like bun from which the glowing face emerges as if from a cornucopia.

Alongside these, Reddy had begun to make lifesized figures which in their abundant sexuality are reminiscent of the *yakshi*s of Bharhut and Mathura. In a marvellously full-bodied golden sculpture simply titled "The Woman" (1995), the traversion of idioms from the classical to the profane is extraordinary. The exaggerated folds of her flesh are marked by intersections which could at the same time be expressions of a ritual diagram. She seems to straddle both the mythic and the real world. While her face is alert, the turn of her body in a theatrical posture suggests an alignment with some translucent sphere. In "Sitting Woman" (1995) the blue figure sits with her legs astride in a posture of having a bath as well as to incite ritual fertility (figure 3). In another magnificent sculpture the woman holds two plants almost as an extension of herself (figure 4).

In coalescing the ritual, mythic, the street and the everyday, Reddy visually surfs many frontiers of art that have emerged in recent times. In many ways his work could be seen as installations which concretely extend into space and invite other realities. Yet the participatory aspect is absent, for Reddy's voluminous masses cannot be honed into but stand apart from the audience. As the artist Gieve Patel states, "their sensuality is serene, in most instances the sexual impulse does not speak of excitement but of fulfilment."[5] The objecthood of Reddy's works places them undeniably in the present and yet their decodifications seem to be heraldic.

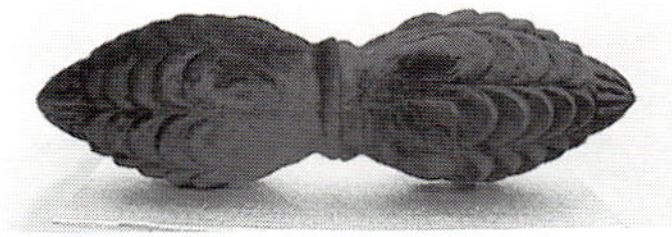

5
Anita Dube
"Seduction", from "Theatre de Sade", a 13-piece sculpture-installation, 1998–99
Glass, velvet; 40 x 12 x 12 cm

Ritual Art

The ritual comes to the fore in many installations in India and creates an expectation of Third World theatre. Yet the street, the bazaar, a Muharram procession, or the paan shop could themselves be considered site-specific art works rooted in popular practices. Ironically when these are imported back to the country as an aspect of internationalism they have been democratized and released from social rigidities. As the artist Anita Dube points out, "This is certainly paradoxical, as is the paradox of a convoluted 'return' – where installation and performance return to our cultural space via this democratised route, as genres to break down 'fine art' hierarchies and straitjackets but not as social ones. It is also ironical that in India, within contemporary art practice, installation and performance methods have been immediately appropriated and again hierarchised by the cultural elite as a marker of their superiority, whereas actually installation and performance should have returned via the

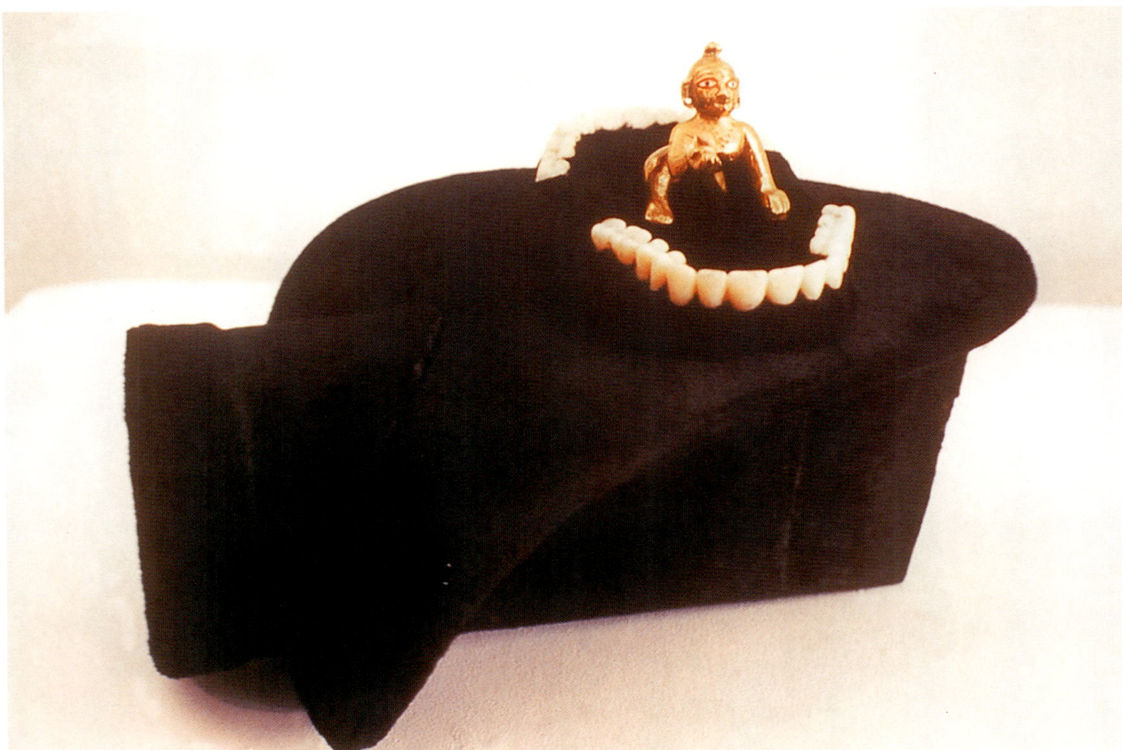

6
Anita Dube
"Victim", from "Theatre de Sade", 1998–99
Wood, dentures, velvet, brass idol

democratic principle to its real life sources in the base, among the ordinary people."[6] Installations which by their very nature break hierarchies and the isolation of "high art" exist in this esoteric space when they are "returned" as it were.

An artist like Anita Dube uses the more intimate and personal aspects of ritual which are carried over to a public site. In a remarkable series in 1997, titled "Silence (Blood Wedding)", Dube uses human bones as her basic armature, embellished with red velvet, sequins, and beads. The jewel-like spectres in the shape of a fan, a garland, etc. indicate a love relationship but with a cutting edge. Dube's involvement with death (her father was a surgeon and died a few years ago from cancer) is in the form of a retrieval where its knowledge creates the passage towards a fuller life. Yet the restoration, as the colour red indicates, is not into complacency but into alternative modes of existence like that of a lesbian or even an Oedipal relationship. As she states, "I wanted to keep the auspiciousness of red within Hindu custom, but also profane this with suggestions of a lesbian marriage, even an incestuous marriage (with one's father for example). So the 'silence' here is a reversal, a rebellion that takes on death and patriarchal cocksureness."[7]

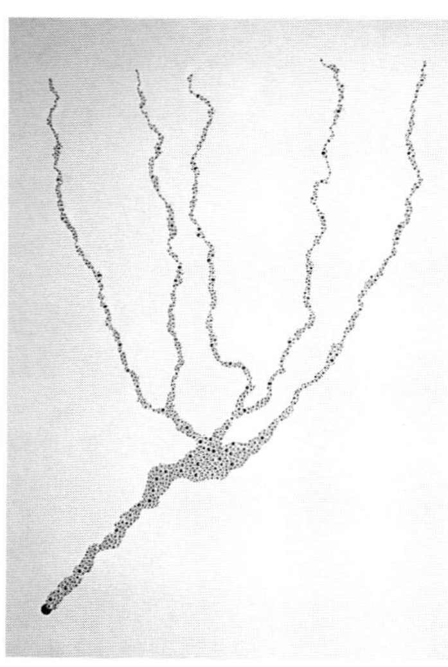

7
Anita Dube
"River/Disease", 2000
Installation with found ceramic copper eyes
Dimensions variable

8
Anita Dube
"River/Disease" (detail)

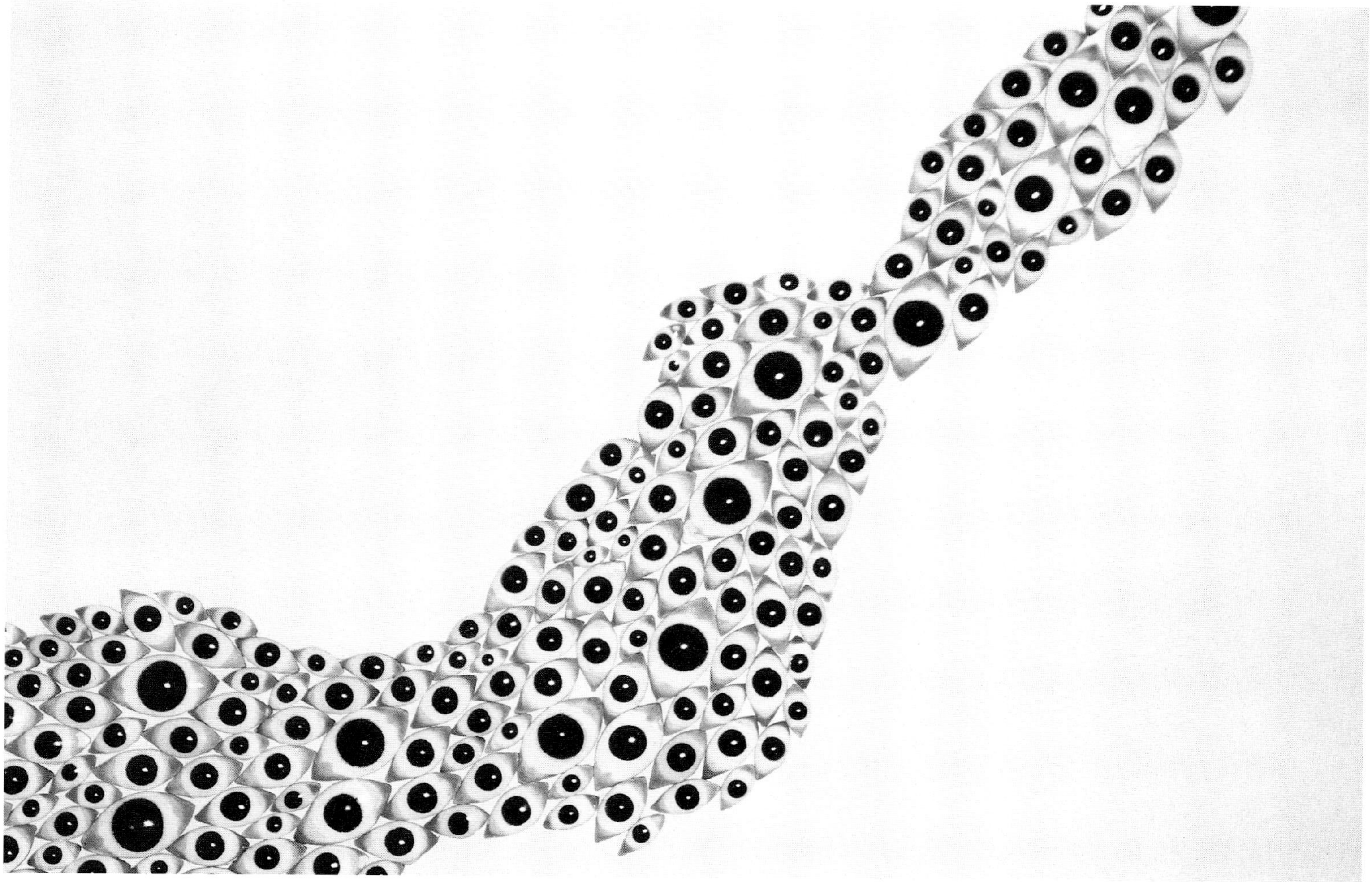

In her recent "Theatre de Sade" series (1999) the dark, threatening side of Eros is revealed where the animal masks and instruments of torture are made in a choking black (figure 5). The most compelling of these are glistening white dentures stationed in black velvet existing of their own volition in an omnipotent state. In a startling juxtapositioning of metaphors she places a golden brass idol of the infant Krishna in the tub of dentures and then positions these over a black square (figure 6). The ritual act of bathing the infant god lovingly performed by women all over India is here counterpoised by the menacing dentures. According to Dube, "For me the world of found objects has opened up new territories, including tradition. So when the context of an object – such as an idol, ritually worshipped in Hindu homes – is critically re-placed, the tension is very palpable. At that very juncture of this terrible juxtapositon is the space for thought in my work, the conceptual space."[8]

The popular aspect of ritual emerges in a work like "River/Disease" (2000), made entirely of ceramic copper eyes which are placed on Hindu idols in Mathura and Nathdvara to "bring them to life". The eyes of varying sizes are placed like a stream moving upwards on the wall (figure 7). These regurgitating, reflecting eyes, now bulging, now subsiding create an uneasy sensation of having a life of their own, each one seemingly alive, separate from the other (figure 8). Perhaps the most public of her works, for Dube these speak of mass migrations, primarily during the Partition of India in 1947 as reflected by the five rivers of Punjab. She states, "The eyes are like people for me and this could speak of large migrations in history. It could be from Kosovo or the migration from Pakistan to India. The sheer vulnerability and the futility of these migrations is expressed by the eyes. It also has to do with the village-city migration which is fraught with despair. Lastly these could be cells growing uncontrollably one from the other like a tumorous disease."[9] As with the rest of her work there is a cutting edge to "River/Disease" for its enticement prepares you for the brutal truth. The seemingly endless proliferation of eyes could be peering into your conscience.

The trajectory from the personal to architectural spaces and to the public arena was accomplished by Dube with the means of found objects. These as she pointed out changed the complexion of her work, inflecting it with subtle nuances which were often beyond her control. These were also works which introduced the popular and the common as an intervention which could provide the same works with several sub-texts.

Street Signs

The cacophony of the street enters the works of the artist Atul Dodiya in a forceful manner. The carnivalesque quality is delivered in a relay of images which pass the memory membrane in several registers. The street signs and movie posters, the small-scale operators of consumerism, the hand-made images sensitive to the smallest fluctuation of public feeling are all grist to the visual mill, and are churned up in a lengthy array. The dynamism of the street provides constant impetus for change, and Dodiya draws upon this in many of his paintings.

"Sour Grapes" (1997), an oil and acrylic work based on a south Indian oleograph found in a Bombay street vendor's display, shows the god Vishnu lying on the mythological serpent Sheshanaga. He is surrounded by a litany of gods praying to him and begging his intervention in saving the world (figure 9). From the navel emerges not the great god Brahma but a polymorphous deity, a conflation of Dodiya's own face with a Picassian cubist portrait. The superimposition denotes the affinity between the three-headed Brahma who can in his wisdom see in all directions and the multiple perspectives of cubism which radically altered art practices. The gaudy clothes of Vishnu as well as his film-hero

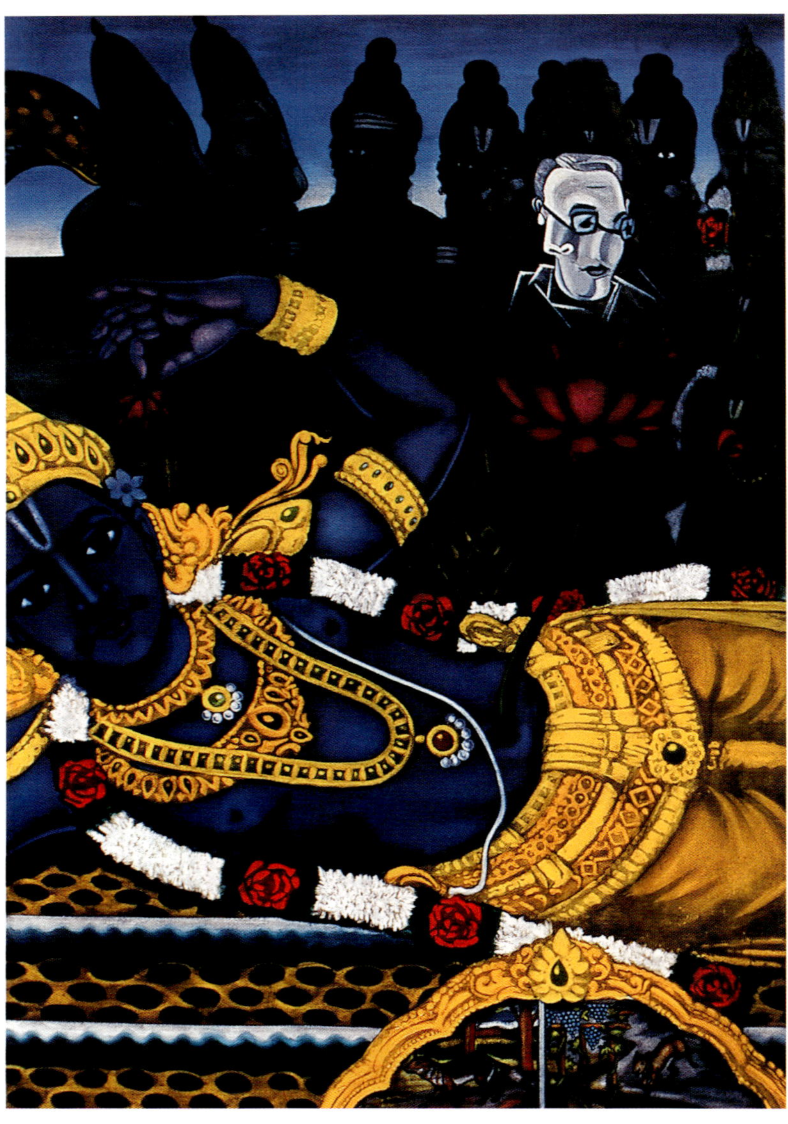

9
Atul Dodiya
"Sour Grapes", 1997
Oil and acrylic on canvas;
175 x 122 cm

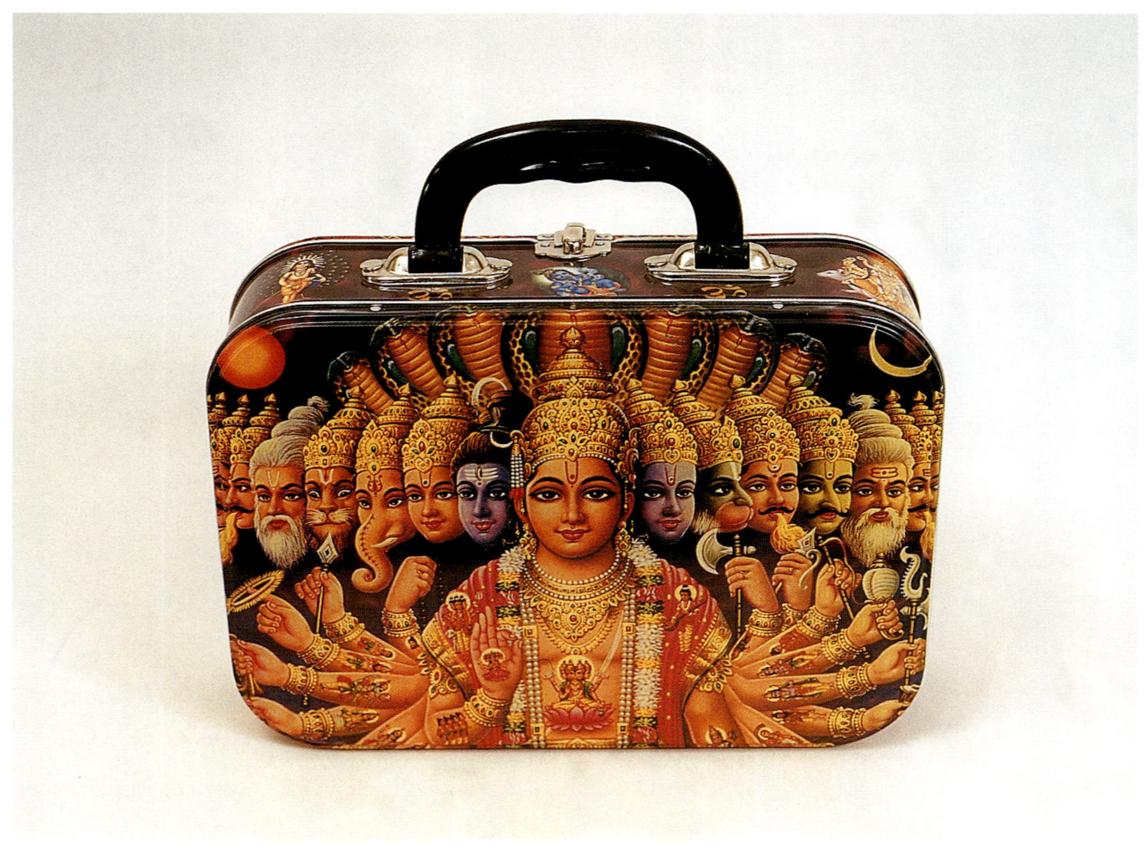

10
"A lunch box with Indian icons"
Tin; 17.5 x 25 x 7.5 cm
Conceived in Seattle, made in
China, and sold at the Brooklyn
Museum in New York

countenance are reminiscent of calendar art and he decontextualizes this by truncating the form and foregrounding it (compare figure 10). The close encounter with an image which is normally seen at a distance relegates it to a primary position. The deep apocalyptic blue which is liminal in places elevates the brassiness of the painting.

The inclusion of the most popular form in Indian art today and experimental practices of European painting with Dodiya's own self-image provide the multiple texts of the painting. Although he has mostly stayed with the medium of painting, for him the canvas is not a mere container of

11
Atul Dodiya
"Fool's Day", 1997
Oil, acrylic, and marble dust on canvas; 183 x 122 cm

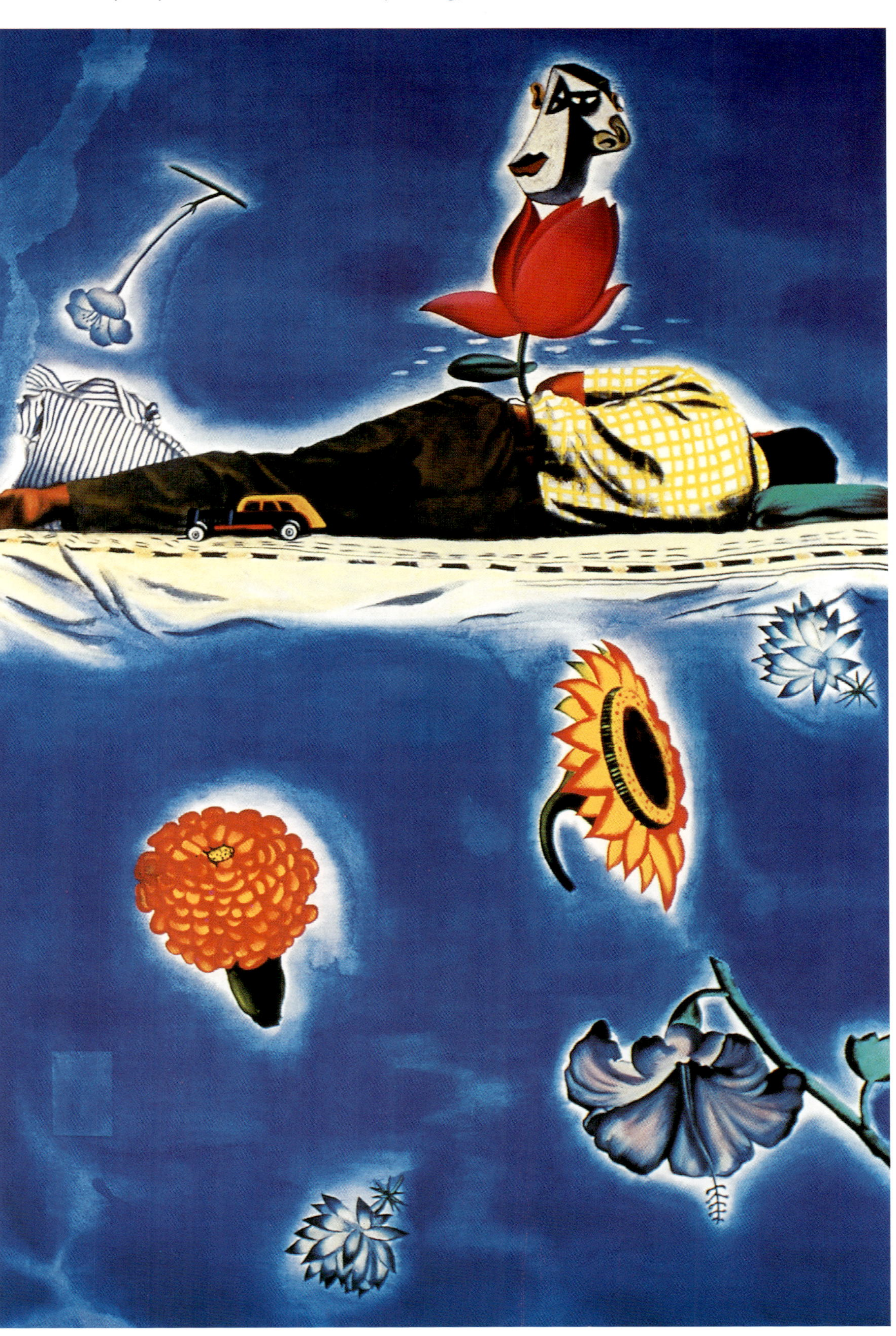

images. Instead it works as a volatile surface which interjects several levels of reality. While retaining its painterly quality, the canvas incorporates elements from conceptual and video art and creates a fluid interactive space within its frame. In an echoing linkage, the supine auto-portrait is far from passive in his case where its inert nature allows for a fluid interaction with his surroundings. In a painting like "Fool's Day" (1997) for instance, the artist's own figure substitutes for the horizontal Vishnu with his back to the viewer. The rosebud which emerges from his navel with a parody of a cubist head keeps watch with its multiple vision (figure 11). The bright flowers scattered all over the picture space faintly evoke Hindu rituals as well as the bright plastic flowers found in pavement

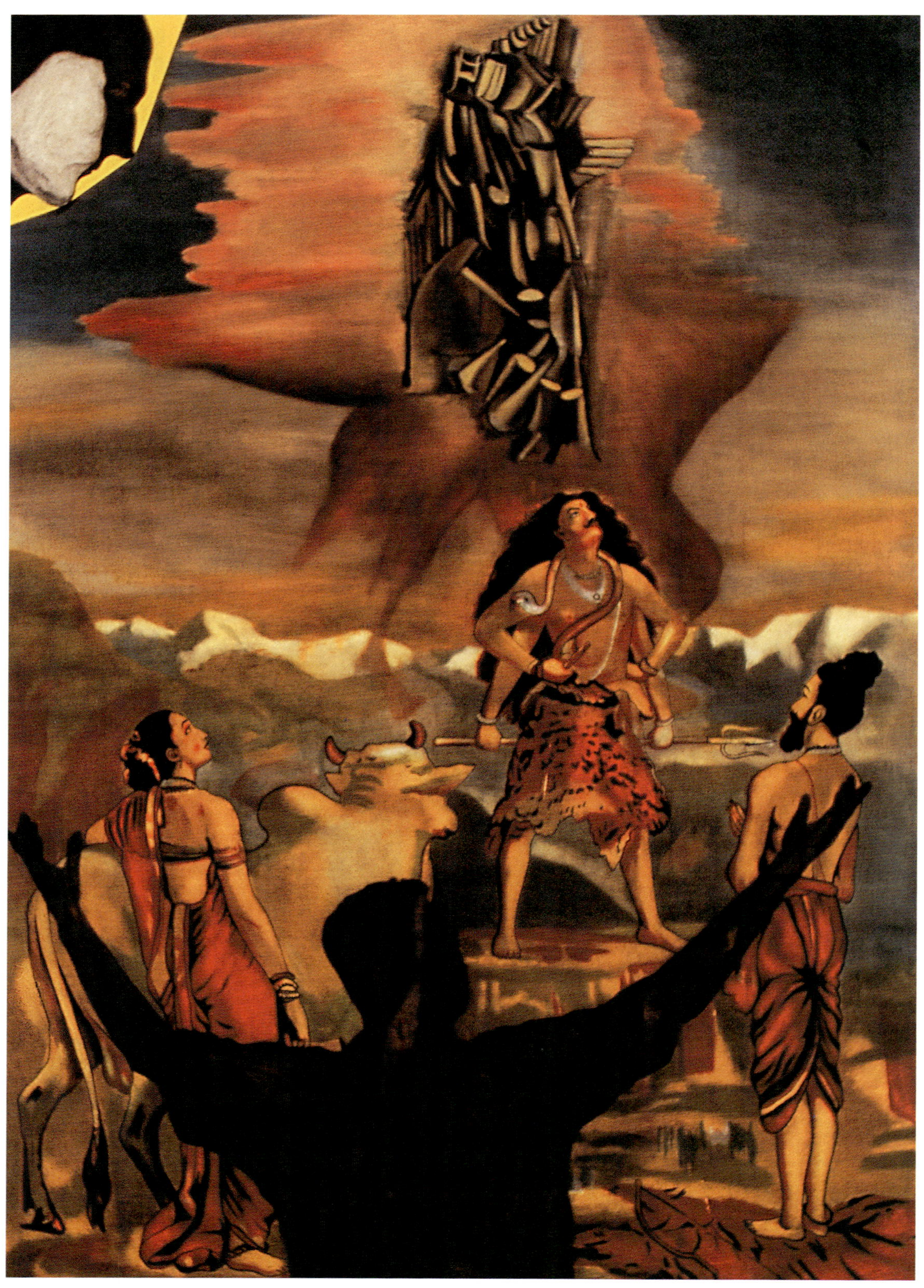

12
Atul Dodiya
"Gangavataran: After Raja Ravi Varma", 1998
Oil, acrylic, and marble dust on canvas; 213 x 152 cm

shops. In cosmic time, Vishnu yawns and turns and a century passes. The small yellow taxi skimming the surface could be negotiating the vast recesses of consciousness suggested by this painting.

The heroes of art history for Dodiya are artists like Marcel Duchamp and his discovery of found objects which questioned modernism's monolithic self-image. But he also resists the Duchampian and Dadaist hegemony by countering it with other inventions from his own memory and history. In "Gangavataran: After Raja Ravi Varma" (1998), the oleograph which has devolved into the comic strip of the present, has the god Shiva awaiting the descent of the Ganga (figure 12). The celestial river in this case has been substituted by the Duchampian "Nude Descending the Staircase" while Duchamp in silhouette gazes at this chimera from memory. The two masters, the binary styles of found objects and street art, the international and the local are evenly matched in this vivid work. Finally the outstretched shadow of the artist himself provides the visual counterpoint which asserts its freedom to reinvent metaphors from history. As the art critic Ranjit Hoskote writes, "He counters the absolutist's desiccated monoism with alternative readings, a plurality of versions; he reclaims tradition from the fossil-worshippers by inserting his own preoccupation into it, revitalising it for the present."[10]

While the original impetus for installations has come from outside, it has at the same time a characteristic rootedness in India. The post-modernist metaphor also stems from the logic of historical and social memory. The usage of street and popular art, the visual seepages from the environment, and the use of waste and recycled material have all served to provide a distinct flavour to site-specific works here. The hybridity, fragmentation, and multiculturalism from the international arena intersect inherent multiplicities creating a fusilladed landscape. Perhaps the heady intermixing of these has led to the burgeoning pluralism of the present. In its formative state it is to be seen if this will lead to sharply defined modes which provide an impetus to future works.

NOTES

1. Partha Mitter, *Art and Nationalism in Colonial India,* Cambridge University Press, 1994.

2. Geeta Kapur, "Dismantling the Norm", paper presented at the "Traditions/Tensions" seminar, Asia Society, New York, 1996.

3. Ibid.

4. Ajay Sinha, "Transfiguring the Ritual Body", *The Art News Magazine of India*, vol. 2, issue 2.

5. Gieve Patel, *G. Ravinder Reddy, Painted Sculpture and Relief,* catalogue for show at Sakshi Art Gallery, Mumbai, 1991.

6. Anita Dube, "Is Installation Relevant to India", *The Art News Magazine of India*, vol. 4, issue 2.

7. Kamala Kapoor, "Sieve-O-Physis, interview with Anita Dube", *Art and Asia Pacific,* issue 26.

8. Ibid.

9. Interview with the writer, New Delhi, May 2000.

10. Ranjit Hoskote, *Atul Dodiya – Recent Works,* catalogue for his show at the Vadehra Art Gallery, New Delhi, March 18 – April 5, 1999.

1
Gu Wenda
"United Nations – China
Monument: Temple of Heaven",
1998
Installations with human hair,
glue, rope. wooden monitors;
approx. 7.3 x 9.1 x 8.2 m
Collection: Artist

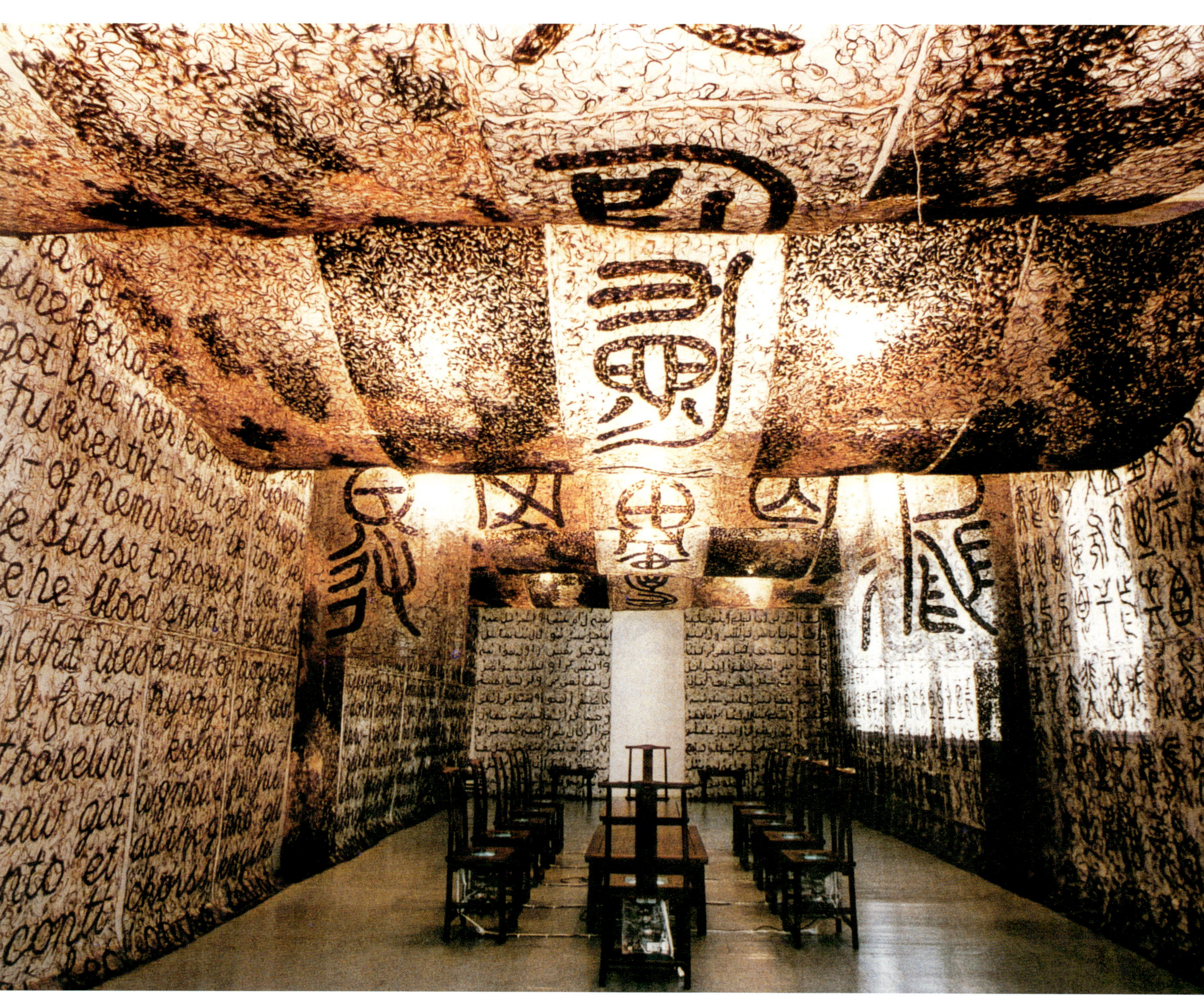

Thomas McEvilley

eurocentrism and contemporary indian art

Nicholas of Cusa, an Italian mystic of the 15th century, is famous for the remark, "God is a circle whose centre is everywhere and periphery nowhere." The thought bears some resemblance to Vedantin ideas in the Indian tradition – as when, for example, Shankara says that Being exists in absolute fullness everywhere: "not different in different things, but one in all its appearances".[1] Then everything is the centre, everything is pure Being: "That art thou, O Svetaketu," states the *Mahavakya* (Great Saying) of the *Chandogya Upanishad* (VI.8.16).

Nicholas's formulation probably was based on Plato, whose ideas had recently been reintroduced to the West, through the commentaries of Plotinus, after almost a millennium of absence (absent because the Christians had deliberately burned them). According to Plato, as understood by Plotinus, every Essence contained all the other Essences, while somehow managing to remain distinctively itself – "different but at the same time not different", as the *Brahma Sutra* (II.3.43) said, or *bhedabheda* (different/non-different) as Nimbarka and Bhaskara would rephrase the idea. So the centre is everywhere in the sense that the centre is the periphery; and there is no periphery in the sense that the periphery is the centre. Each disappears into the other (or the Other).

But in the actual history of embodied selves and nations, that ideal seems distant or unattainable. What happens in history is a cruel parody of it. During the colonial era, for example, the nations of western Europe felt that they and they alone constituted a centre for the world. Everything else was periphery. This was expressed in Hegel's declaration that "World History happens in Europe." As Plato observed, it seems that the ideal of sameness-in-difference cannot be concretely attained in space-time so much as dimly sensed behind it. The infinite interpenetration of the Essences becomes a random here-and-there and now-and-then penetration of one thing by another. That is the low-down truth of a world that is cut off from the Essences and cannot realize them directly.

Nevertheless, something like Nicholas's idea has been stated as both the premise and the goal of the post-colonial period, as if it somehow could escape the bad news of history. Sameness-in-difference has been seen as an ideal for the relationship of different cultures in the same world. Each would contain something of all the others while yet remaining itself. The god of such a world might well look at it and exclaim, as Plotinus exclaimed at the vision of the Essences: "Each is all and all is each and the glory of it is infinite!" But that god, that unifying stream of Being which carries all things along toward its inwardly-cherished goal, appears today in the guise of Late Capitalism, the transnational unifier that creates, as its model of multiculturalism, the international food court in metropolitan airports, where the burrito and the gyro and the pita sandwich coexist for the nourishment of all.

Eurocentrism to Americentrism

In the colonial period the western European powers held the reins of the rest of the world – at least so far as their wealth went. All reins went back to Europe as all roads once led to Rome – and all money found its way there eventually, too. Meanwhile, all canons of normality were to be based on European ways of doing things: thinking, appreciating, making art, writing books, having a certain skin colour, and so on. The cultural facade masked the economic engine, obscuring the howls of machines and the weary cries of workers with waves of beautiful music.

Today that overt and unashamed brand of Eurocentrism has mostly disappeared; it survives in the West only in the political and cultural right wing. Elsewhere the colonial era lingers in less violent residual effects such as the maintenance of art world hegemony in the West. In the colonial era the West believed in its own artistic hegemony – believed, that is, that its artists' work was superior in quality to the efforts of the rest of the world. Today it is not artistic hegemony per se, based on a hierarchy of quality, that remains in the West (only diehard colonialists such as the art critics who appear in the right-wing American journal *New Criterion* would still make that claim), but what might be called "art world hegemony" lingers still in New York City.

In terms of Eurocentrism, New York is an extension of Europe or a surrogate for it, and Eurocentrism now takes the form of Americentrism. In the 20th century, America, for better or for worse, crossed its Rubicon and definitively attached itself to the end of European history, as if the linear central line of history as conceived by Hegel had simply swerved across the north Atlantic to a new centre which was really just a proxy for the old one. So America's position is highly ambiguous. Conceived in the 18th century as a place that would be outside of history and free of its inherited travail, when it entered World War I, and especially World War II, on the side of the western European powers it lost that status to a considerable extent, becoming an extension or surrogate of Europe.

On the other hand, America is the only major nation that is a nation entirely of refugees – nomads, hybrids, and so on – that is, of supposedly post-modernist people. And, since 1966, an important date in the history of the early development of post-modernism, American immigration laws have ceased to favour Europe and the tide of the American population is turning, with seeming inexorability, to Asia and to the so-called Second and Third Worlds. A recent show on American art in the 20th century, curated for the Royal Academy in London by Norman Rosenthal and Christos Joachimedes, presented the situation like this: that Europe carried the ball of history, moving it toward the goal, till World War II when it more or less lost it, dropped the ball as it were, or was about to drop it and at the last second passed it to America. America then caught the ball of the forward edge of civilization (supposedly) and carried it onward, filling in (supposedly) until Europe could recover, whereupon America was expected to pass the ball back again. This recovery happened in the 1980s, when first the New German Painting, then the Italian transavantguardia, then the New British Sculpture, appeared and were applauded as signs of Europe's evidently reinvigorated cultural health. But by this time the response was not so predictable as these European curators had thought it would be. America's loyalties are increasingly divided between its European cultural origins and its ever-growing orientation toward the Third World, from which most of its new citizens arrive. It is not so certain that America will, or can, just pass the ball back. Some Americans may try to pass it back while at the same time others try tossing it over their heads into the Third World.

Multicultural Modernism

So today, to say "art world hegemony" resides in New York does not necessarily mean it is at Europe's disposal. By "art world hegemony", rather than "artistic hegemony", is meant the infrastructure of an art system: art schools, galleries, magazines, publishers, and auction houses. But this art infrastructure by itself seems a mere shell of the lively activity that it contained not long ago, when American art was, with some justification, seen as embodying the forward edge of art history at least in the West. Now it is a neutral set of equipment in which anything can be processed, and it is precariously balanced between the First and Third Worlds. One day it may rebond itself with Europe, or tear itself farther away toward its emerging Asian connection (17 per cent of Americans are now of Asian extraction). Meanwhile it maintains the infrastructure as if idling or on hold, waiting till something about the world situation comes clear again in the post-colonial turbulence.

So today New York is an empty set of equipment, waiting; without new grist for the mill it might soon wither away. Meanwhile the shell is kept alive by the fact that certain cities in the West remain the chosen centres of residence for artists from all over the world. It is only partly an aftermath of colonialism that artists such as Masami Teraoka of Japan, T.F. Chen of Taiwan, Gu Wenda of China, Ouattara of Cote d'Ivoire, Shahzia Sikander of Pakistan, Alexander Kosalopov of Russia, and countless others from virtually everywhere in the world, live today in New York City. Somewhat comparable lists of artists could be made up for London and Paris, but with the difference that each would reflect the list of colonies those nations once held. For the United States, however, this situation is only in part the aftermath of western European colonialism, inherited by America along with Europe's wars; it is in at least equal part the result of America's own role as an immigrant nation whose edges are increasingly melting into those of the Third World.

2
Shahzia Sikander
"Our Racial Veils", 1994
Vegetable colour, watercolour, dry pigment, tea wash on *wasli*; 30.5 x 20 cm

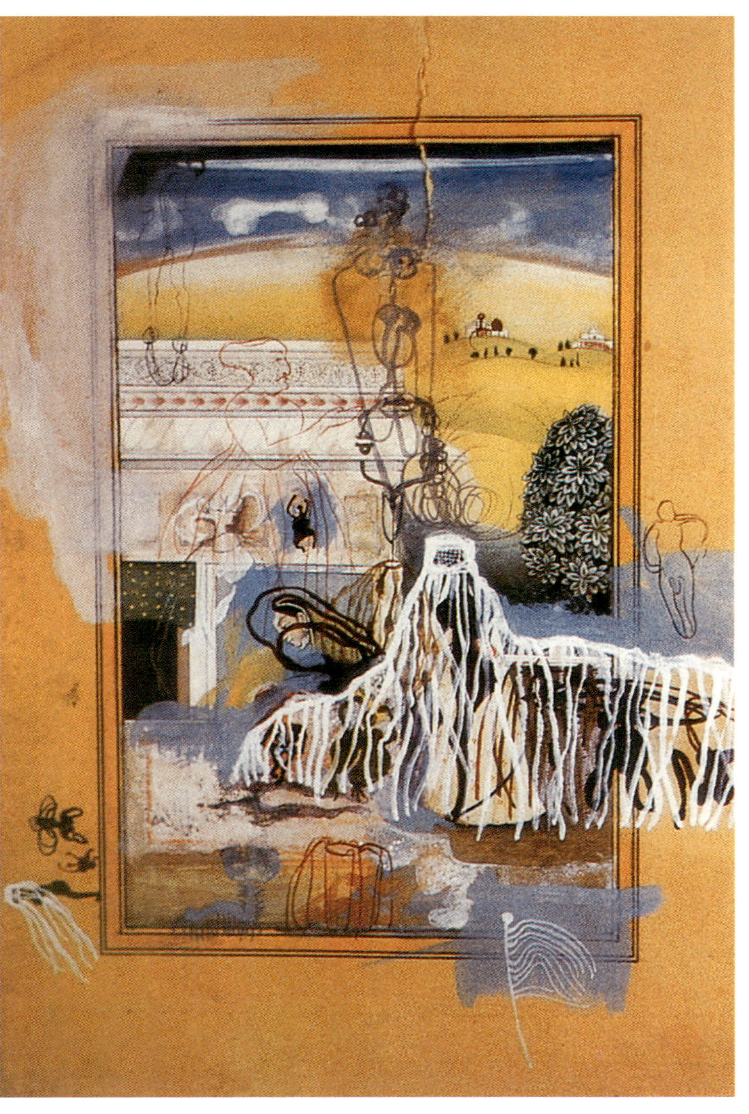

In the age portrayed in, say, Ousmane Sembène's films, a colonial who ended up in some Western urban centre would be working in a menial job and living in the kind of social invisibility that novelist Ralph Ellison defined as the situation of the African American.[2] Today the citizen of a previously colonized society resident in the West may instead be living and working as a creative individual whose self-expressions find an appreciative audience. In the colonial era there were a few colonial artists who managed to occupy positions of respectability in Western urban centres, but

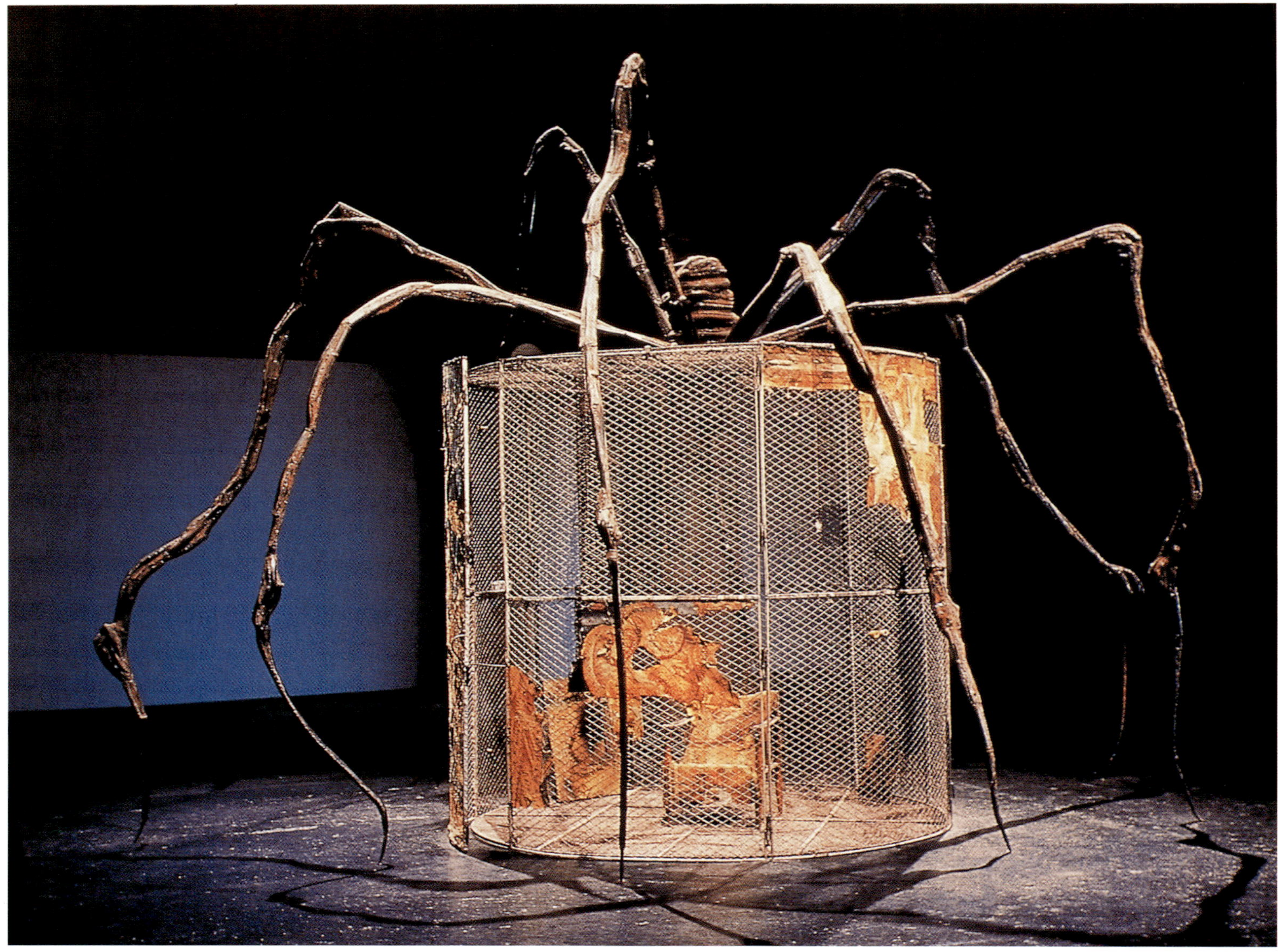

3
Louise Bourgeois
"Spider", 1997
Steel and mixed media;
4.4 x 6.7 x 5.2 m

in order to find an audience who would take their work seriously, it was necessary for them to work in heavily Westernized modes. Thus, as Yashodhara Dalmia writes, "It has often been contended of the Modernists, that much of their work was imitative of western artists and particularly of the School of Paris painters."[3] It had to be imitative in order to be acknowledged at all. Today, that is not the case: in New York, London, or Paris, exhibitions of work from other traditions can receive appreciative and educated reviews in several newspapers or magazines without pretending to be something they are not.

Today the United States is sharply divided into parties of multiculturalists and xenophobes. Most art publications – but not all – are of the multiculturalist persuasion. Each tends to have one or more writers who have a special interest in the previously colonized world. (Eleanor Heartney at *Art in America* or Holland Cotter at the *New York Times* are examples.) These and other writers with similar commitments approach the art of the rest of the world with a combination of careful scholarship and eager appreciation. On this level of cultural discourse something like the metaphysical ideal of mutual interpenetration can indeed happen, as artists from different sides of the world become interested in one another's work and influenced by it not so much in imitation as in creative interaction with their own. In the famous era of "primitivism" early in the 20th century, Western artists such as Picasso were interested in, say, African art because of how it interacted with their own – but this interest was not mutual. Today in India, China, Thailand, Taiwan, Japan, Indonesia, the Philippines, and elsewhere in Asia, as well as many nations of Africa and Latin America, one finds artists who are interested in what Western artists are up to, and influenced by it to an extent, but not to the extent of burying their own tradition and their own inheritance. A corresponding interest in artistic modes from other traditions is found in the West.

So various options seem to be on the table. On the one hand, the atmosphere is pretty good in Western centres right now for artists from around the world. Mohan Samant, an Indian artist of significant achievement who has lived in New York for many years and has felt excluded and ignored, might not find the welcome so cold if he were arriving today. Not only is the United States less rabidly xenophobic, there are in addition more highly developed networks of diaspora populations from around the previously colonized world ready to offer support to arrivals from home.

For multiculturalism is still advancing in the West, though more slowly than was anticipated about fifteen years ago. The *New York Times* in January 2000 announced that Beth Israel Hospital would soon open a clinic for Chinese Medicine – an event that could not have been imagined a generation ago. Developments of this type are happening steadily but slowly as the nationalist categories of modernism gradually dissolve. The relaxing of American immigration quotas in 1966 led to large non-Western populations in virtually every American city of more than 250,000 and many smaller ones. The attitude towards them is not very negative anymore except in right-wing fundamentalist Christian parts of the country. Mostly they are appreciated today for their particularity rather than resented for it.

A View from the American Academy

An insight into where the situation is right now can be attained through comparing editions of the art history textbook most commonly used in American universities for the last twenty years or so, H.W. Janson's *History of Art*. Despite its uncompromisingly universalist title, the book is a history only of Western art, not of art in general. The title retains the colonialist attitude – that Western art really is art while other traditions around the world somehow missed it. According to Kant's *Critique of Taste* (1790) a cultural product was real art only if it was a direct or "pure" expression of the present sensibility of the artist at the moment of its making. (The ultimate expression of this idea, under Clement Greenberg's intensification or exaggeration of it, was Action

4
Nilima Sheikh
"Speaking of Akka-2" (detail), 1999
Tempera on Sanganeri paper

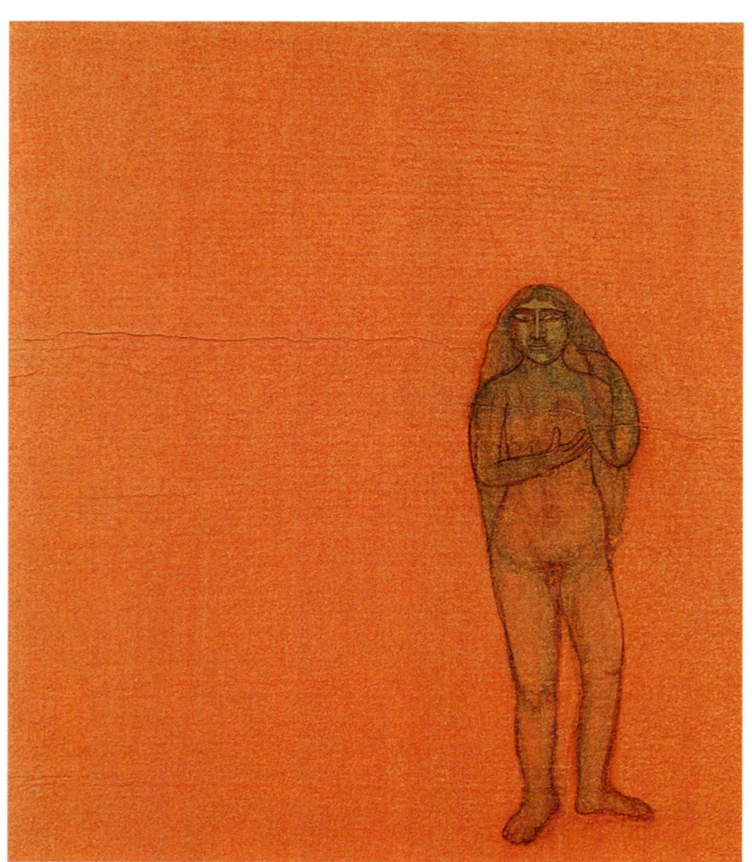

Painting). That theory pretty much eliminated all art that was deeply involved in a tradition – including Indian art. Hegel, in his *Phenomenology of Spirit* (1806) and even more his *Philosophy of History* (based on a series of lectures of 1821) added to Kant's insistence on sensibility the mandate of progress or innovation. An entity was only to be considered real art if it was conceived and executed with the motive of pushing the envelope of form that had been left by the last generation. Again, art from traditional societies is pretty much eliminated.

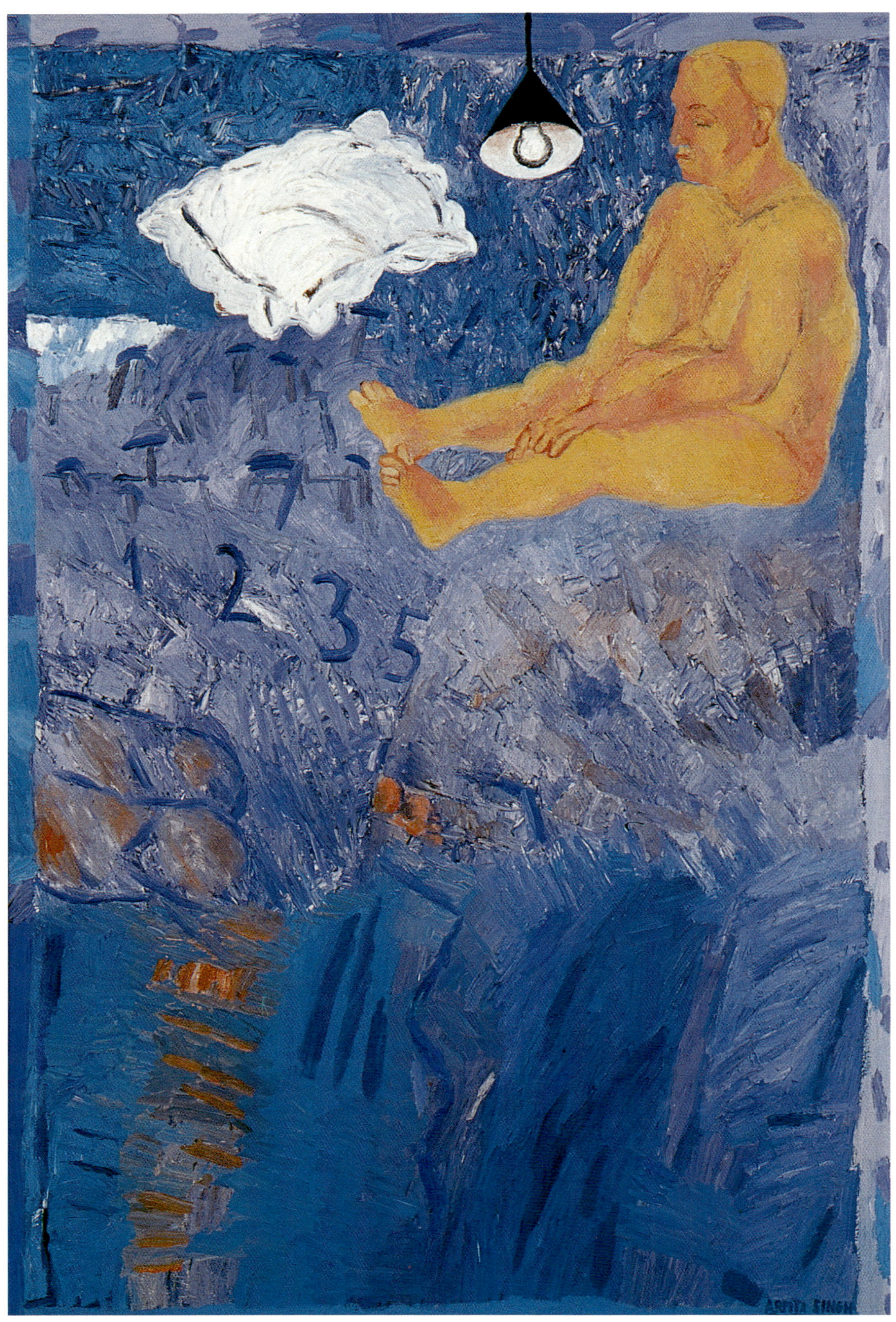

5
Arpita Singh
"Woman Sitting –
The Dissolving Body", 1995
Oil on canvas; 178 x 119 cm
Private collection

The American counterculture of the 1960s and '70s was in essence an anti-European movement, born from horror of war and disgust at colonialist depredations. It awakened much Western interest in non-Western traditions, and in response Janson's *History of Art* at some time in the '70s introduced, in the back of the book, a small section on Asian art which dealt only with a handful of canonical masterpieces from eras sufficiently distant to be considered classical. Nothing contemporary from the rest of the world could be even imagined as a possible inclusion. To do that would truly be, as one English critic said of the 1989 French multiculturalist exhibition *Les Magiciens de la Terre*, the end of Western civilization.

That is because "contemporary" is an especially loaded word in the modernist view of history. It does not mean simply that an art work was made at the present time, but that it is based on a study of the Western art tradition, possesses an awareness of the critical discourse surrounding that tradition, and is created with the purpose of contributing to that tradition and that discourse. So there couldn't really be a "contemporary art" that was made by a non-Westerner unless he or she had gone to school in the West and been initiated into its systems of thought.

Since history, on the Hegelian view, is always moving forward, there must be one edge of it which is the forward edge, the cutting edge, the edge that represents the whole daring project of progress and control of the future. Contemporary thus cannot be simply a chronological term; it carries on its shoulders the heaviest weight of meaning that Western civilization has to offer: the contemporary is where progress comes from. If the mandate of the contemporary is not carried out with full awareness of its meaning, progress will not happen, history will lose all meaning, and civilization, on the Hegelian modernist view, will have failed. And the proper execution of the mandate of the contemporary is to be in the hands of the West, which feels it has won it by demonstrating the principle of willing developmental change.

Meanwhile a part of the attitude that Edward Said called "Orientalism" is that the West can strengthen its grip on the rest of the world, while seeming, somewhat deceptively, to be appreciative of it, by the simple stratagem of admiring its ancient cultures. The point is that this admiration can then be used against the contemporary condition of the same societies, as a sign that they have degenerated; maybe they once had the spirit of civilization but they lost it, and so on. As the interest in multiculturalism grew in the West throughout the '80s, Janson enlarged the section of his book dealing with the ancient classical cultures of the East and tacitly denigrating the contemporary.

But by 1999, spurred by a series of post-colonialist exhibitions and the discourses surrounding them – *Primitivism, Magiciens, Africa Explores, Traditions/Tensions*, etc. – and fuelled by the impressive display of capitalist knowhow among the so-called Little Tigers of Asia, an increasing interest in living Asian artists could no longer be ignored. This was not often a deep interest, and was usually tainted by pure commodificative display – but in terms of getting into the art history books that could only help. Sometime in 1997, for example, *Art News* magazine, the most commercialized of the New York art magazines, but still a major one, had a call-out on its cover reading, "the hottest young artist in Asia". The absurdity of proclaiming a single "hot" artist out of all of vast Asia didn't worry anyone, nor the odd (once, anyway, it would have been odd) insistence that this artist be young.

As a part of post-modernist revisionism in the '80s the Western art world had pretty much deconstructed or jettisoned its own past. We found we were no longer interested in our canon of mature contemporary artists. Who cared about Richard Diebenkorn or Helen Frankenthaler anymore?

Led by a hungry gallery system, the market sought and lionized ever younger new artists, seeking to control the manufacture of a new canon, which could be expected to control art market money for at least a few years. So it was inevitable that when the desire arose, also out of market forces, to incorporate some Asian artists into the network, it would be framed as a search for unknown young geniuses. This was the way the market was to work in the post-*Magiciens* era – by letting one artist in at a time, and treating him or her as inevitable ("the hottest") at his or her moment. (As I recall, it was the Indonesian Heri Donó whom *Art News* proclaimed in this way.)

By this time, Janson's son (who now had inherited the book as a family business) saw it was no longer feasible to cover only classical Asian art and act as if contemporary Asian art did not exist – as if Asia were still, as Hegel had insisted, ahistorical. Yet neither he nor anyone on the staff knew enough about it to write the needed section – and anyway it seemed unwise to rush into taking such a momentous step. So they simply removed the Asian section from the book altogether! Now, instead, there is a note saying that they feel the earlier approach – the Orientalism of dealing only with the ancient – will no longer suffice, and they are considering their next move. One day, evidently, a new section on Asian art will appear that will somehow attempt to include at least the modern and perhaps some hint of the contemporary too. So now Asia is omitted from the book, as it was at the beginning – but this time it is omitted out of respect rather than dismissal.

Post-Modernism and a Global Language

There seems to be general distrust in India of the sea-change of attitude that many Westerners call post-modernism. It is as if the Westerners' renunciation of modernism was a trick by which they hoped to keep it all for themselves. As W.J.T. Mitchell said, the post-modern faction in the West "may find itself preaching a rhetorical de-centring and de-essentializing to cultures that are struggling to find a centre and an essence."[4] Nevertheless, the reality of the idea may come through when Indian or other non-Western artists arrive in the West and find interest in their work primarily among those who regard themselves as post-modernists. To us in the West modernism is still seen as yearning, however covertly, for colonialism and enforced Western hegemony; post-modernism, in contrast, not only accepts but celebrates the end of colonialism and the dawning of a differently arranged and more multivocal geopolitics. But just in the last decade or so a significant

6
Surendran Nair
"Forty Winks"
Oil on canvas

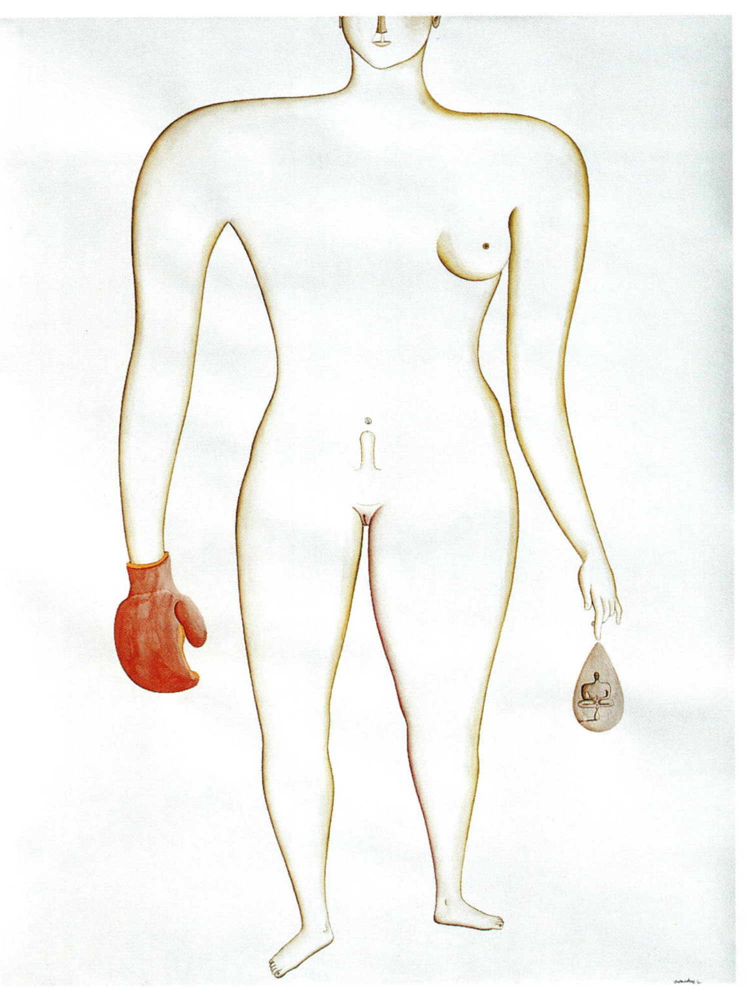

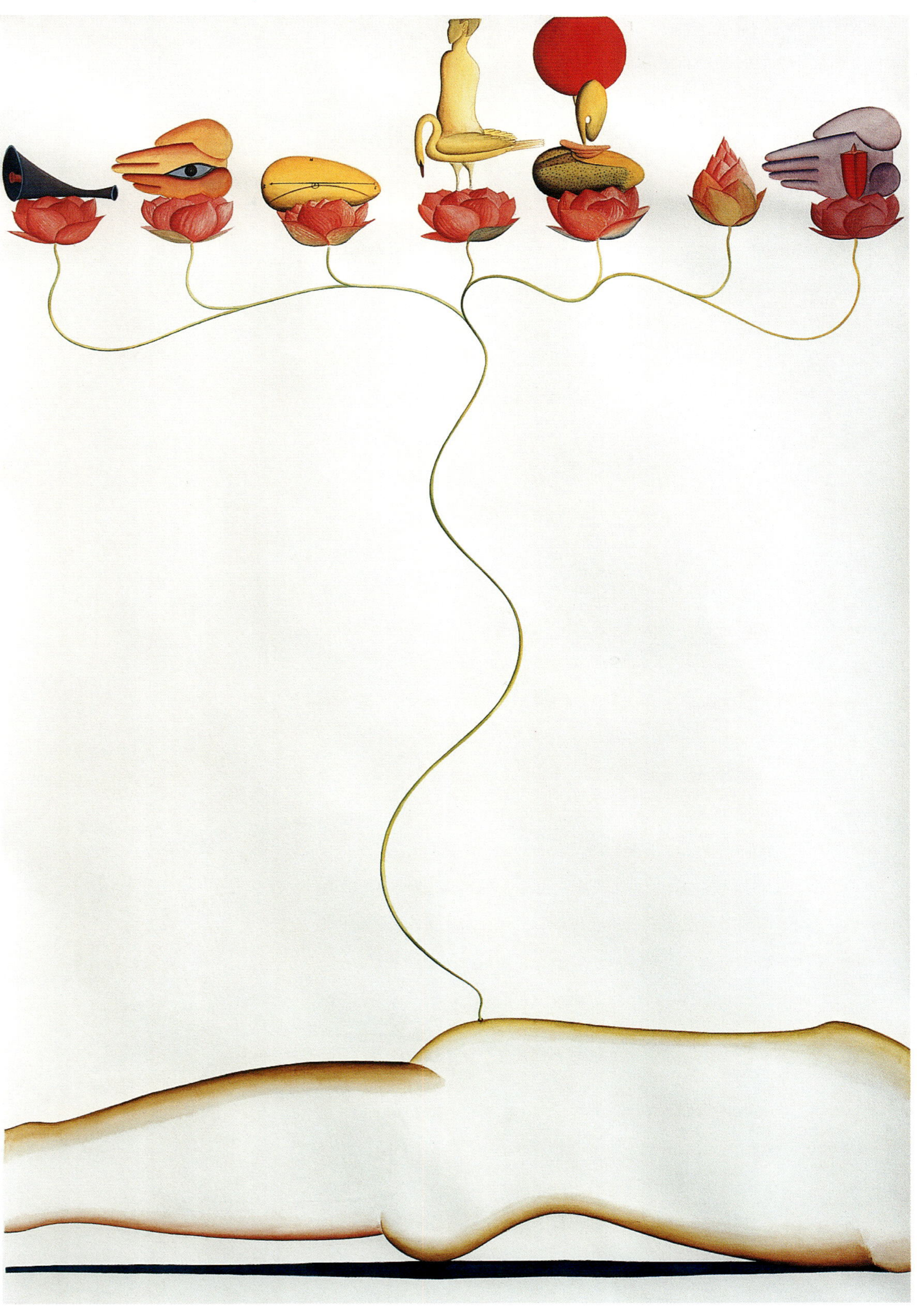

7
Surendran Nair
"Forty Winks 1"
Oil on canvas

change in the picture has occurred. Suddenly the vision of post-modernist globalism as a mutually fertilizing cultural interpenetration seems already to have passed, before it even became familiar.

In the 1980s, talk of post-modernist globalism imagined (for example) African-American jazz musician Roland Kirk playing the didjeridoo in Texas while Indian classical musician L. Subramaniam plays ragas on the western violin – and so on, in a global cultural picture where the centre is in fact a little bit everywhere. But when the news media speak of globalization today they mean something very different: the onward flood of late capitalism sweeping cultures aside or burying them beneath its seemingly inexorable advance. The expectation of a cultural globalism has been drowned by the raw fact of an economic globalism rushing over it. It is no longer culture which seems to be leading; though it may still be in the picture, it is following along behind. As the West eagerly purchases commodity goods from the newly producing industries of the previous Third World, it also becomes interested in its art. No longer necessarily Eurocentric, this interest will follow wherever the capitalist action goes. During the 1980s, when goods from East Asia flooded Western markets, interest was whetted for Indonesian, Chinese, Thai, and Korean art. This interest slackened after the temporary collapse of Asian stock markets in the middle '90s, but will probably return as the market does. This new mode of globalization seems to be capitalism running its course like a juggernaut that has hurtled through history but has not yet worn itself out; it is not truly global in the cultural sense that was often in the air in the '80s. Africa, for example, is being left out this time, though after *Magiciens de la Terre* in 1989 it was African artists who most immediately attracted attention in Western markets. That was still a wave of cultural globalism that was like a premonitory tremor foretelling the fiercer and mightier wave of capitalist globalization unleashed in the '90s. Cultural preferences will have less to do with it now than it once seemed. A vast mechanical process seems to be taking over.

In the colonial era the western European nations thought they could abruptly terminate other cultural traditions and quickly replace them with their own. Any day now people around the world would, as Hegel anticipated, be dressing, talking, and thinking like 19th-century Prussians. But cultural identity proved much harder to eradicate or redefine than had been expected. In the New World, enslaved Africans, made to turn away from the Yoruba religion to Christianity, invented Santeria, a crypto-form of Yoruba made to look like Christianity. Santeria is still alive four hundred years later, and with it something of African identity, not only in the Caribbean and Brazil but in neighbourhoods in New York, Los Angeles, Miami, and other Latinized North American cities.

Today the Western nations no longer attempt to force the rest of the world into their configurations. As Simon During said, "Postmodern thought [is] that thought which refuses to turn the Other into the Same."[5] But still, as nomadic cultural interactions swarm about the expanding surface of global capitalism, there will be a gradual mingling of cultural identities as their confrontations erode cultural boundaries and seepage occurs. In the age of global capitalism, cultures will still be homogenized, but at a slower rate

8
Sudhir Patwardhan
"Tree", 1996
Oil on canvas

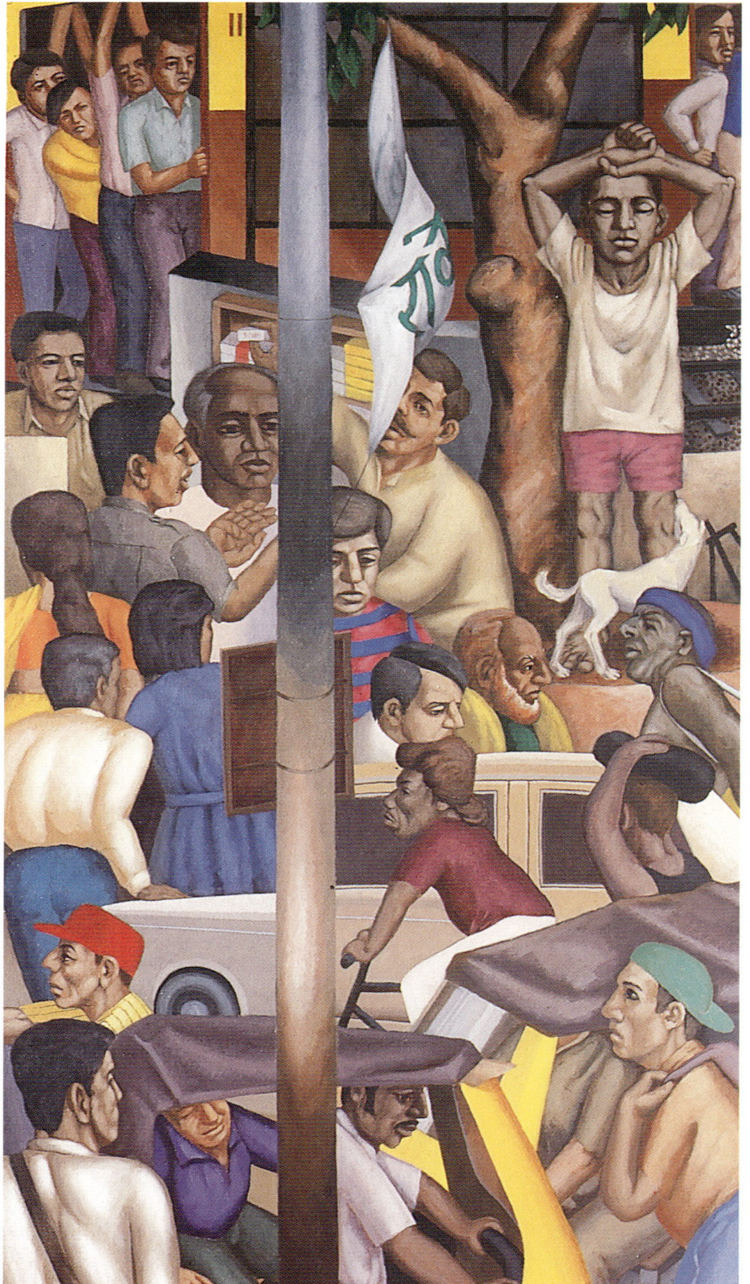

than envisioned in the colonial era. There may be a period when the cultures of the shrinking world will maintain themselves self-consciously pure, but that purity will be artificial, or at least artificially maintained like a hothouse flower. Meanwhile the living culture will still be carried along on the wave of homogenization. Cultures will leave museum displays of themselves behind them as they disappear into a future whose identity cannot yet be seen or imagined. Perhaps the great question is, what language will people speak at that time?

For better or for worse, English is rapidly becoming the global second language and spawning myriad hybrid or pidgin or pastiche forms of itself: Indonesian English, Senegalese English, Brazilian English, and so on. (Or perhaps one should say "American" rather than "English", since it seems less the lingering effect of the British Empire than the contemporary effect of American pop culture that is spreading the language so far afield.) English has thus become denaturized, or neutered; it is no longer exactly English per se.[6] The English of Shakespeare and Milton is becoming more distant, less taught in universities; it appears less relevant as a model for young writers.[7] The reality of the hybrid forms of English is overshadowing the reality of English-as-English, and it no longer seems true, as it once did, that "for the post-colonial to speak or write in the imperial tongues is to call forth a problem of identity, to be thrown into mimicry and ambivalence"[8] – or, as Chinua Achebe said, "it looks like a dreadful betrayal".[9] The Irish, a colonized people whose own language was all but crushed and exterminated by the English, have since made English their own. Most lists of the greatest 20th-century authors in the English language would feature Irish writers – James Joyce, William Butler Yeats, John Synge, Samuel Beckett, and others. England itself cannot boast as distinguished a list of modern English authors. The imprint of Indian culture has also been deeply left upon the English language and its tradition of letters. First there was the period when "captive Greece her captor Rome held captive", when English colonialists were so struck by the power and coherence of the Indian tradition that – in a mixture of Orientalism and inspired self-discovery – they all but adopted it, becoming Indologists, elevating Sanskrit to a pinnacle of prestige in Europe almost comparable to its traditional stature in India, and so on. The list of authors from the Indian subcontinent who have written English with distinction is hardly less impressive than that of the Irish: from the generation of Rabindranath Tagore, Ananda Coomaraswamy, and Swami Vivekananda, to that of Nirad C. Chaudhuri and Sarvepalli Radhakrishnan, and finally that of Gayatri Spivak, Homi Bhabha, and others.

"Post-colonialism," writes During, "is the need, in nations or groups which have been victims of imperialism, to achieve an identity uncontaminated by universality or Eurocentric concepts and images." This "need" may be somewhat less urgent in India than elsewhere, due to India's enormous cultural prestige, the equal of any, and due to the neuterization of English through American post-colonial, pop-cultural hegemony. (When I was in China a few years ago people were standing all night in long lines in the streets outside music stores where Michael Jackson's new album was expected to go on sale the next day.) Still, it is felt nevertheless, as the India of the BJP, the Ayodhya riots, and Hindu fundamentalism is in danger of developing an "official nationalism" with "imposition of cultural hegemony from the top, through state action."[10]

Spivak takes an attitude toward post-modernism similar to that taken by African-American authors such as Bell Hooks and Cornell West: that Western discourse ostensibly designed to shift the discursive centre toward the colonial periphery and affirm the previously colonized subject is in fact "the result of an interested desire to conserve the subject of the West, or the West as subject. It is, in effect, what, in the Civil Rights Movement, was called tokenism. The thrust of pluralized subject-effects gives an illusion of undermining subjective sovereignty while often providing a cover for this subject of knowledge. The much publicized critique of the sovereign subject thus actually inaugurates a Subject."[11]

On this view, post-colonialist multiculturalism is a form of neo-imperialism – another attempt by the West, less overtly violent but, in compensation, sneakier – to anchor the world's discourse in the sound of its voice. Those previously colonized peoples who participate in the discourse become Uncle Toms (Gunga Dins); they have been fooled yet again. As Spivak puts it, "Certain varieties of the Indian elite are at best native informants for first-world intellectuals interested in the voice of the other."[12] In contrast, the optimistic view of Chinua Achebe sounds laboured in its sentimentality: "Let every people bring their gifts to the great festival of the world's cultural harvest and mankind will be all the richer for the variety and distinctiveness of the offerings."[13]

Yet it is true, as Kachru says, that "the domains of English have been restructured [so that] people ask is English really a non-native (alien) language for India, for Africa, for South East Asia?"[14] Raja Rao answers the question somewhat ambiguously: "English is not really an alien language to us. It is the language of our intellectual makeup – like Sanskrit or Persian was before – but not of our emotional makeup."[15] The question may soon enough become academic. Though English is now becoming the global second language, and though American (or African-American) popular culture is sweeping the world, that is only for the moment. By 2050 will Chinese be the global language?

Indian Modernism

Geeta Kapur's call for an Indian modernism points up some difficulties of the situation. In the era of the Progressives it was assumed that modernism meant something that not only had happened in the West but also was inalienably or essentially a part of it; so to become modern one had to become Western.[16] That is how Hegel saw it, how Husserl and Heidegger saw it – and how the Progressives saw it too, before it was widely realized that the values of Hegel were about to pass away. But the idea that modernism, because it was invented in the West, must carry the trappings of Western culture with it, seems questionable. Does a syllogism work only in the culture that formulated it? Modernism, as a system of social, political, and economic relations, would seem to be a structural pattern in which a great variety of cultural contents could be arranged. So a modernism that does not grovel to Western hegemony and carry along with it the baggage of Western cultural influences should be possible.

At the same time, the phrase Indian modernism might seem a contradiction in terms, since modernism was supposedly international in its attitude. One can also imagine an argument that Western cultural patterns that have emerged out of modernism itself over the last few centuries may be argued to be more innately modernist than those that have emerged out of non-modernist cultures through recent impact of modernism. But modernist internationalism was so tilted toward Eurocentrism that it was a one-way relationship. And if Western culture has recreated itself by a saturation in modernism, so can others.

In terms of visual arts a relevant distinction lies in the implications of different genres. Modernist internationalism put its full weight behind the cultural sign of Western easel painting. That genre more than any other represented the West and its illusory sense of mission (its "civilizing mission"). As the representational painting seemed to open like a window on the wall, it pointed to the realization of space in the depth axis through worldwide exploration and colonization. With its endless pictures of Christian scenes ("God is on our side") and its idealized portraits of merchant princes and equestrian conquerors it promoted the colonial activity, which subsequently it maintained in place through its pictures (like Delacroix's "Death of Sardanapalus") of Asia as decadent and febrile. The easel painting was like the flag on the mast of the slave ship, and obeisance to it was the cost that a non-Western artist had to pay in order to have his existence even acknowledged. The recent spate of installation art is much more in line with the multicultural movement. Inspired as much by the ritual practices of non-Western cultures as by the natural history museum's dioramas, it involves elements from the

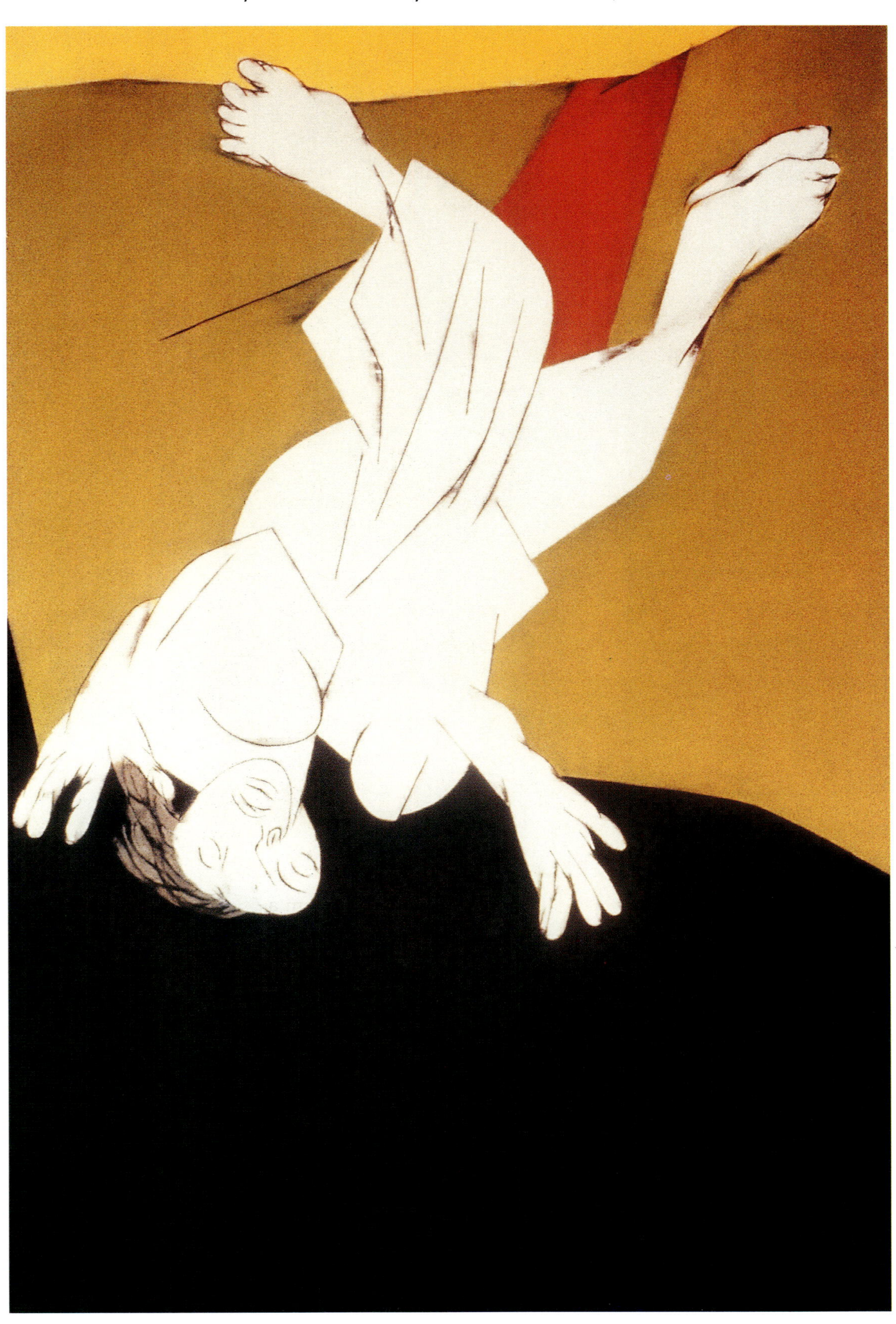

9
Tyeb Mehta
"Falling Figure", 1987
Acrylic on canvas

maker's culture and signs of his or her identity passing through the nomadic initiation. It does not especially stand as an emblem of the West or its claimed hegemony.

Still, post-modernist pluralism will inevitably become involved in a process of global homogenization. Though it once refused to call the different the same, still, in time it will iron out the differences just by mixing and mingling them in the vast blender of capitalist commodification. Internationalist modernism, with its banner of abstract painting leading the charge, attempted to developmentally force the homogenization of the world; post-modernist installation and other forms of multicultural art, carried on the cresting wave of late capitalism, may accomplish the same end more slowly, without the uncomfortable feeling of developmental forcing.

From the 1940s to the 1960s India was involved in the process of using art to embody a conception of its identity. The activity was ambivalent, as there were two sides to it that contradicted one another: first, the Progressives attempted to assert their identity as Euro-modernist on the grounds that modernism was international and applied to them as much as to western Europeans. Second, the New Delhi Triennale was founded in 1960, the first (or one of the very first) Third World recurring exhibitions of international contemporary art. The ambivalence is in how they were acted out. On the one hand the Progressives became modernist with a repression in their work of much of their own tradition; they in effect declared themselves part of the First World, or declared the First World to be ideologically universal. On the other hand, the New Delhi Triennales remained committed to India's position within the Third World (and somewhat the Second), exhibiting works from, say, Mongolia and Yugoslavia rather than France and America.

Now that phase is long past. What situation has replaced it? Today India has established an ambiguous hold on contemporary art. It is ambiguous because on the one hand contemporary art is firmly established in India, has numerous estimable practitioners, some critics and gallerists, and a few collectors both here and abroad. On the other hand, Indian contemporary art is not widely recognized outside of India as a functioning and in some ways exemplary part of the global situation. While Asian capitalism was thriving in the 1980s the Western art world was relatively eager to regard and receive its products. But India has never unambiguously been a part of Asian capitalism.

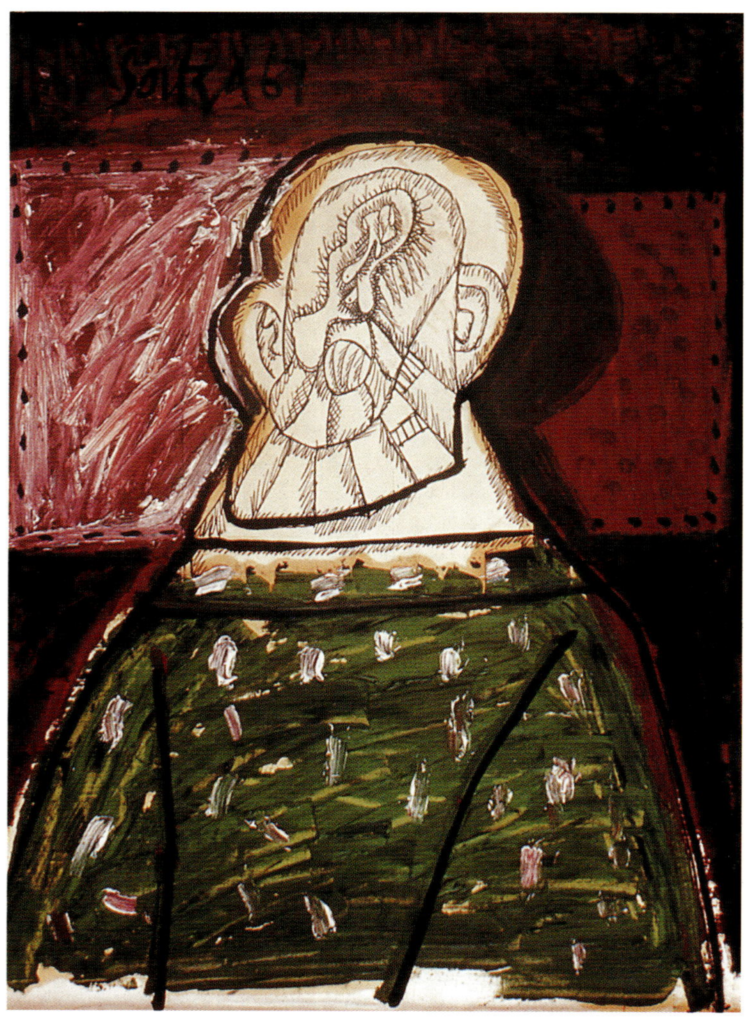

10
Francis Souza
"Head", 1964
Oil on canvas
Collection: Kumar Gallery, New Delhi

India still has to deal with the question of whether to make art that proclaims its identity as part of the First, Second, or Third World. And it still is uncertain on this point in its own mind. Economically and socially much of its population belongs in the Third World. Its government has long kept up a tenuous linkage with governments and cultures of the Second World. Its artists and its art system, insofar as it exists, seem to see themselves primarily in terms of the First World.

Which direction will be most useful to it today? India is one of the nations in the world which have possessed since antiquity cultures which might be described as Totalities. The other one, China, has managed to destroy its links with its own cultural history and today participates in the contemporary world without a supporting foundation of self-knowledge based on its past. This leaves a special position that India alone holds in the world today which may open for it options not available everywhere. If an Indian modernism could arise which would protect India from the depersonalizing capitalist mode of globalization it would be welcome. As a tradition increasingly serves purposes other than its own extension, it withers at the root. Whether Indian culture will maintain its living roots while exfoliating in the hybrid atmosphere of transnational capitalism remains to be seen.

NOTES

1. Surendranath Dasgupta, *A History of Indian Philosophy*, 5 vols., Delhi, Motilal Banarsidass, 1975, vol.1, p. 446.

2. Ousmane Sembène (b. 1923), Senegalese labour union activist, writer, and film director, is best known for his historical-political works with strong social comment.

Ralph Ellison, *Invisible Man*, New York, Vintage, 1947.

3. Yashodhara Dalmia, "Modernist Inventions", in Bina Sarkar Ellias, ed., *Fifty Years of Indian Art*, Mumbai, Mohile-Parikh Centre for the Visual Arts, 1998, p.113.

4. W.J.T. Mitchell, "Postcolonial Culture, Postimperial Criticism", in Bill Ashcroft, Gareth Griffiths, and Helen Tiffin, eds., *The Post-Colonial Studies Reader*, London and New York, Routledge, 1995, p. 477.

5. Simon During, "Postmodernism or Postcolonialism Today", in *The Post-Colonial Studies Reader*, p. 125.

6. I mean something somewhat different from what Braj B. Kachru means when he speaks of the "neutrality" and the "neutralization" of English ("The Alchemy of English", in *The Post-Colonial Studies Reader*, p. 292). I mean that the language has lost the kinds of power and attraction associated with gender: it has lost sexiness, sexuality, sexual power.

7. Ibid.

8. Cited by Ngugi Wa Thiong'o, "The Language of African Literature", in *The Post-Colonial Studies Reader*, p. 285.

9. Ibid.

10. Partha Chatterjee, "Nationalism as a Problem", in *The Post-Colonial Studies Reader*, p. 165.

11. Gayatri Spivak, "Can the Subaltern Speak?", in *The Post-Colonial Studies Reader*, p. 24.

12. Ibid., p. 26.

13. Chinua Achebe, "Colonialist Criticism", in *The Post-Colonial Studies Reader*, p. 61.

14. Kachru, "The Alchemy of English", p. 294.

15. Raja Rao, "Language and Spirit", in *The Post-Colonial Studies Reader*, p. 296.

16. Discussed by Kapur at the conference, "Fifty Years of Indian Art", at the Mohile-Parikh Centre for the Visual Arts, Mumbai, January 1996.

1
Anish Kapoor
"As if to Celebrate I Discovered a Mountain Blooming with Flowers",
1981
Mixed media; 96 x 309 x 304 cm
Collection: Tate Gallery, London

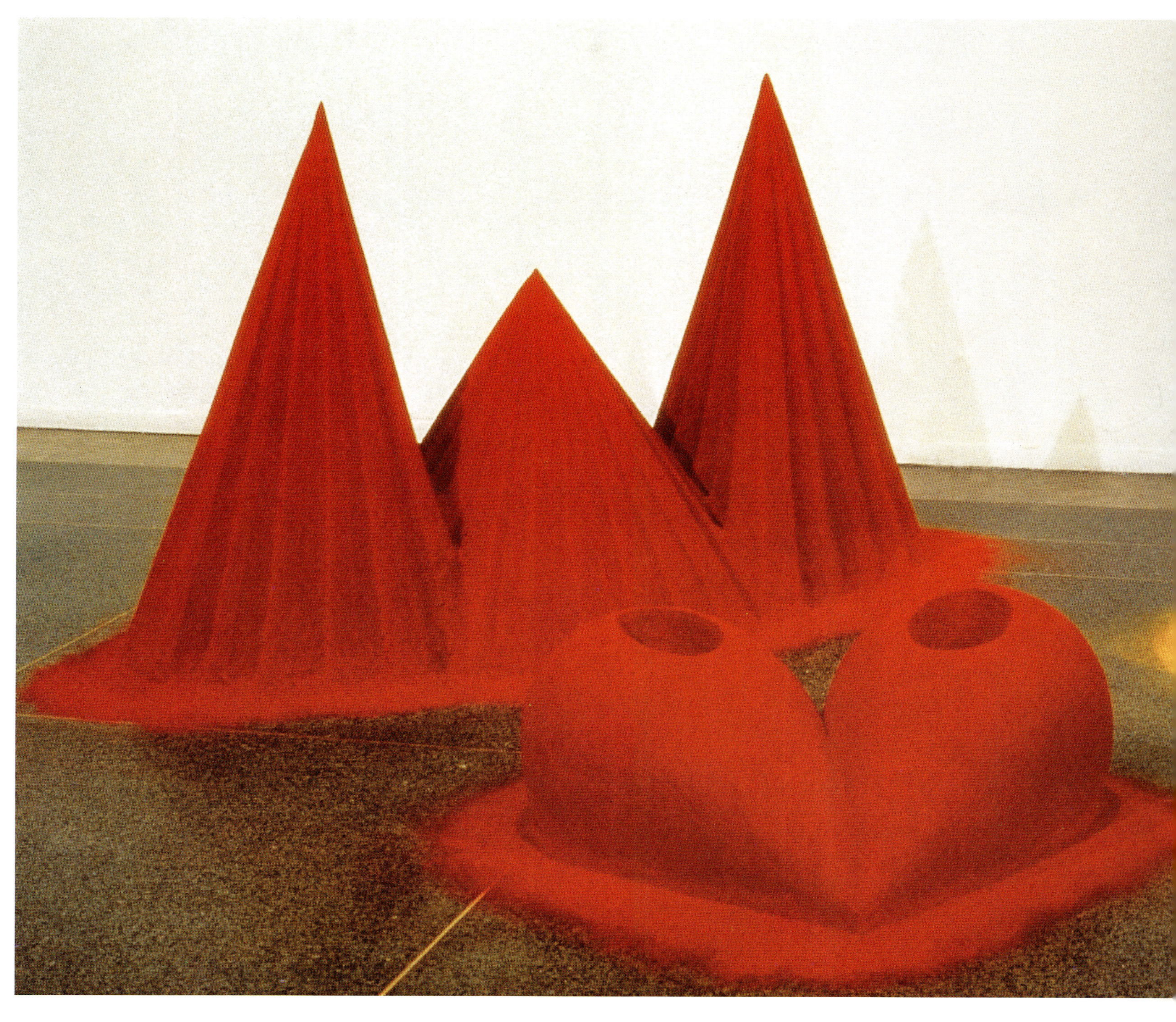

John Clark

asian modernisms

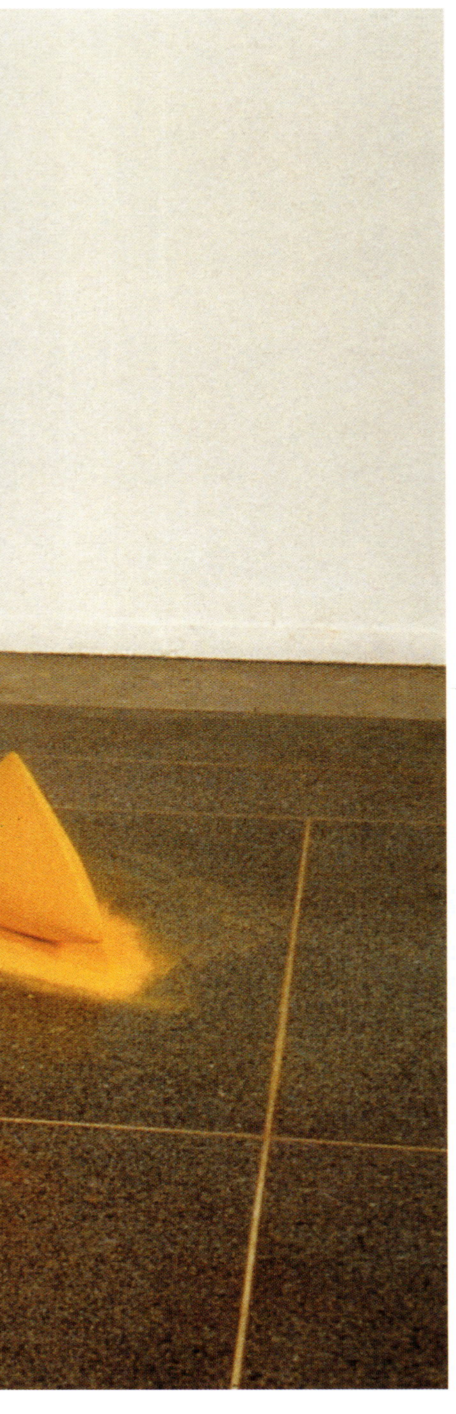

Location

At the end of the 1990s it is relatively facile – for someone in Euramerica[1] – to consider that various kinds of modern art works and artists from the non-Euramerican world have been accepted within it or have begun to be so. This seems to be particularly the case of Asian artists who have been seen at *Les Magiciens de la Terre*,[2] at the Venice and Sao Paulo Biennales, and who are increasingly the subject of country[3] or area-specific[4] shows, or the major component of others.[5] Such acceptance might also be taken to mean the incorporation of modern Asian art into the bounding intellectual paradigms of modernity and its histories which were supposedly invented in Euramerica: the position of the centre may have moved, but it is still the centre.

This essay does not accept either of these premises. Other positions can be briefly but directly brought into focus if we consider two Asian artists of Indian origin and the intellectual constructions around them. Anish Kapoor is an artist of Indian origin residing in London, who has been exhibited at the Venice Biennale in the British pavilion and is the subject of "major" critical overviews by leading Euramerican curators and critics.[6] N.N. Rimzon is an Indian artist residing in India who has been exhibited abroad but who has not been the subject of such a Euramerican catalogue.[7] The one is subject to Euramerican discourses which privilege themselves by the incorporation of difference. The other is subject to no such Euramerican gaze but remains, however, formally cognate and qualitatively related to the work accepted in Euramerica, as "Indian" or in another discourse. Yet the latter has been seen in other sites outside both India and Euramerica, in for example Australia. This differentiation is between a vertical, uni-central model of art assimilation to Euramerican canons, and a horizontal, polycentral discourse between differently constituted centres, none of which claim to assimilate, nor indeed reconstitute, a canon.

The difference of position derives ultimately from Euramerica's claim to have invented, and therefore to retain purchase on, modernity. This claim, whilst true in a rather simplistic developmental history, disappears the moment it is accepted that modernity invents itself everywhere it is required for a new relativization of the pasts of any given culture or group of cultures. The principal condition is that these cultures need to – and are capable of – carrying out this relativization. It is a relatively easy step from this position to the future-oriented, projective relativization of modernism, or, further, to the involuted and eclectic re-relativization of modernity itself some call post-modernism. In the quite precise language of fashion and the street it is also called "retro".[8] Seen this way modernity

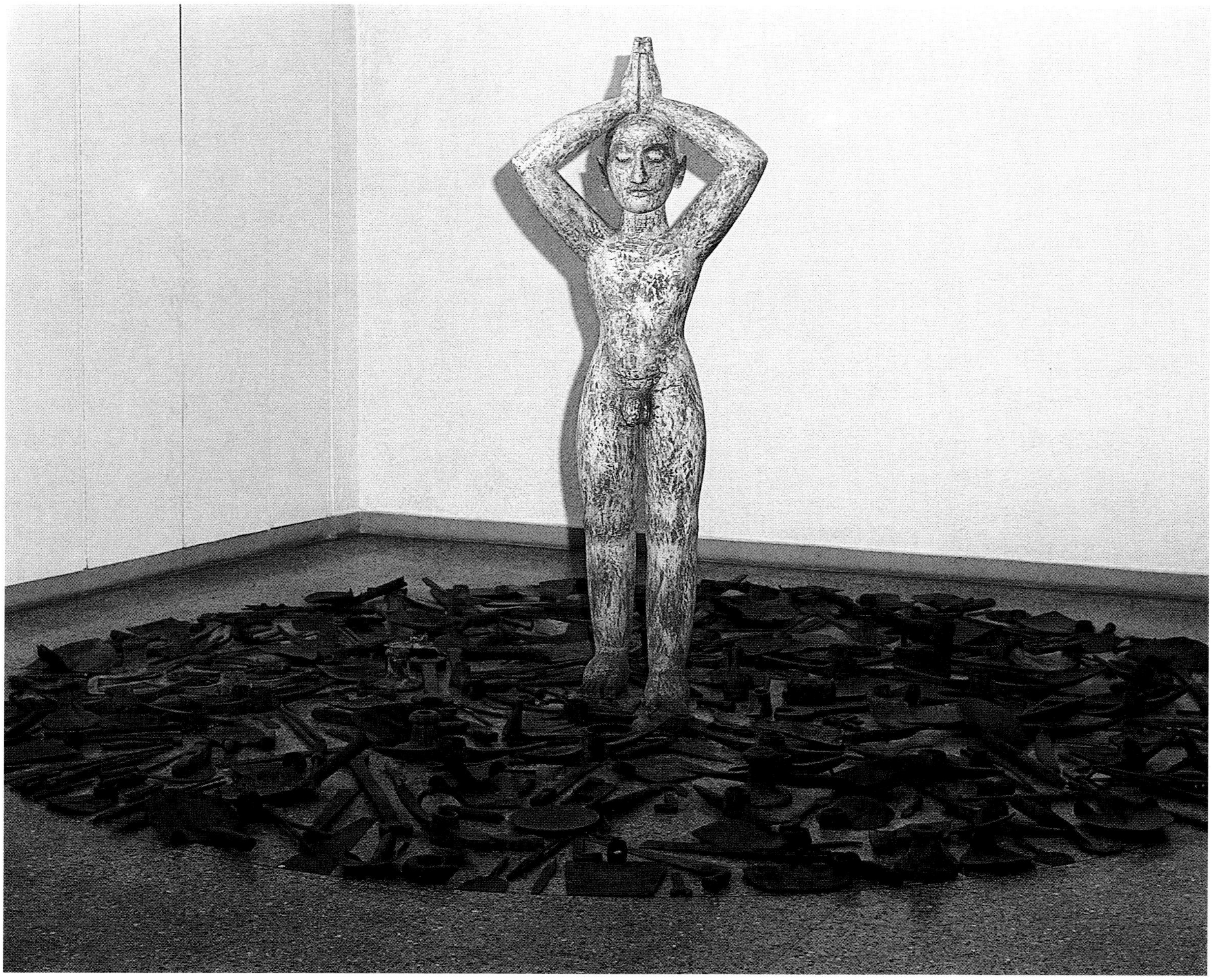

2
N.N. Rimzon
"The Tools Resin", 1993
Marble dust, fibreglass, and iron;
4 x 4 x 2 m

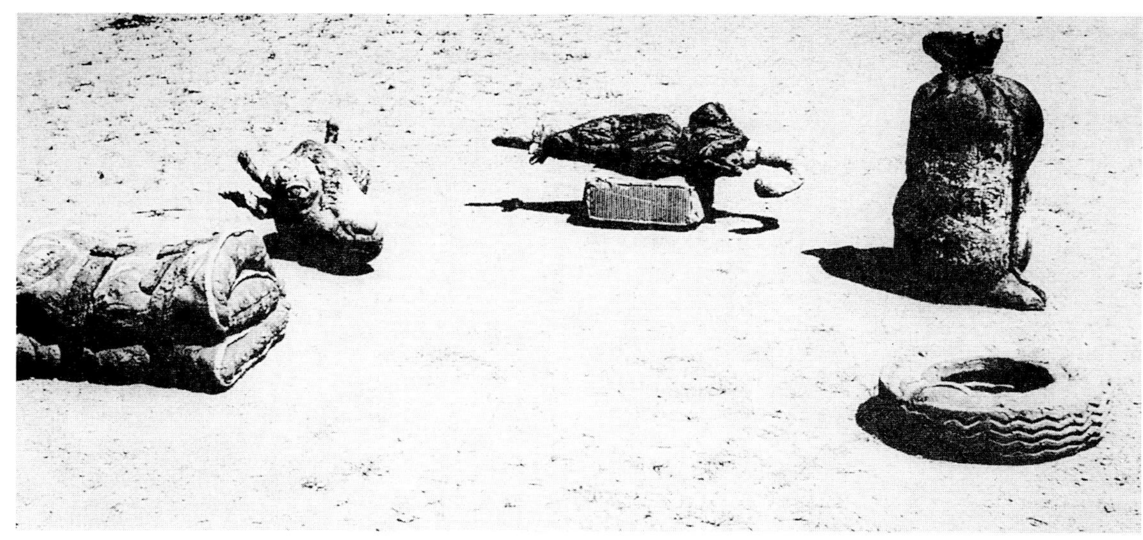

3
N.N. Rimzon
"Departure" (Still Life), 1985
Plaster

belongs to Asian artists because they work in societies and cultural discourses which require it. Modernity does not operate by the privilege of transfer from Euramerica or by the valuation of Asian modern art works and artists through their being accepted in Euramerica. Even before we approach the phenomenon of globalization, it is sensible to see how basic this difference of approach to modernity must be to one which privileges Euramerican origin.

Affiliation

But if modernity belongs to Asian art cultures because of their own demands, what kind of modernity is it? How did it come into being? How is it to be recognized from inside any particular Asian art culture or from without? If modernity is not owned by "The West", does that mean the kinds of modernity found in, say, some Asian art cultures are different, new, or radically other?

The affiliation of such modernity may be constructed in at least three ways, the full implications of which are yet to be explored. One is to see it as contestatory, as in a dialectical relation to that which has occasioned or imposed modernity, "The West". This is the colonial/post-colonial dimension of modernity, where modernity arises as a trajectory of subaltern counter-appropriation or rejection and revolt. It implies, at least theoretically, a lack of authenticity or own demand driving Asian modernity because external stimulus is a necessary cause.

A second affiliation is to group modernities in a family of species which have derived from an *ur*-species. This is a model of affiliation where the branchings of a tree are seen to derive from common

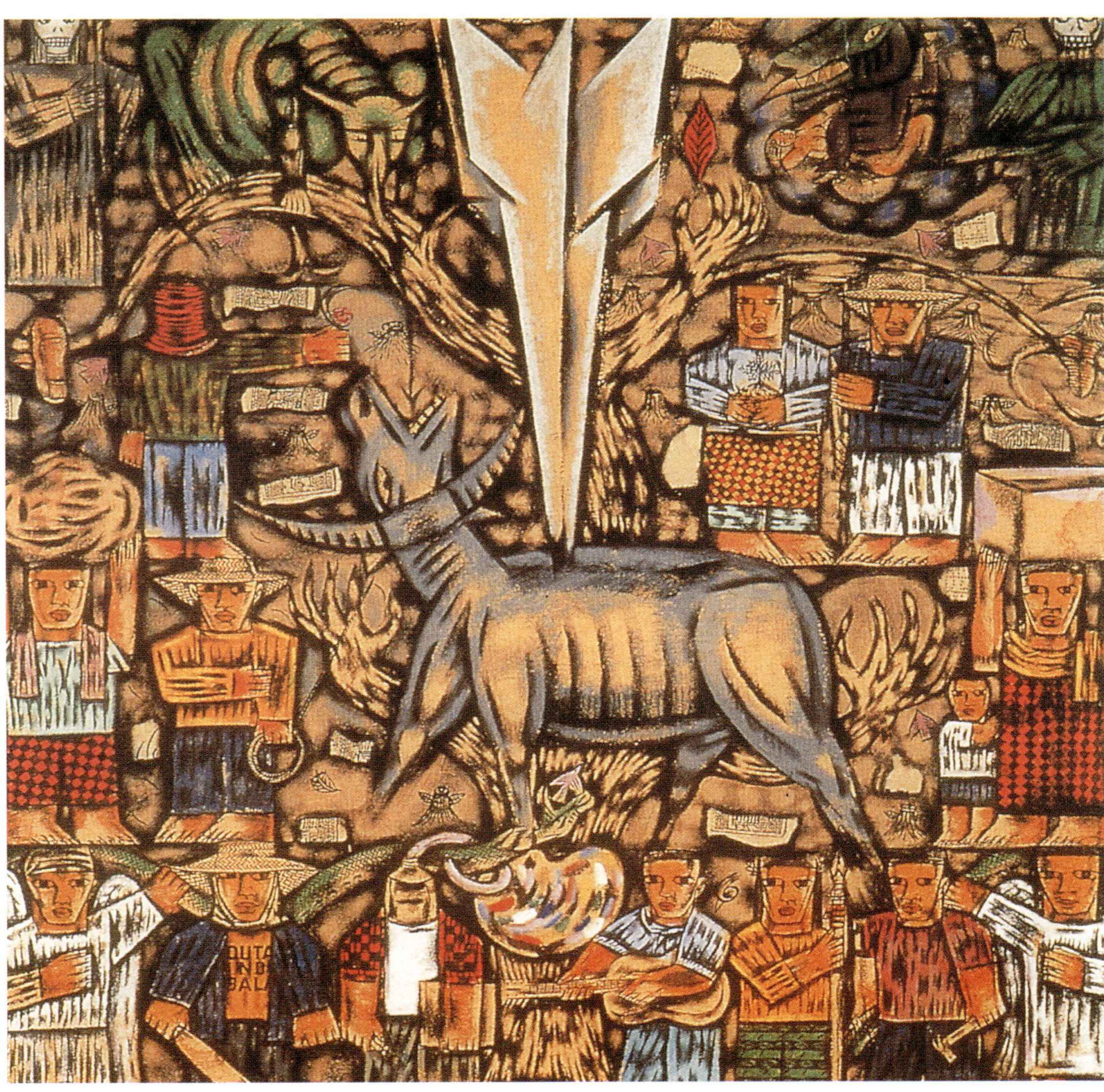

4
Alvardo Nunelucio
"Beginning without End", 1990
Oil on canvas; 2.44 x 2.44 m
Collection: Singapore Art Museum

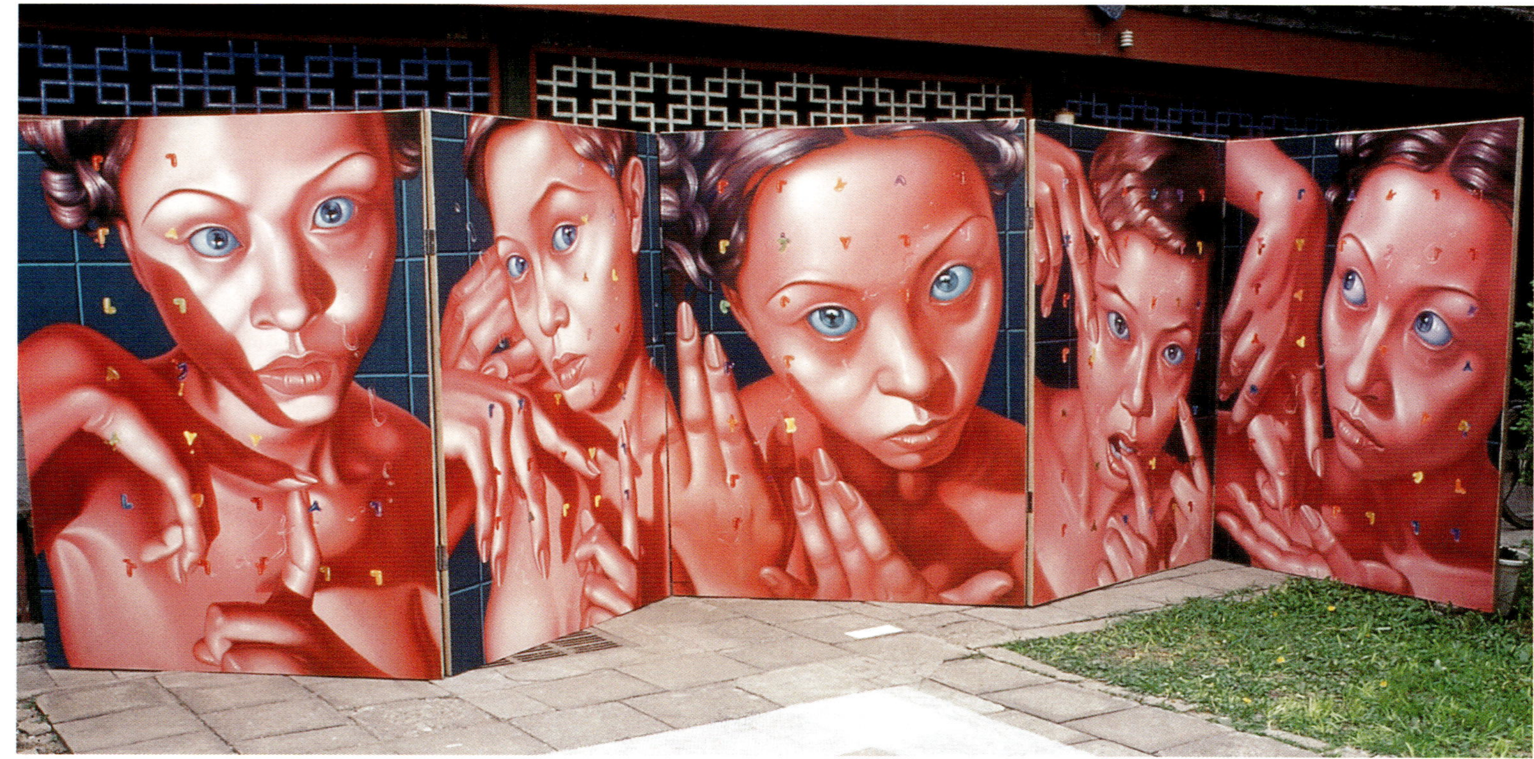

5
Chen Wenbo
"Testing" series, 1999
Oil on canvas;
200 x 150 cm each
Photograph: John Clark

ancestors whose different sub-branchings represent (in a Darwinian evolutionary model of development)[9] the adaptations of the species to different conditions in different localities. A variant of this model is to accept the notion of species branching but to see these (in Gould's revisions)[10] as not in a hierarchical tree but in various bunchings of variation from the same original set of species which exist in parallel and not in a single hierarchy.

A third model of affiliation is to see modernity in art along the lines of different languages in dialogue under conditions of heteroglossia (as in Bakhtin).[11] The dialogistic relation of such art discourses, that is their perpetual mutual relativization, may be interpreted as a fundamental condition of modernity. Affiliation is given because of common relativization, however it is achieved. Relativization can operate through the modes provided by colonial domination (India), internal self-development (Japan), and various kinds of quasi-sovereignty which seek to maintain the unitary identity of discourses even as they are broken down by contact from without (China).

In art history it has been relatively easy to overlook the different implications of these models of affiliation, because of the transfer of styles and their ideological constructs from "The West" to Asia. The transfer and overlaying of technical and symbolic values has taken attention away from the meaning of these transfers from within, and from the way authenticity has been created from a wholly new and constructed "tradition" at this interface.

"Tradition" has often been hermeneutically opposed to "modernity" when the "traditional" has only been made possible by the "modern". But even as the "modern" has been relativized by its transfer from "The West", so the neo-traditional has been secondarily relativized by its constructed discursial difference from the "modern". Thus have modern Asian art discourses been constructed not along the lines of a single "East/West" split but at least by a process of primary and then secondary relativization – which I choose to call "double othering".[12] This process can act as a relativization or "othering"[13] between a distancing of the neo-traditional *Kannon the Compassionate Mother* by Kano Hogai, 1888, from its "Japanese" pasts, and further by its separation from the position of near-contemporary "Western-style" work like *Kannon Riding on a Dragon*, by Harada Naojiro, 1890.

Histories

Relativization of the past may be the historical position of modernity whose marker is the caesura in local discourses created by the wholescale transfer of "Western" academy realism. Such a position has tended in the discourse of interpretation to render the onset of modernity as a radically historical disjunction. But on closer examination on the historical record in the discourse of art works[14] it may easily be seen that modernity in several Asian art cultures such as Japan or India did not start with the transfer of "Western" realism, and indeed had a long antecedence in many proto-modern features of art discourses and in the structures of the art world. One cannot also ignore the longevity of the linkages between the prehistories of modernity in Asia and Euramerica. There is thus neither a caesura in cultural relations nor an absolute rupture in the way art discourses are related to their pasts. It seems that part of the reason why there is a tendency to create such interpretive caesuras is a reflection or reduplication of the levels of binary structures habitual to the Euramerican world, such as imperial/metropolitan and colonial/local. This world has not been noted for its creation of discursial spaces defined between multiple centres and histories.

Furthermore, what one might call the habitual Euramerican interpretive mode has tended to see the inward movement of academy realism in a linear series of stages such as transfer, assimilation, and transformation. This view has concealed or de-privileged the various kinds of relativization implicit in such processes for an Asian art world. It has concealed how many features of modern and modernist modes of art discursial change were present inside these transfers. Perhaps the largest shift in art-historical interpretation required by modern Asian art is one away from the notion of transfer marked by the dissemination of models of stylistic development. Interpretation, whether exogenous or endogenous to any art discourse, should move to understanding a range of processes of relativization as imbricated within the complex term modernity/modernism/post-modernism. In this complex, any particular stylistic model or congruence is probably the least signifying element for the endogenous art discourses involved. The discursial space has to be left for a kind of co-option by local movements of an international one, and I would argue this is often found even very early in the transfer of realism. The co-option is not principally of the local by the central which would be the habitual (and still colonial) perspective. Such a

6
Gaganendranath Tagore
Untitled, 1920–25
Ink on paper
Collection: Kasturbhai Lalbhai

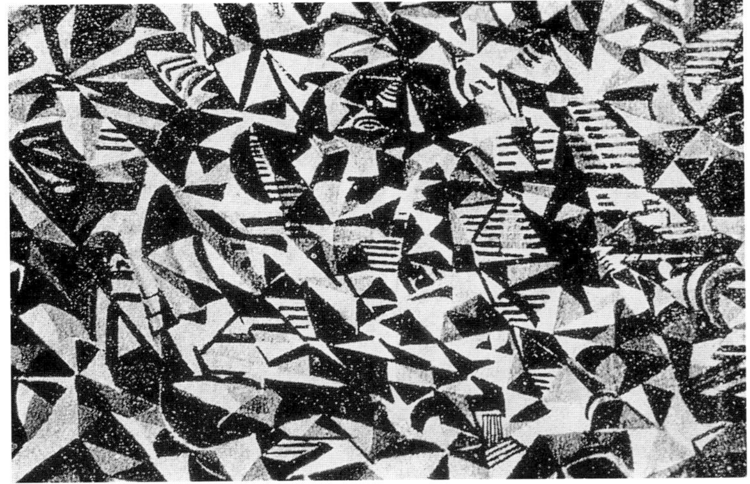

position also possibly accounts for the perverse late- or post-modernist pleasures to be derived both endogenously and exogenously from 1990s' Chinese "popism" such as in the work of Zhang Xiaogang, a discourse which cynically manipulates a surface conventionality in order to sequester – I would argue – a subversive parody safely within.[15]

Nations

For most Asian cultural discourses the modern began with the relativization of the past provided by the historical break of colonial or neo-colonial rule. As importantly, it also began by the reaction against this in the form of an anti-colonial movement and independence struggle towards the founding of a new state. However hegemonic the new state became in claiming domain over many kinds of society and cultural discourse within it, such states claimed to have founded the nation, to have integrated many discourses under their umbrella, and in most cases to have provided the leader of the people. The modernist striving for a desired future articulated between a leader and a people became a frequent subject for pictorial representation. This has historically been so much the case that one might postulate the thematic of modern Asian art to have been the allegorizing of the new nation through representing the new leader, and often of the very people who supported him. There is no doubt that as these *male* figures seek to articulate the masculinist privilege of serving the nation,[16] so alongside them the *female* figure of the mother, or of multiple types of women as a repository of a variety of national values, or of a leader of the masses in the self-sacrificing figure of a toiling intellectual, acts as a feminizing counterpart,[17] even if this counter allegory can only rarely be described as feminist in intention.

Two conditions seem to have changed the possibility for this type of national allegory. One is the success of the movements under or against colonialism, where nationalism survived as a strategy for creating a repertory of ideal figures in a national imaginary under the conditions of a rapidly de-colonizing world. This can provide a kind of semantic exhaustion where the use and reuse of a particular metaphor, like Chairman Mao as Great Helmsman, turns into a saturated metonym, a kind of image coinage where value – or metaphorical weight – resides in the currency system, not in any particular image. A second, and usually consecutive, condition is found where the colonial or the reaction against it only survives as a dim echo in a national imaginary now preoccupied with negotiating the post-colonial terms of its relation to a globalizing world. Thus stand the agonized, repeated faces of Philippine peasants in works by Alvorado Nunelucio looking out in the individualized frames of their images.[18] Through the slightly hallucinatory effect of their black outlines and primary colours they flicker, in a way like alternative TV pictures, to subvert the very fractionating forces which place them in a world economy and split them off from their former lateral solidarity in the possibility of a Philippine "nation".

Mediators

Art history, at least any history of modern art, cannot at least escape the possibility it will serve as a cultural critique, even if it is not explicitly so intended. Any exogenous or endogenous construction of a modern, modernist, post-modernist, or simply contemporary art in Asia is going to privilege some kinds of art against others. But in a world brought into close communication within and between art cultures, the figures who have normally provided for these kinds of assessment in various functional domains – critics, curators, journalists, art historians – with modern art are always serving to re-position the "new".

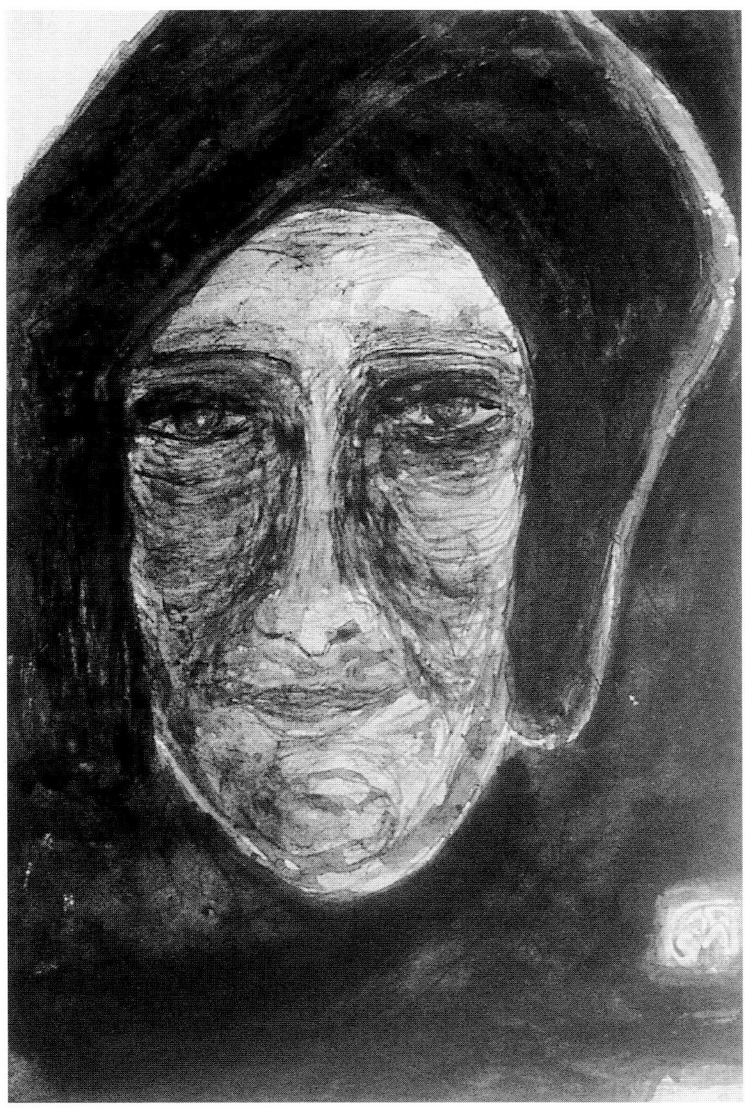

7
Rabindranath Tagore
"Face"
Ink on paper; 27 x 41 cm
Collection: National Gallery of Modern Art, New Delhi

The endogenous role of a critic, curator, or dealer in mediating and sometimes forming a group of conceptual perspectives around a cohort of disparately arranged artists is well known in Euramerica. It has also been a significant feature of Asian modernity, such as the role played at different times by Geeta Kapur in India,[19] Li Xianting in China,[20] or Nakahara Yusuke in Japan.[21] The important feature of such critics, however well informed they may be about international and exogenous art movements or by their own personal experience, is that they work from inside a set of cultural discourses which are their own centre. But the late 20th century has seen the advent of more specifically "interface" critics, curators, and dealers who mediate supposedly scarce knowledge and works from the endogenous to the exogenous levels. There is no doubt this particular position has played a significant role in the mediation of particularly East Asian art cultures to international art exhibitions, and here the role of Nanjo Fumio[22] and recently of Hou Hanru in China is prominent.[23] Whilst there can be no doubt such mediators, or "doorkeepers"[24] play an important role in inserting different types of Asian art into Euramerican discourses which otherwise might ignore them, they also manifest a minority opinion or a selective representation against the very complexity of the endogenous discourses they purport to represent to the exogenous. In other words, for an art history of modernity which includes Asia as one range of non-Euramerican practices, it would be fallacious to assume this could wholly or even partially be based on the art introduced from such mediators to the international level, even under the shifting rubric of "contemporary practice".[25] The hard but rewarding work of looking from inside at each endogenous discourse is the base for such an art history of other modernities, not the post-facto hypothesizing of such a history from such works as have been articulated on exogenous levels.

Some will argue that the global, exogenous level of practice, of the distribution of works and of the career-cycling of artists has long ago penetrated down to the local endogenous level. This is an unexceptional objection. Many artists, some the most rooted in their endogenous discourses such as Rabindranath Tagore, have continuously paid attention to international levels, even as these were earlier structured by the very world colonialism they were trying to see a way for their cultures to escape from. If the modern involves relativization of the past, and modernism the elevation to the plane of a formal subjectivity of an orientation to different futures, and if we were to attribute hermeneutic sovereignty to the global level, then that relativization would disappear or become a mere simulacrous imitation of itself. This would be to reproduce – even from a supposedly progressive position – the structure of central superordination over the local – now abstracted onto a "global" level – which the rich variety of practice made possible by modernism had the potential to resist, subvert, or at least circumvent. Whatever we conclude to be the role of globalizing forces in the late 20th century, an Asian history of modern art would first have to construct what conceptually and pragmatically links its own discourses.

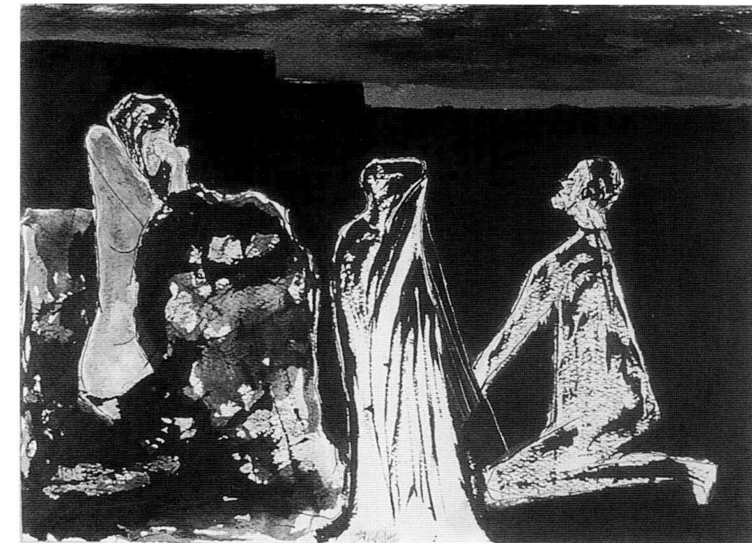

8
Rabindranath Tagore
"Three Figures"
Ink on paper; 29.2 x 22.2 cm
Collection: National Gallery of Modern Art, New Delhi

NOTES

1. This terminology, although perhaps unfamiliar, is necessary. Once the non-technological cultural products of "The West" were adopted, adapted, and transformed outside "The West" the location of their geographical origin no longer constituted a privileged civilizational autonomy. One pernicious legacy of direct colonialism is that the cultural products transferred to the world from "The West" are somehow always to be denied their *authenticity* to those who adopted them under its duress in places not in "The West", at least seen from the position which I shall now locate in *Euramerica* or characterize as *Euramerican*. For fuller exemplification see my *Modern Asian Art*, Sydney, Craftsman House and Honolulu, University of Hawaii Press, 1998.

2. See Jean-Hubert Martin, ed. and curator, *Les Magiciens de la Terre*, Paris, Centre Georges Pompidou, 1989.

3. See for example, Gao Minglu, ed., *Inside Out, New Chinese Art*, Berkeley, University of California Press, 1998.

4. See Apinan Poshyananda, et al., *Traditions/Tensions: Contemporary Art in Asia*, New York, Asia Society Galleries and Sydney, The Fine Arts Press, 1996.

5. See Hou Hanru and Hans Ulrich Olbrich, *Cities on the Move*, Ostfildern-Ruit, Verlag Gerd Hatje, 1997.

6. See Homi K. Bhabha and Pier Luigi Tazzi, *Anish Kapoor*, London, Hayward Gallery and Berkeley, University of California Press, 1998; Germano Celant, *Anish Kapoor*, London, Thames & Hudson, 1996. Celant barely refers to Kapoor's Indian origins.

7. For early Rimzon material see A. Dube, catalogue essay for *Seven Young Sculptors*, New Delhi, Kasauli Art Centre, 1985. See also Victoria Lynn, "The art of N.N. Rimzon", *Art and Asia Pacific*, vol. 3, no. 2, 1996.

8. Art-historically speaking, modernity, modernism, and post-modernism do not form a series of clear-cut tripartite stages, but tend to overlap, particularly if there is a relative freedom to eclectically modify styles whose sources do not yet operate a bounding hegemony, such as the "syncretic" architecture of early Meiji Japan.

9. Darwin's position was as follows: "Thus modern forms ought, on the theory of natural selection, to stand higher than ancient forms. Is this the case? It seems that this answer must be admitted as true, though difficult of proof." Charles Darwin, *The Illustrated Origin of Species* (abridged and introduced by Richard Leakey from the sixth edition of 1872 including comments which update Darwin's theories or his evidence), London, Faber & Faber, 1979, p. 174.

10. For Stephen Jay Gould, *Wonderful Life: The Burgess Shale and the Nature of History*, London, Penguin Books, 1989, p. 47, "The maximum

range of anatomical possibilities arises with the first rush of diversification. Later history is a tale of restriction, as most of these early experiments succumb and life settles down to generating endless variants upon a few surviving models."

11. Since it seems so directly indicative of the problems raised here, please allow a somewhat lengthy citation from Bakhtin's "Discourse in the Novel", found in M.M. Bakhtin, *The Dialogic Imagination* (tr. C. Emerson and M. Holquist), Austin, University of Texas Press, 1981, pp. 284–85: "But internal dialogization can become such a crucial force for creating form only where individual differences and contradictions are enriched by social heteroglossia, where dialogic reverberations *do not sound in the semantic heights* of the discourse [as happens in rhetorical genres] *but penetrate the deep strata of discourse*, dialogize language itself and the world view a particular language has...", my italics.

12. For a discussion see John Clark, "Yoga in Japan: Model or Exception? Modernity in Japanese art, 1850s–1940s: an international comparison", *Art History*, vol. 18, no. 2, June 1995, pp. 253–85.

13. See John Clark, "Gendai Ajia no Bijutsu gensetsu ni okeru 'Taka'", "Othering in Modern Asian art discourses", translated into Japanese from a Tezukayama Gakuin workshop paper of 1996, published in Shimamoto Kan and Kasuya Makoto, eds., *Bijutsushi to Tasha*, Kyoto, Kôyô, Shobô, 2001, pp. 39–67.

14. See Chapter Two on "Prehistories" in John Clark, *Modern Asian Art*.

15. See John Clark, "Histories in the Modern", in Graeme Murray, Meg Syme, and June Knight, eds, *Reckoning with the Past: Contemporary Chinese Painting*, Edinburgh, Fruitmarket Gallery, 1996, pp. 17–20.

16. See Julia Andrews, "Chairman Mao goes to Anyuan", in *Painters and Politics in the People's Republic of China: 1949–79*, Berkeley, University of California Press, 1994, pp. 338–42.

17. For a feminist understanding of Ravi Varma see Geeta Kapur, "Ravi Varma's Unframed Allegory", in R.C. Sharma, ed., *Raja Ravi Varma: New Perspectives*, New Delhi, National Museum, 1993.

18. See his work "Duta Indi Bala" (Land not bullets) in the catalogue of the *First Asia-Pacific Biennale*, Brisbane, Queensland Art Gallery, 1993, p. 31.

19. Among Geeta Kapur's important earlier writings are *Pictorial Space: A Point of View on Contemporary Indian Art*, New Delhi, Lalit Kala Akademi, 1977; *Contemporary Indian Artists*, New Delhi, Vikas Publishing House, 1978 (Souza, Kumar, Padamsee, Husain, Khakhar, Swaminathan); and *Place for People* (text for exhibition), Bombay, Jehangir Art Gallery and New Delhi, Rabindra Bhavan, 1981.

20. Li Xianting's activities may be glimpsed in English through his historical essay in V.C. Doran, ed., *China's New Art post-1989*, Hong Kong, Hanart TZ Ltd., 1993, and the essay, "The Imprisoned Heart", *Art and Asia Pacific*, vol. 1, no. 2, 1994.

21. For an indication of his position see Nakahara Yusuke et al., *Europalia 89: Japan in Belgium*, Gent, Museum van Hedenndaagse Kunst, 1989.

22. See Nanjo Fumio and Dana Friis-Hansen, *Transculture*, Tokyo, The Japan Foundation and Fukutake Science & Culture Foundation, 1995. Nanjo was very active in the 1980s in introducing Japanese contemporary art abroad. See in particular, Kathy Halbreich, Kômoto Shinji, Nanjo Fumio, and Thomas Sokolowski, *Against Nature: Japanese Art in the 1980s*, New York, New York University Grey Art Gallery, 1981; Kondo Yukio, Nanjo Fumio, and Peter Weiermaier, *Japansischer Kunst der Achziger Jahre*, for the Frankfurter Kunstverein, Edition Stemmle, 1990.

23. Hou Hanru was the Chinese adviser for *Les Magiciens de la Terre* and has since been active as a curator of modern Chinese art in Europe working from Paris. See his essays "Departure Lounge Art", *Art and Asia Pacific*, vol. 1, no. 2, 1994; "Beyond the cynical: China avant-garde in the 1990s", *Art and Asia Pacific*, vol. 3, no. 1, 1996; "Towards an 'Un-Unofficial Art': de-ideologicalisation of China's Contemporary Art in the 1990s", *Third Text*, no. 34, Spring 1996; "Entropy; Chinese Artists, Western Art Institutions: A new internationalism", in J. Fisher, ed., *Global Visions: Towards a new internationalism in the Visual Arts*, London, Kala Press, 1994; "De 'décrire la réalitié' au 'théâtre du monde'. L'art Chinois depuis 1979" (traduit par J. Lacoste), in Harry Belleter, ed., *Face á l'Histoire*, Paris, Centre Georges Pompidou, 1996. See also *Cities on the Move*, note 5 above, and his conversation with Gao Minglu in *Inside Out*, note 3 above.

24. On "doorkeeping" see John Clark, "Art and its 'others' – recent Australian-Asian visual exchanges", in Maryanne Dever, ed., *Australia and Asia: cultural transactions*, Surrey, Curzon Press, 1997, and also Chapter Eleven of my *Modern Asian Art*.

25. Thus catalogues like *Cities on the Move*, note 5 above, in a tendency followed by the recent catalogue Gilda Williams, ed., *Cream*, London, Phaidon, 1998 (which declares itself to be "a portable exhibition in a book"), increasingly resemble telephone books where the artists' works become a kind of conceptual address and the name of the artist a fantastic, unfathomable number.

ACKNOWLEDGEMENT

This article first appeared in *Humanities Research*, no. 2, 1999.

1
Diego Rivera (1886–1957)
"Pan-American Unity" (detail), 1940
Fresco; 6.74 x 22.5 m
Photograph courtesy of the City College of San Francisco

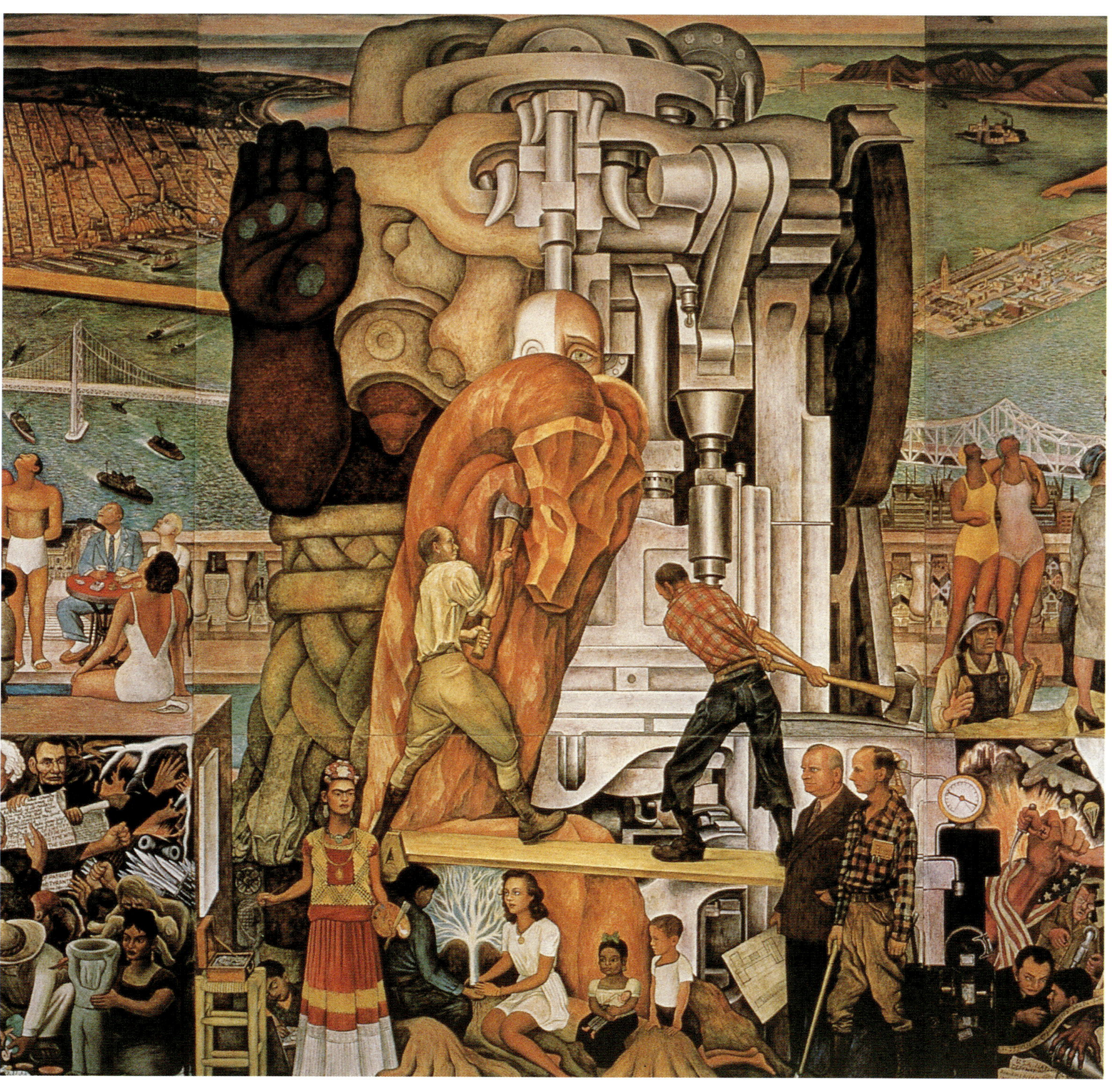

John H. Bowles

an indo-mex smorgasbord from the united states of modernity

The poet Gertrude Stein once declared the United States to be the oldest nation in the world. Why? Because it had been the first to modernize.[1] What then does this oldest modern nation and present "global superpower" represent to modern artists of Mexico and India, two old societies that have come late to modernity? I would like to explore this theme by briefly considering a few paintings.

An Odd Utopia

"Your engineers are your great artists," Mexican muralist Diego Rivera once proclaimed while visiting the USA. "These highways are the most beautiful things I have seen.... In all the constructions of man's past, pyramids, Roman roads and aqueducts, cathedrals and palaces, there is nothing to equal these. Out of them and the machine will issue the style of tomorrow."[2]

A lifelong communist, Rivera was both politically critical of the US and deeply admiring of its modern cities, engineering, and industry. Consider the central detail from his immense "Pan-American Unity" mural, painted for San Francisco's 1939–40 Golden Gate International Exposition (figure 1). A dominating central image combines the features of a gigantic stamping press (as used for automobile production) with those of a famous monument of the Aztec earth goddess Coatlicue ("She of the Serpent Skirt") – a composite colossus of writhing snakes, venerated through human sacrifice, and "...wearing a grisly necklace of severed hearts and hands.... A monument of cosmic terror."[3] According to the artist: "In this mural I projected the idea of the fusion of the genius of the South (Mexico), with its religious ardor and its gift for plastic expression, and the genius of the North (the United States), with its gift for creative mechanical expression. Symbolizing this union – and focal point of the whole composition – was a goddess of Life, half Indian, half machine."[4] The mural also reflects Rivera's apprehension over the growing threat of European fascism, and his eagerness to promote friendship between American democracies. In the upper left of this illustration an upraised hand gestures reassurance (like an *abhaya mudra*); it rises "...up out of a machine as if to ward off the forces of aggression, symbolizing the American conscience reacting to the threat against freedom, in the love of which the history of Mexico and the United States were united."[5]

Exploitation and Defiance

Seven years before Rivera painted "Pan-American Unity", another major Mexican modern master visited California and painted a mural using Christian sacrificial iconography to convey a far more critical and defiant message. The story goes that when the Plaza Art Center commissioned

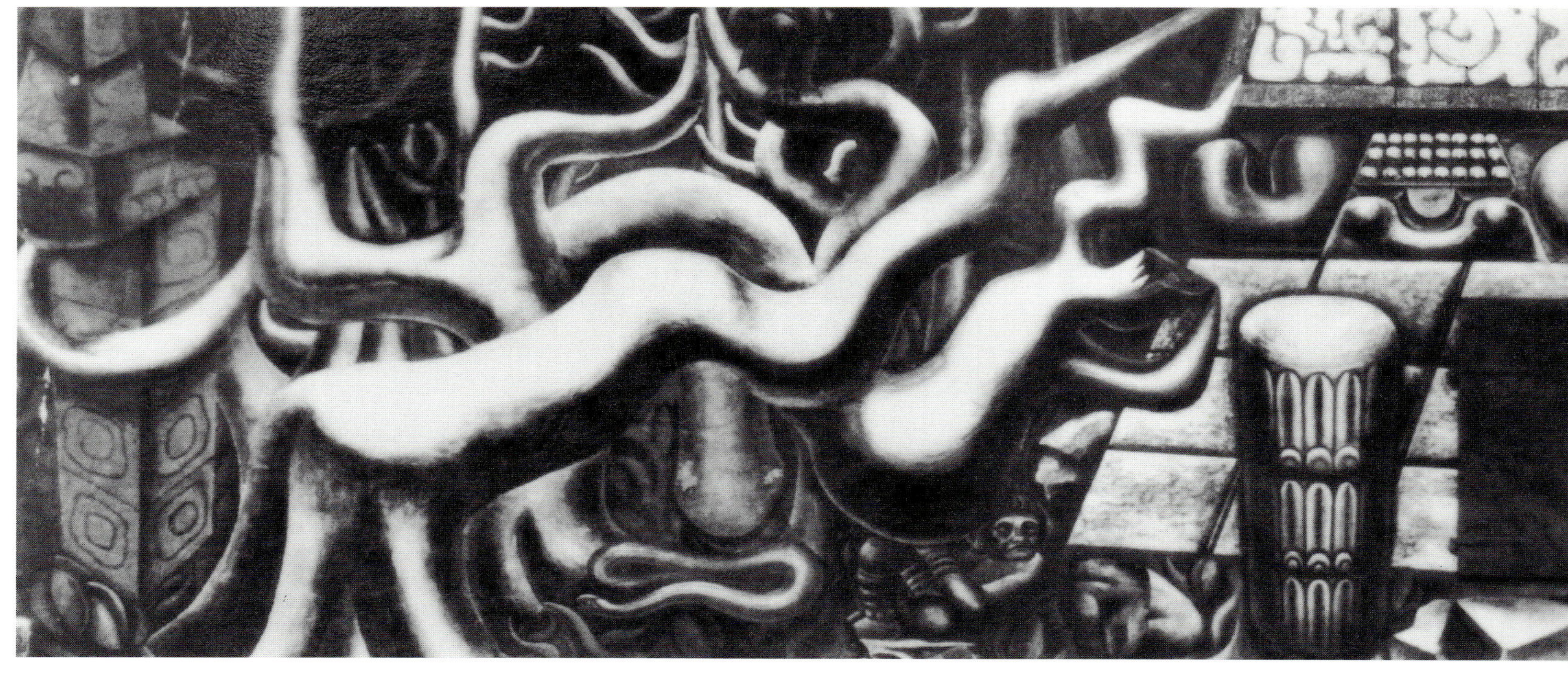

2
David Alfaro Siqueiros
(1896–1974)
"Tropical America"
Mural on Olvera Street, Los Angeles, 1932 (whitewashed; presently under conservation)
Fresco; 4.88 x 24.32 m
Photograph courtesy of El Pueblo de Los Angeles Historic Monument

the 35-year-old David Alfaro Siqueiros to paint a mural entitled "Tropical America" on a wall above Olvera Street (located in the Mexican historic heart of downtown Los Angeles), the community expected something colourful, exotic, picturesque, and innocuous. Instead what they got was a shocking scene of victimization (figure 2), featuring a crucified indigenous Mexican surmounted by the bald eagle (the USA's national emblem), which in turn is being targeted by a couple of armed Mexican peasant revolutionaries (shown at far right). The background features a pre-Columbian temple midst a jungle strewn with ruins and fallen idols. As succinctly stated by art historian Shifra Goldman: "The Spanish conquistador has been supplanted by 'Yankee money'."[6] Siqueiros' anti-imperialist mural so offended certain community leaders that it was whitewashed, and what now can be seen of the original work is the black and white photograph here reproduced.[7]

Siqueiros was known for his personal courage and activism on behalf of the impoverished masses. In his youth he served in the Mexican Revolution and the Spanish Civil War and, like Rivera, became a lifelong communist. Both artists served on the Communist Party of Mexico's Executive Committee, but of the two Siqueiros was by far the more doctrinaire and politically active. During 1925–30 he gave up painting to become the Party's Secretary and pursue various revolutionary activities.[8] The Mexican government repeatedly imprisoned him for his subversive activities, and at different times he was deported from – and denied entry by – the US. His passionate political concerns (often targeting

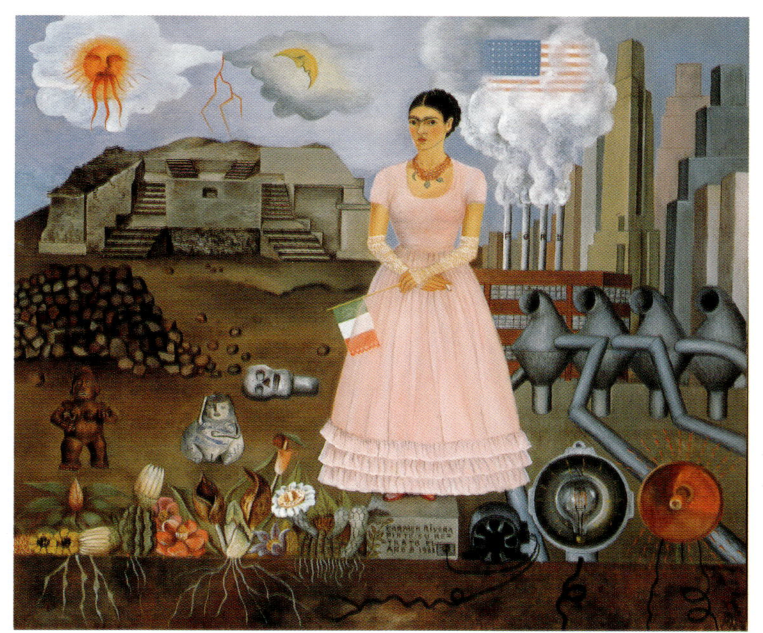

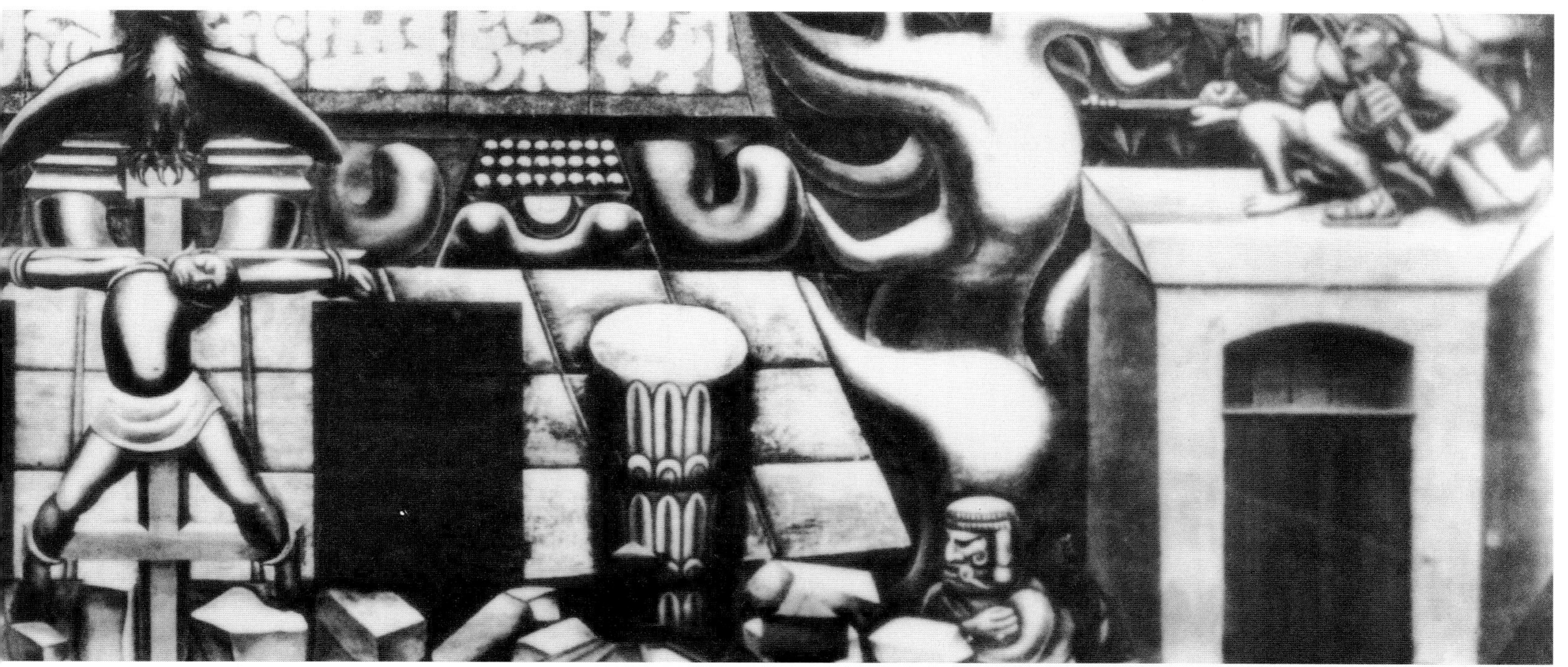

US racism and capitalistic exploitation of Mexican workers) parallels his bold artistic style – which has been criticized for often lapsing into "overdramatic gestures and bombast".[9]

Disenchanted Resentment

Frida Kahlo painted her 1932 "Self-Portrait on the Border Between Mexico and the United States" (figure 3) while living in Detroit (where she stayed with her husband Diego Rivera, who was then engaged in a large mural project for the Detroit Institute of Fine Arts).[10] Its setting is both surrealistic and symbolic. The landscape at left represents Mexico (note the pyramid and deified sun and moon in the background, and broken idols and vegetative growth in the foreground); and on the right the US (represented by the background skyscrapers and the flag hovering over the belching smokestacks of Ford's Detroit factory, as well as the loudspeaker, light bulb, and other mechanical devices in the foreground). At first impression the artist looks demure and ladylike (formally coiffed and wearing long gloves, jewellery, and a full-length fancy dress). But on closer inspection one notices Kahlo's defiant stare, along with the cigarette and Mexican flag she holds, and the fact that she is bra-less – all signalling her angry resentment at being stifled by an alien culture and a difficult husband.[11] Unlike Rivera's integrative vision of "Pan-American Unity", Kahlo emphasizes the differences between traditional Mexico and modern US – divisions that seem irreconcilable.

Appreciation in New York

Our next illustration (figure 4) shows a Mexican artist's view of New Yorkers appreciating Mexican art. The setting: an exhibition opening at New York's Museum of Modern Art. The year: 1940. The Artist: renowned Mexican caricaturist Miguel Covarrubias. The celebrities: movie star Greta Garbo, artists Georgia O'Keeffe and Roberto Montenegro, photographer Alfred Stieglitz, archaeologist Alfonso Caso, and assorted millionaires such as Edsel Ford, Mr and Mrs Henry Luce, and various Rockefellers – to name but a few. The centrepiece: the Aztec colossus of Goddess Coatlicue (the same as previously depicted by Diego Rivera (see figure 1). How to interpret all of this? How about "New

3
Frida Kahlo (1907–54)
"Self-Portrait on the Border Between Mexico and the United States", 1932
Oil on metal, 32 x 35 cm
Private collection
See Acknowledgements on page 125

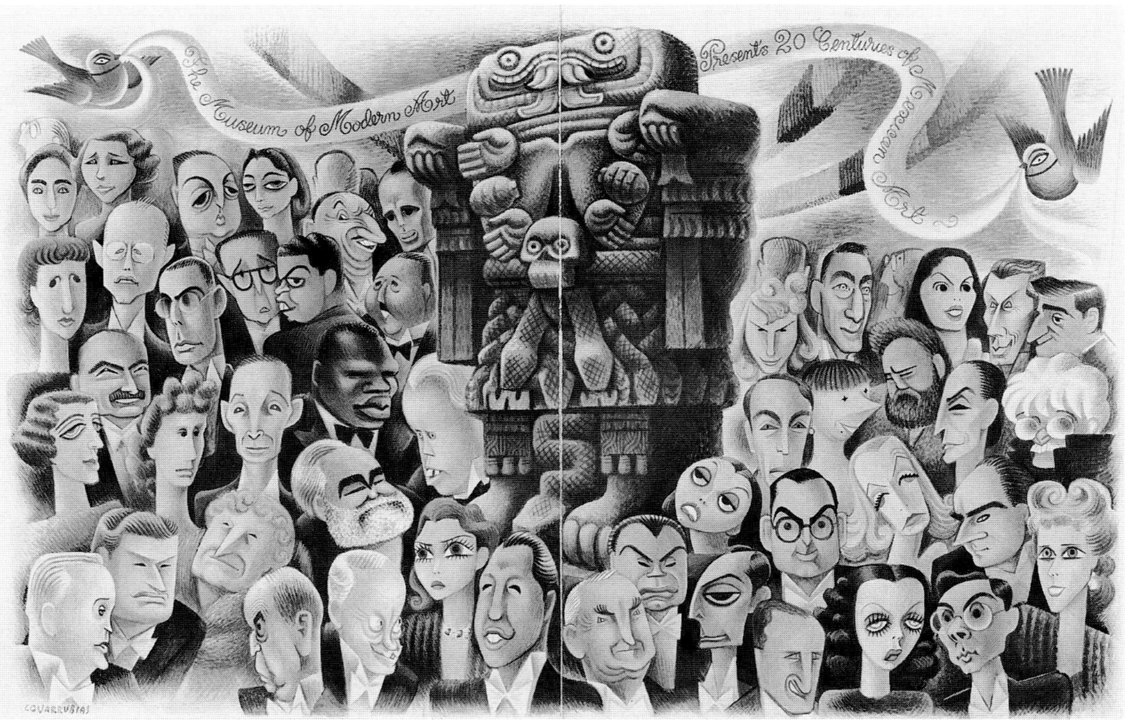

4
Miguel Covarrubias (1904–57)
"Twenty Centuries of Mexican Art at the Museum of Modern Art", 1940
Watercolour; 38 x 57 cm
Yale University Art Gallery, Gift of Senora Rosa R. de Covarrubias

York Goes Mexican" – the title of the *Vogue* exhibition review accompanying the picture's first reproduction.[12] The review starts with a lively account of the town's new rage for Mexican fashion – from pets (miniature Chihuahua dogs), food and beverages (tortillas and tequila), to dances and clothes (the rumba and tango,[13] and sombrero, rebozo sarape...). Stereotype after stereotype. Thus a grand "Twenty Centuries of Mexican Art" exhibition inspires an enthusiastic "South of the Border" fad – Ole!

US museums and galleries produce sensational popular exhibitions, which in turn generate temporary "crazes". One year it's Mexico, another it's Egypt, and thereafter Japan – and each time a new ethnic fashion boosts sales of related merchandise, the art itself "appreciates" in value, and more and more cultures become commodified and consumed by the consumer culture. Meanwhile, most real "diversity" gets progressively glossed over, trivialized, assimilated, and homogenized. Almost all, that is. If the truth be known, what isn't easily digested simply gets marginalized, rejected, ignored – even (on rare occasions) destroyed. See the gentleman with wavy hair in the lower left corner? That's Nelson Rockefeller, who had just recently commissioned Diego Rivera to paint a large mural at the Rockefeller Center in midtown Manhattan – and then ordered it to be demolished because it included a depiction of Lenin. As Rivera later lamented: "Thus was free expression honored in America."[14]

Nightmares

Now, an artwork of a very different sort by contemporary Huichol tribal artist José Benítez Sánchez. Entitled "Dream-Visions at the Edge of Darkness" (figure 5), it shows the artist making his first trip to the US in order to prepare for an exhibition. However important such recognition was for Benítez as an artist, as a Huichol his spirit was deeply unsettled by this visit to the "...dark edge of the world, [...] so-called because the United States is beyond the world controlled by the Huichol Ancestors... [and] therefore, corresponds to the underworld that the sun goes through when it sets...."[15] Depicted in a continuous narrative format, the artist first appears seated atop a moth-like aircraft (shown in the lower right-hand corner), and thereafter haunted by disturbing nightmares (including visions of "Spirits of the High Hills" (of Berkeley) and the "Lagoon" (San Francisco Bay) – as well as his own Ancestral Spirits commanding him to return home to perform penitential rituals.[16] His misgivings are characteristic of many traditional societies, where the taboos against distant travel protect and reinforce endogamous, psychological, and religious identity.

Paraphrasing Herbert Read, ethnographer Juan Negrín explains that "Art is the creative therapy through which José Benítez Sánchez reconstitutes his fragmented psyche"[17] – a fragmentation in which modern forces of dominant world culture certainly play a major role. Yet the same "outside culture" also introduced the manufactured materials necessary for creating Huichol "yarn paintings". Here, as elsewhere, the mixed blessings of modernity both spiritually challenge and materially facilitate contemporary traditional arts – for better or for worse.[18]

Confronting Mickey Mouse

Contemporary artist Enrique Chagoya focuses his work on highly charged themes of social and political conflict by ironically juxtaposing icons and styles clearly associated with traditional Mexico and modern USA. His imagery frequently depicts confrontations between American and Aztec

5
José Benítez Sánchez (b. 1938)
"Dream-Visions at the Edge of Darkness", 1975
Original wool yarn painting; 100 x 122 cm
Photograph courtesy Juan and Yvonne Negrin

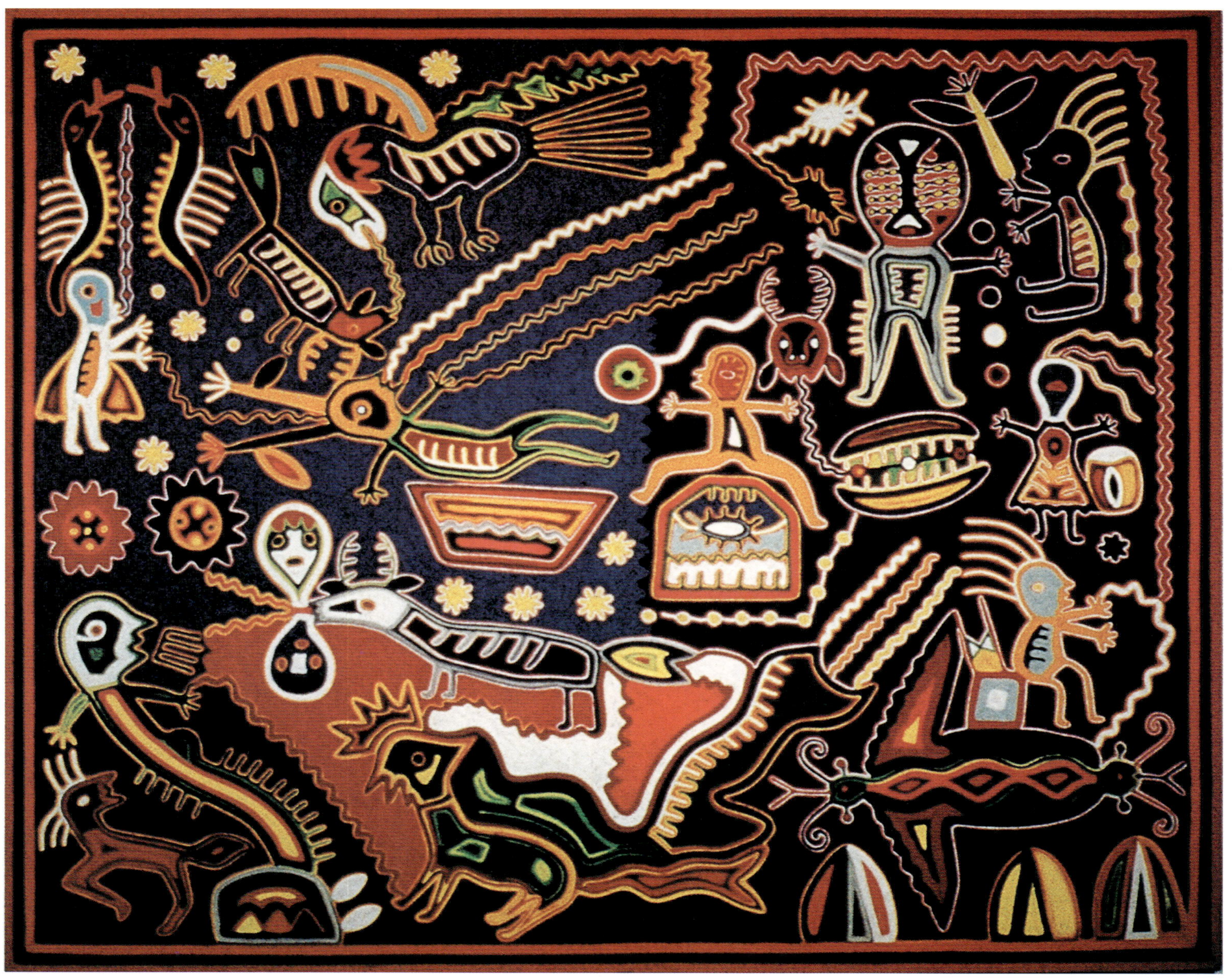

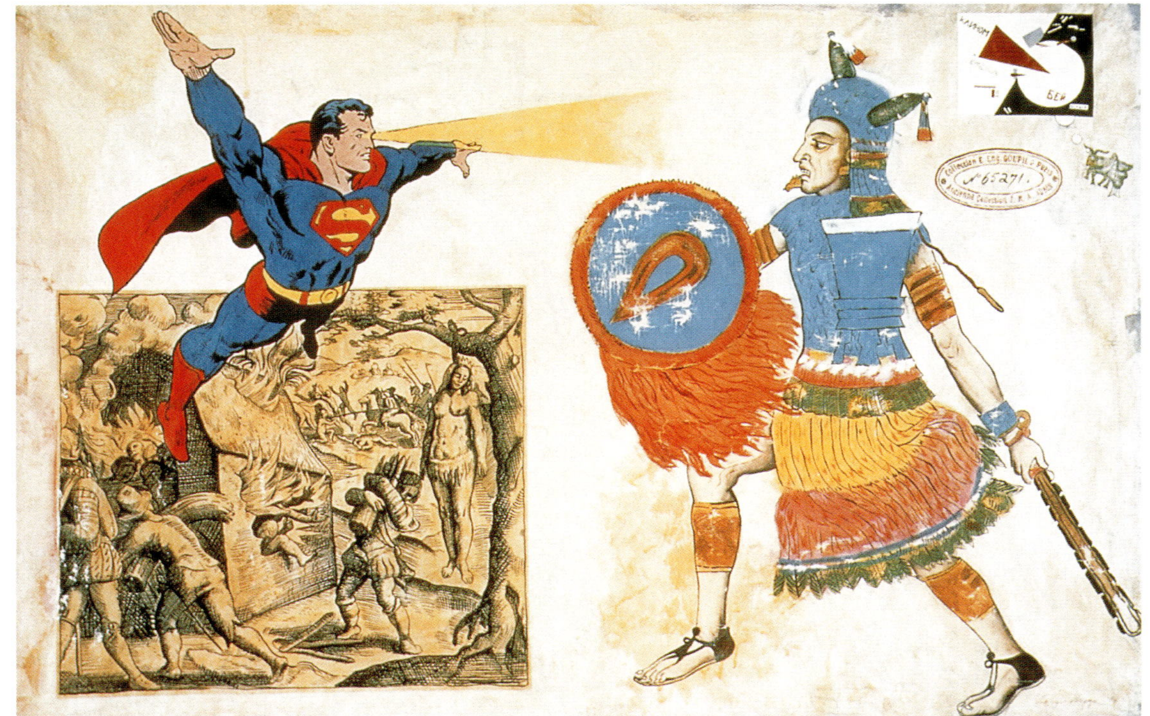

6
Enrique Chagoya (b. 1953)
"Uprising of the Spirit", 1994
Acrylic and oil on amante paper;
122 x 183 cm
Courtesy of the Los Angeles
County Museum of Art

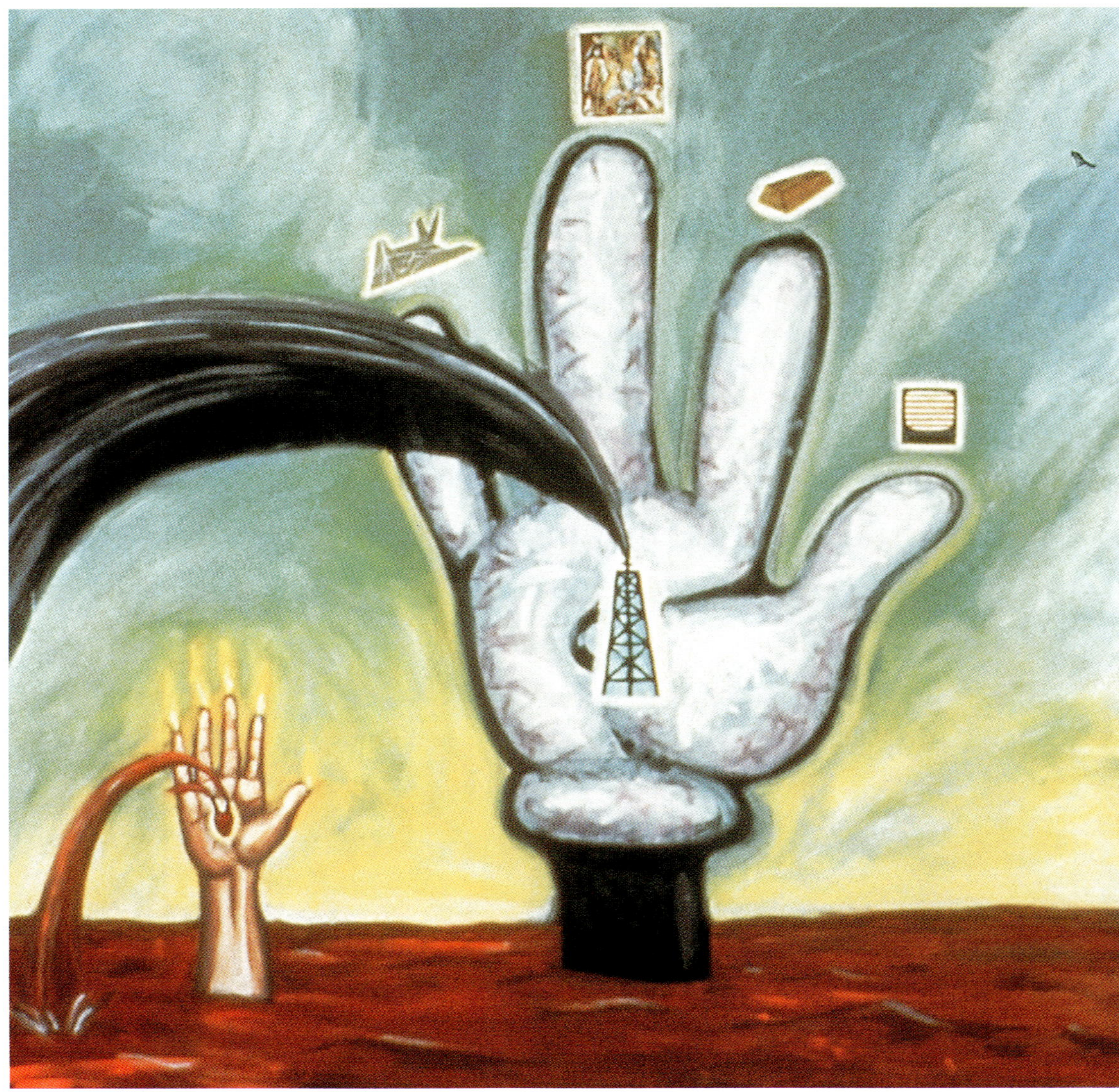

7
Enrique Chagoya (b.1953)
"Hand of Power", 1993
Oil on galvanized steel;
122 x 122 cm
Artist's collection
Photograph courtesy Gallery
Paule Anglim, San Francisco

heroes: codex-style battles between Aztec warriors and invading US tanks; Superman versus the poet-king Nezahuacoyotl (figure 6). Visions of Mickey Mouse also recur, variously manifest as: threatening colossus overshadowing some diminutive Mexican figure; a tasty sacrificial victim bound and ready for devotee consumption; or – in "Hand of Power" (figure 7) – an appearance of Mickey's gloved four-fingered hand, which dwarfs and parodies a martyred human hand derived from Catholic votive imagery. Blood flows from the stigmata of the latter, while from Mickey's palm arises a gushing oil derrick, with fingertips graced by stealth bomber, a television set, a gold ingot, and a commodified Picasso "masterpiece".

A native of Mexico City, Chagoya's political activism was initially sparked by the internationally infamous 1968 student massacre in the city's central Tlatelolco Plaza. He became involved with subsequent protests,[19] drew political cartoons, studied sociology and economics at the Autonomous University of Mexico, and immigrated to the US in 1977 – where he received a B.F.A. from San Francisco Art Institute and an M.F.A. from the University of California, Berkeley. Chagoya now teaches art at California State University, Hayward, and became a US citizen in 1995.

Chagoya's caustic post-modern cultural pastiches express his social concerns regarding racist policies and attitudes against legal and illegal Mexican immigrants living in the US, as well as the broader issues of the US military interventions, exploitative economic relations, and damaging cultural influence upon Mexico and other Central American nations. Such subject matter likewise interests many other Mexican and Mexican-American artists, working in various media, and on both sides of the border.[20]

8
Ganga Devi (1928–91)
"The Washington Monument", 1986
Inks on paper; 55 x 76 cm
Courtesy The Crafts Museum, New Delhi

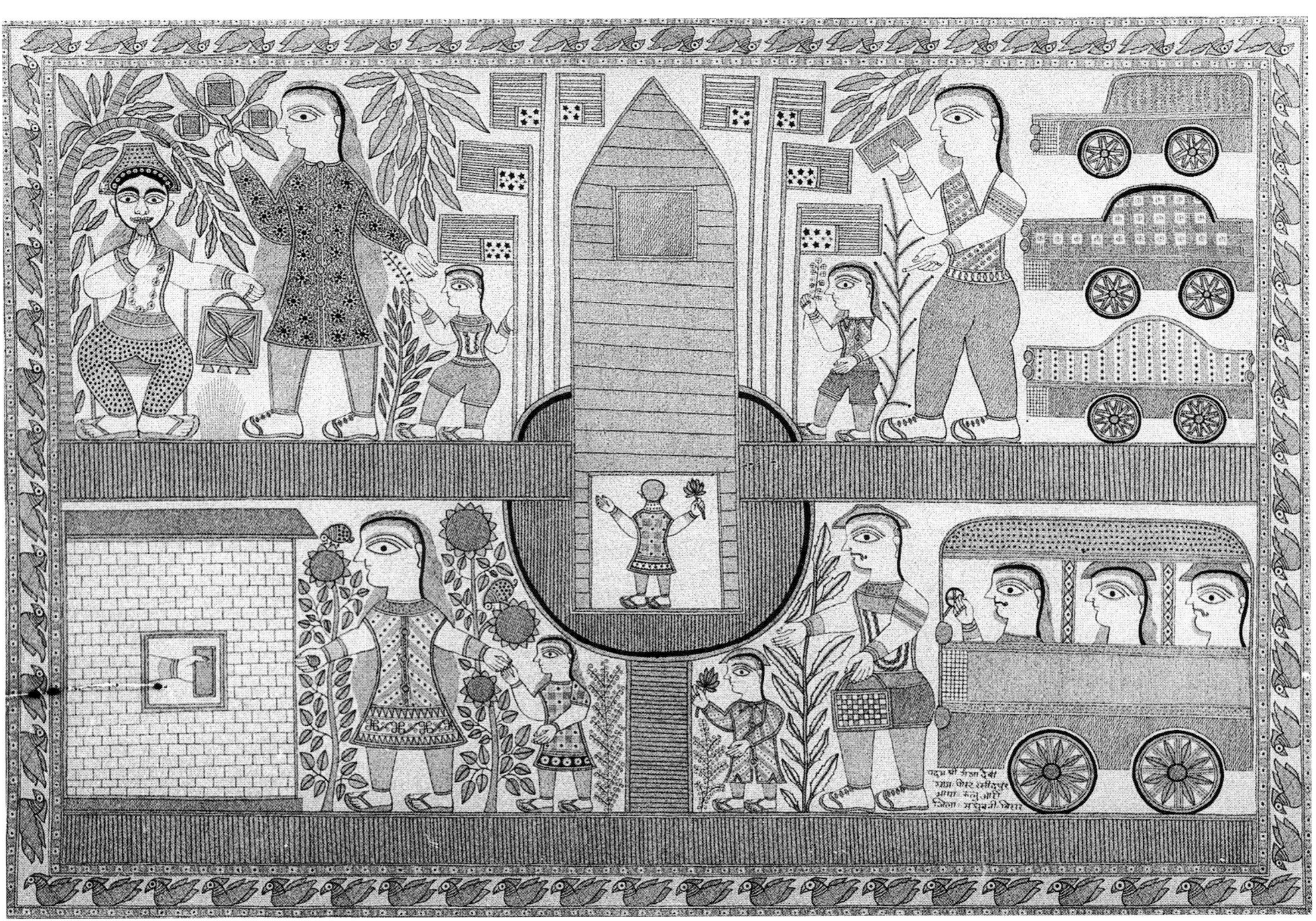

"...You Deal with the Hand"

According to political artist/activist Guillermo Gomez-Pena, popular blockbuster exhibitions from abroad attempt to "...use art as conservative diplomacy and as a means to create a conflict-free image of a country for the purpose of seducing investors and promoting cultural tourism."[21] In 1985–86, the US and India jointly produced a grand "Festival of India" which featured exhibitions and related cultural programmes presented at over thirty different institutions throughout the United States (including museums, universities, and performing arts centres).[22] Many visual and performing artists were invited to participate in these programmes – including several tribal and folk artists – whose responses to the experience varied considerably. According to Jyotindra Jain: "While most returned home laden with American wrist watches, cameras, radios, tape-recorders, and thermos flasks bartered for their 'Oriental Ware', [Mithila artist] Ganga Devi came back almost empty-handed but charged by the experience of this 'completely different world'. Later, the experience led to her remarkable 'American Series' of paintings."[23] In the picture from that series here illustrated (figure 8), Ganga Devi uses continuous narrative to depict her visit to the Washington Monument: buying her ticket at a booth (at lower left), and then entering the central monumental obelisk surrounded by US flags (depicted flying upside-down).

Years after she returned from the US, Ganga Devi characterized that "completely different world" as a place where "...everyone is carrying a shopping bag, men do the domestic work while the women go to offices to work". Also, "In America often you do not have a direct contact with people. Mostly, a hand comes out of a counter or a window, takes away your money and after a while comes out again to hand over your ticket. You do not see the person; you deal with the hand."[24] This specific sense of modern alienation seems quite a natural response from a rural artist from Bihar, a state still mired in feudal oppression – customarily applied in various *personal* ways.

Playing to the Gallery

M.F. Husain's paintings on political themes range from his evocative 1972 depiction of Mahatma Gandhi to a more suspect portrayal of Indira Gandhi as the goddess Durga riding a tiger (painted after her 1975 Emergency proclamation). Most recently – in response to the fighting in Kargil (Kashmir) – Husain appeared before some 15,000 patriotic spectators assembled in a New Delhi stadium, where he executed an enormous painting of an Indian soldier atop the Himalaya, with the Republic's flag flying in the background. This public "performance" was accompanied by band music – to which Husain synchronized his brush strokes; upon completion, the painting was ceremonially presented to Prime Minister Vajpayee.

Such background information about Husain's iconographic inspiration can perhaps shed some light on his 1976 "Washington and Arjuna" (figure 9), painted in honour of the USA's bicentennial celebrations. Here the artist substitutes Washington for Krishna and attaches a US flag to Arjuna's chariot. Does this playful commingling of popular icons have some deeply provocative significance? Or does Husain's religious and political iconography simply follow the ever-changing winds of politics, patronage, and popular sentiment? And how does Husain's inherently difficult position – being a prominent Muslim artist at a time of rising Hindu nationalism – affect his choice of subject matter? These are awkward but perhaps necessary questions to ask about India's most internationally recognized contemporary artist.

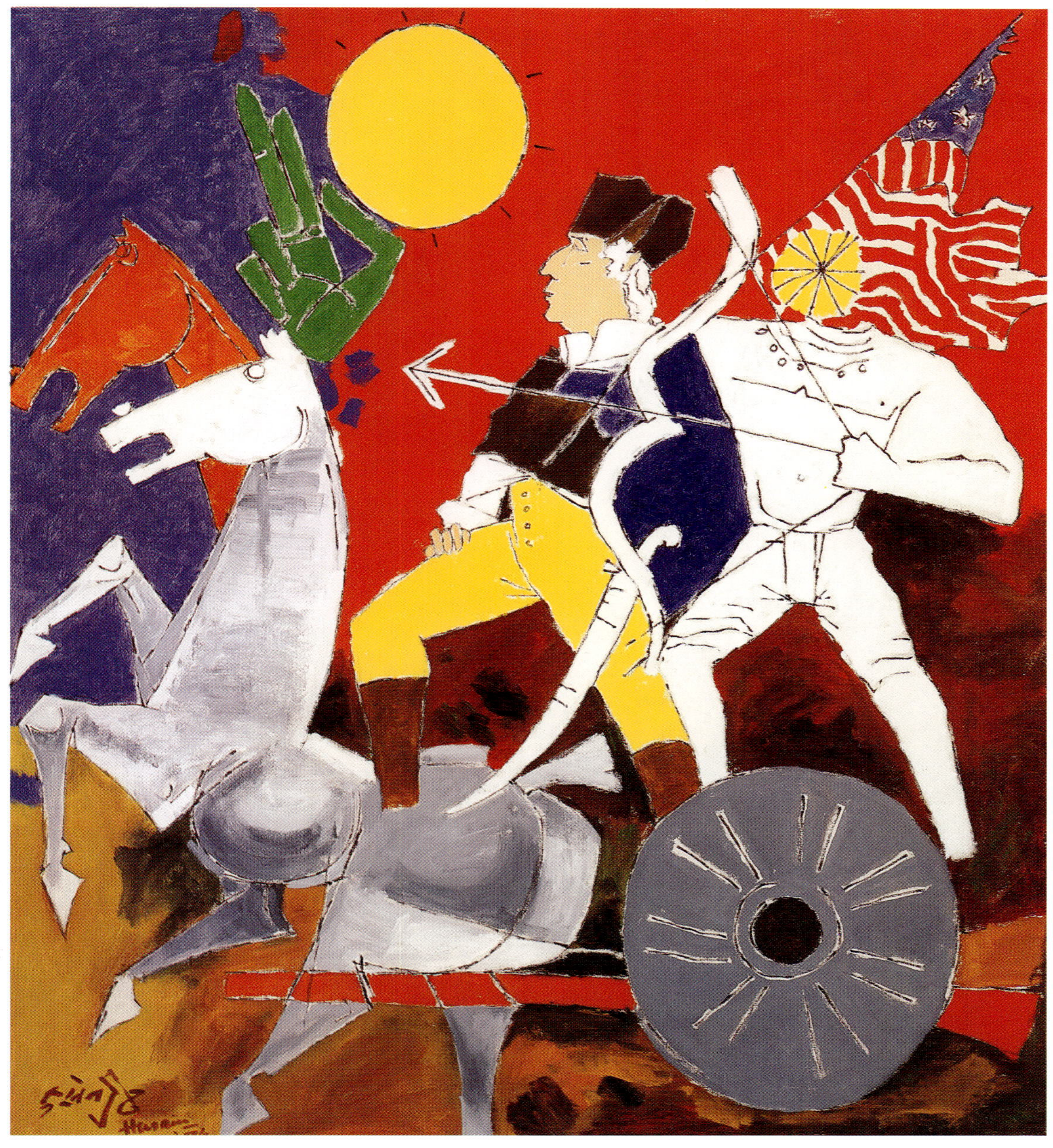

9
M.F. Husain (b. 1915)
"Washington and Arjuna", 1976
Acrylic on canvas;
141.6 x 123.2 cm
Photograph courtesy Peabody Essex Museum, Salem, Massachusetts

Incidentally, "Washington and Arjuna" is one of over 3,000 artworks in the world's largest private collection of contemporary Indian art – established in Massachusetts by the late Chester Herwitz and his wife Davida. It was seeing Husain's artwork, and then meeting the artist, which first "hooked" Mr and Mrs Herwitz into almost forty years of enthusiastic collecting.[25] And so continues a long-established Indian tradition of "courtly" patronage by powerful foreign elites – with US collectors, museums, galleries, and auction houses assuming leading roles. The influence of such US patronage has yet to be fully analysed.

Long-Distance Nostalgia

The journey from Chital village in Gujarat to New York City is a long and rather unusual one, especially for an artist. Vinod Dave is the youngest child of an ayurvedic doctor who was less than enthusiastic about his son's determination to become an artist. Dr Dave was acquainted with the hardships of that vocation (he knew a traditional painter of religious icons, whose only payments seemed to come as gifts of food and grain), and urged his son to become a civil engineer. For a few months young Vinod attended a science college at Rajkot. But he persisted with his wish to study art and eventually his father reluctantly consented and provided some modest support for Vinod to

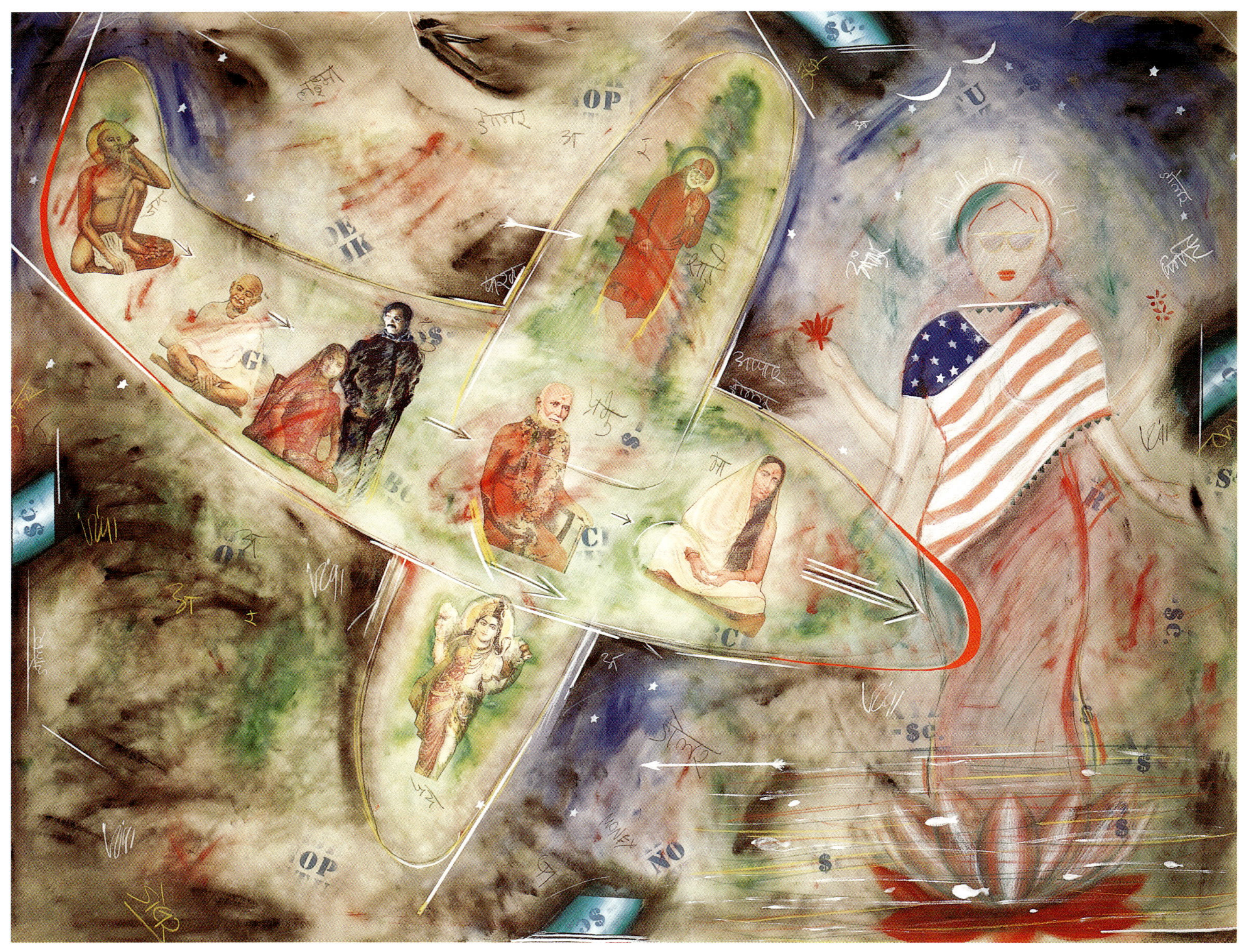

10
Vinod Dave (b. 1948)
"Pushpak Viman (Chariot of Lord Rama)", 1991
Mixed media on canvas; 203.2 x 259 cm
Herwitz collection, Peabody Essex Museum, Salem, Massachusetts

study studio arts at Baroda's Maharaja Sayajirao University. Scholarships and teaching positions followed, first in India and then in the US. Vinod Dave recently became a US citizen, and now pursues his vocation in the competitive and stimulating art world of New York City.

Dave's success has not come without struggle. Although he continues to exhibit his work in India (and elsewhere in Asia and Europe), his greatest patronage remains in the US. Collectors Chester and Davida Herwitz have acquired hundreds of his works, including three especially commissioned series on subjects of mutual interest. One of these series features 25 large "Icons of Deities" inspired by various religious traditions – mostly Hindu but also Jain, Buddhist, Muslim, etc. – but no Christian "icons" (Chester Herwitz emphatically objected to Dave's inclusion of any Christian imagery – a matter of earnest but respectful dispute between artist and patron).[26] "Pushpak Viman (Chariot of Lord Rama)" (figure 10) depicts an aircraft loaded with an odd assortment of Indian jet-setters (including Ardhanarishvara, a Hindi movie star, Mahatma Gandhi, the artist himself, and various celebrity gurus) – all about to arrive in America, signified as Lakshmi sporting a new set of attributes: sunglasses, a stars-and-stripes sari/*choli*, a "Statue of Liberty" crown, and a green dollar-and-cents flag. Dave has mixed feelings about life in the US: "Coming here has made me go back to my own culture; physically I may be living here, but in imagination I live there. When I was in India I took everything for granted, but when I came here I started to become nostalgic, and my work became more 'Indian' in subject matter and spirit.... When you are hungry, only then do you realize the true value of food."[27]

The Temptation of Deserts

This visual smorgasbord presents some of the diverse ways in which modern Mexican and Indian artists depict the US – as well as certain ironies regarding their patronage and national identity. Consider, for example, the radical differences between depictions of the US and Mexico as illustrated here by Rivera, Siqueiros, and Kahlo – all three contemporaries with similar Stalinist politics.[28] Also the astonishing irony of Rivera and Siqueiros' US patronage: both undertook important mural commissions in the heart of major US cities (Siqueiros in Los Angeles, Rivera in San Francisco, Detroit, and New York) during the conservative 1930s and '40s (and, in Rivera's case, patronized by such leading capitalists as Ford and Rockefeller). A significant incentive for accepting such projects in the US was the abatement of government commissions in Mexico; yet, as previously noted, readily forthcoming US patronage could also entail limited "freedom of expression", beyond which murals could be censored by whitewashings or demolition (as happened at Olvera Street in Los Angeles, or Rockefeller Center in New York).

And then there's the case of Chagoya and Dave, two contemporary artists who deeply identify with their respective nations of origins; yet both have recently become US citizens. As a US citizen, Chagoya continues to vigorously challenge prejudicial US policies and attitudes against Mexicans and Mexican-Americans; by contrast, Dave – who immigrated from a nation renowned for its long history of communalism – was instructed by his chief US patron to refrain from including Christian imagery in a series of paintings especially commissioned to celebrate India's religious diversity.

The "non-political" works of José Benítez and Ganga Devi express the alienation felt by two traditional artists attending US exhibitions of their work. Ironically, such popular exhibitions of contemporary tribal and folk art reflect modernity's delight in celebrating the very diversity of cultures inherently antithetical to trans-global "development". Meanwhile, Husain makes light mockery of India's eagerness for American-style modernity and development – by replacing Arjuna's charioteer with a foreign, less spiritual hero – the one also depicted on the US dollar bill.

Significantly, politically critical representations of the US rarely appear in works by Indian artists, but often recur in paintings by leading Mexican and Mexican-American artists (represented here by Siqueiros and Chagoya). Basic history and geography account for Mexico's greater wariness of US encroachment on various fronts: political, military, territorial, economic, and cultural. After all, the unneighbourly US invaded Mexico and "acquired" half of its territory in 1848;[29] and more recently Mexico surrendered its economic autonomy to the North American Free Trade Agreement – now widely blamed for further impoverishing the Mexican masses for the benefit of North American business interests.

Although the US and Mexico share the only clearly visible boundary line between the so-called "First" and "Third" Worlds, such lopsided superpower relations can now be seen operating long-distance too. Everywhere the "developing world" gets hooked on US bank loans, arms, and problematic aid, and hankers after Hollywood movies and fast food. India has now experienced nearly a decade of "economic liberalization", which has brought Indian artists closer to the global economy and India itself closer to the US – which is at the forefront of this economy.

How will Indian artists respond to these changes? With alacrity, accommodation and assimilation – or with a more critical consciousness that's articulate, revealing, judicious, and distinctive? Just as many of today's tribal and folk artists get trapped into churning out decorative but soulless "ethnic" and tourist art, likewise talented and urbane contemporary artists can be tempted into following fashionable vogues promoted by financial speculation. These trends are now being further facilitated by the "gatekeepers" of artistic recognition – institutionalized hierarchies of art specialists serving museums, galleries, and all manner of media. And the whole process is becoming more streamlined and efficient every day. Major auction houses, as well as cyber-savvy artists and dealers, are increasingly marketing all sorts of artwork on the internet – a trend that now seems destined to accelerate.[30] This of course is the logical next step for the "globalization" of contemporary arts.

One has to ask: whose interests do these trends really benefit – and who is being excluded from those benefits? What about those artists who can't – or won't – vend their wares in competitive, intellectually articulate, self-promoting ways easily translated into high-tech, affluent, globalized/American-style appreciation? How will they be known? Can highbrow discourse on "post-Modernism" and "multiculturalism" effectively champion the recognition of those who – without calculating ambition – still aspire to express themselves in non-"global" idioms?

As Octavio Paz wisely warns: "...one must not confuse the hegemony of the marketplace with fruitfulness, imagination, and the power to create."[31]

NOTES

John H. Bowles wrote this essay for Marg in 1999.

1. Gertrude Stein, "Why Do Americans Live In Europe", *Transition*, No. 28, Fall 1928, p. 97.

2. Bertram D. Wolfe, *The Fabulous Life of Diego Rivera*, New York, Stein and Day, 1963, p. 277.

3. Mary Miller and Karl Taube, *The Gods and Symbols of Ancient Mexico and the Maya*, New York and London, Thames & Hudson, 1993, p. 64.

4. Diego Rivera and Gladys March, *My Art, My Life – An Autobiography*, New York, The Citadel Press, 1960, p. 151.

5. Ibid., p. 152.

6. Shifra Goldman, "Siqueiros' Ámerica Tropical", *Art Journal*, 1974.

7. In 1932, a third of the mural was initially whitewashed (viz., that which was easily visible to pedestrians from the nearby street). Then, sometime after 1938, the entire mural was whitewashed and the whitewashed surface left exposed to the sun and elements for many decades. The now deteriorated mural is presently undergoing conservation, made possible by the Getty Conservation Institute and a grant from the United States National Endowment for the Arts.

8. Antonio Gonzalez Reynoso, *David Alfaro Siqueiros – an exhibition catalogue*, Los Angeles, Plaza de la Raza, 1985, p. 32.

9. Octavio Paz, *Essays on Mexican Art* (tr. Helen Lane), New York, San Diego, and London, Harcourt Brace & Company, 1933, p. 121.

10. Rivera's murals at the Detroit Institute of Fine Arts celebrate the city's factories and modern technology.

11. Kahlo would later both divorce and remarry Rivera in 1940.

12. Frank Crowninshield, "New York Goes Mexican", *Vogue*, July 15, 1940, No.12, pp. 38–41, 81–82.

13. Both dances evolved from combined non-Mexican traditions: the tango's origins are Spanish/Argentine/Cuban, and rumba's origins are Afro-Cuban.

14. Diego Rivera and Gladys March, *My Art, My Life*, p. 128.

15. Juan Negrín, *The Huichol Creation of the World*, Sacramento, E.B. Crocker Art Gallery, 1975, p. 35.

16. Ibid., pp. 29–33.

17. Ibid., p. 33.

18. See John Carey, "An Iconography of Vision", *Temenos*, vol. X, London, 1989; Nelson H.H. Graburn, ed., "Ethnic and Tourist Arts", *Cultural Expressions from the Fourth World*, Berkeley, Los Angeles, and London, University of California Press, 1976; and Seldon Rodman, *Artists in Tune with Their World, Masters of Popular Art in the Americas and Their Relation to the Folk Tradition*, New York, Simon and Schuster, 1982.

19. Chagoya directly participated in the subsequent student protests of 1971 (also violently suppressed by the government). See Elizabeth Pepin, "Beyond Borders, Enrique Chagoya's Life in the American Salad Bar", *Juxtapose*, vol. 17.

20. For example, see: Clair F. Fox, *The Fence and the River, Culture and Politics at the U.S.-Mexican Border*, Minneapolis and London, University of Minnesota Press, 1999; and *La Frontera/The Border, Art About the Mexico/United States Border Experience*, ed. Kathryn Kajo, San Diego, Centro Cultural de la Raza and Museum of Contemporary Art, 1993.

21. Guillermo Gomez-Pena, "The Free Art Ågreement/El Tratado de Libre Cultura", *The Subversive Imagination: Artists, Society, and Social Responsibility*, ed. Carol Becker, New York, Routledge, 1994, pp. 215–16.

22. See *Festival of India in the United States 1985–86*, ed. Leta Bostelman, New York, Harry N. Abrams, Inc., 1985.

23. Jyotindra Jain, *Ganga Devi: Tradition and Expression in Mithila Painting*, Mapin, Ahmedabad, in association with The Mithila Museum, Niigata, Japan, 1997, p. 114.

24. Quoted by Jyotindra Jain, ibid.

25. Susan Bean, *Timeless Visions, Contemporary Art of India From the Chester and Davida Herwitz Collection*, Salem, Peabody Essex Museum, 1999, p. 8.

26. Author's personal communication with the artist, November 6, 1999.

27. Ibid.

28. It should be noted that while all three artists were aligned with Stalinism for most of their adult lives, Rivera and Kahlo also "lapsed" for some years into an affiliation with Leon Trotsky and his politics, which became a matter of public debate between Siqueiros and Rivera in the mid-1930s. It might also be noted that both artists were implicated in Trotsky's assassination.

29. Viz. the 1848 Treaty of Guadalupe Hidalgo.

30. "Sotheby's and the Cybermasses", *The Economist*, January 29, 2000, vol. 534, no. 8155.

31. Octavio Paz, *Essays on Mexican Art*, p. 300.

ACKNOWLEDGEMENTS

The writer wishes to acknowledge the kind assistance of Julia Bergman, Virginia Fields, John Listopad, Stephen Markel, and Pankaj Mishra.

Jamini Roy
"Sita on the Fire", 1947
Tempera
Collection of Mulk Raj Anand
Reproduced from *Marg* 2/1, 1947

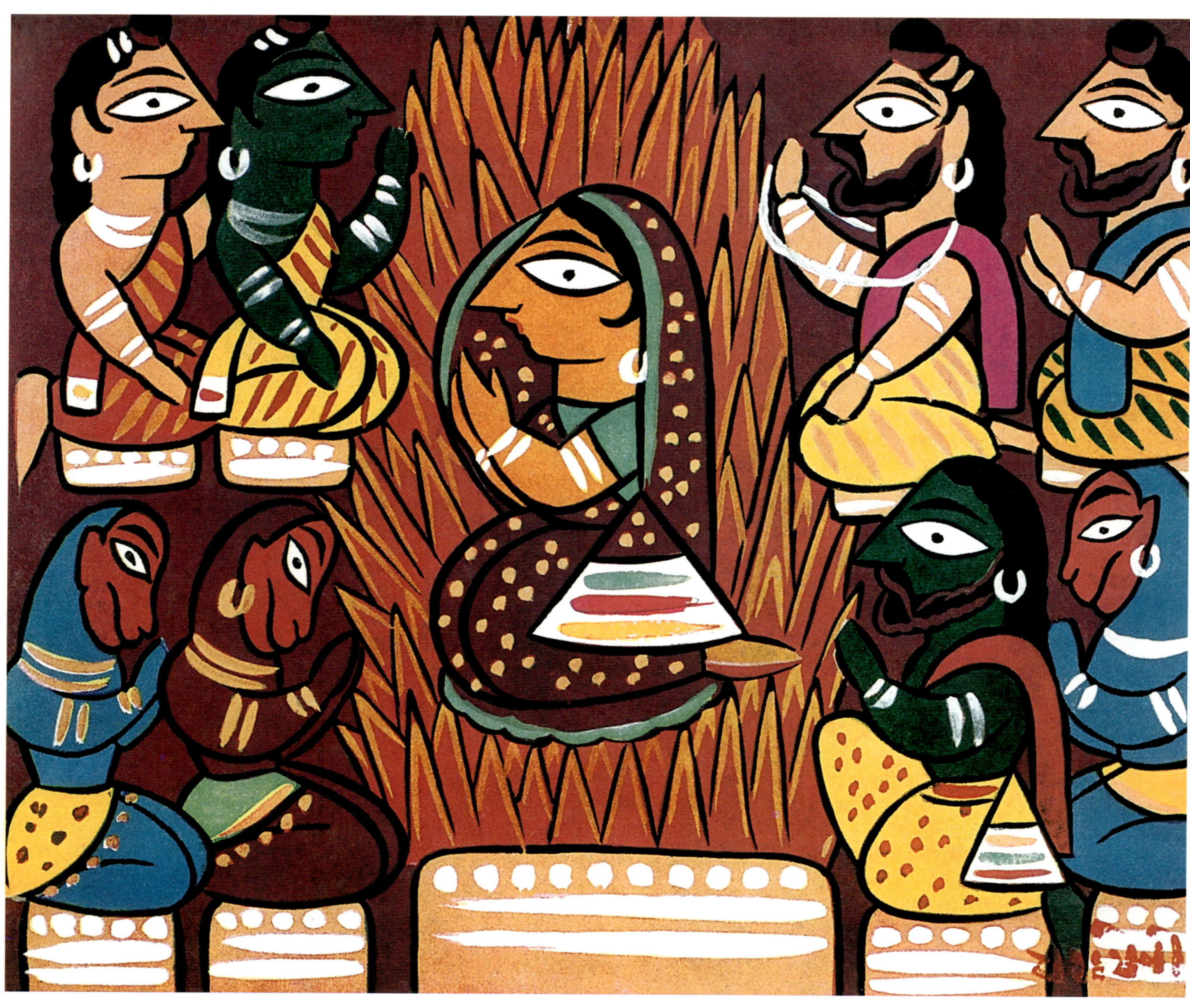

reflections

"Indian Painting" by Rudolf von Leyden

On the one side we find the painters who are determined to continue a truly Indian tradition in art by using a certain formal idiom that was developed either in the classic period of Indian painting or in the medieval schools of miniature painting. They are fond of the languid beauty of the curvaceous line, of fine colour washes and often of a devotional attitude in the subject or attitude of their works. One has called this group the "Bengal School" because it grew out of the great revivalist movement of the Tagores. Another traditionalist group draws on the primitive vigour of folk art with its strong rhythms of form and colour patterns. One could say that this group also originated with Jamini Roy in Bengal where a colourful art life existed in the villages of the Bankura district and in other parts of that lovely country right into modern times. There are many cross-currents between this group and the modern painters who also like strong contrasty patterns. Another group of Indian artists has adopted the more representational styles of Western art. Here we find those who adhere to the strict naturalism of the academic tradition and those who paint "impressions" of nature in oil or watercolour. They have made these various styles entirely their own.

A third group of contemporary Indian artists goes usually by the name of "The Moderns" with a capital "M". Although they have derived many of their ideas from the various styles of modern art that have stirred the art world of Europe for the last fifty years or so, they are really speaking individualists who try in every manner or style to come to terms with the world that surrounds them. They believe that great emotional power and significance is contained in the very elements of painting, namely colour and form, and that they can be used almost in the pure or abstract state to convey the feelings or ideas of the artist. They have, therefore, discarded to a very large extent the appearance of things and use, what the layman calls, distorted and "unnatural" forms. As they follow their own individual visions and inventions it is not always easy for the average friend of painting and art to understand their work. But that should be no reason to call them bad artists. On the contrary, among them are found some of the most original and even most truly Indian painters of today.

Courtesy *The Times of India Annual,* 1953

"Instituting the Nation in Art" by Tapati Guha-Thakurta

One can argue that the year 1947 is in itself of little relevance in the history of Indian art: It marks no major point of rupture or break, still less any notable shift in artistic ideologies or directions. If anything, the '40s in Calcutta and Bombay most decisively signalled the passing of the age of nationalism in modern Indian art, and the disengagement of artists from the demands of nation, history and tradition. Even in writing the history of the recovery of India's artistic past – in charting the course of museums, collections or art historical trends – there is little that spotlights the year or the period as notable landmarks.

Yet, it is in this context, that I wish to rethink the uses, meanings and deployment of art at this symbolic juncture in the life of the nation. I wish particularly to highlight the way the invocations of a "national art" at this point, in marked contrast to earlier invocations, objectifies and memorialises the past in sharp dissociation from the present. The event and the surrounding practices I focus on in this essay are marked, I find, by one resounding absence: the absence of the "Modern" in this image of the nation's art. Such an absence becomes easily naturalised in the event (as it does in my essay), as the attention centres on celebrated notions of "history" and "heritage" that halt the narrative of India's achievements well before the "Modern" age. It becomes particularly instructive here to return to the scene of the 1948 exhibition in the premises of the new Rashtrapati Bhavan in New Delhi – to explore the way the new nation-state sought one of its main ritual forms in the spectacle of a national art heritage that remained enshrined in the past and fixed in the space of exhibition and museum galleries.

Courtesy *Fifty Years of Indian Art,* Mohile-Parikh Centre for the Visual Arts, Mumbai 1997

"Profane and Sacred: Style, Criticism and Ideology" by John Clark

In the 1973 essay on "New Images in Indian Art: Fantasy" the late Jaya Appasamy noted that in Indian art "juxtapositions of the real and unreal are quite traditional", where "fantasy has never been a separate category of art". She identified certain kinds of fantastic reality present in the individual and lonely creations of certain artists whose work is "not devoted to social reality or the presentation of didactic views or ideas". But for Geeta Kapur the fantastic was also seen as the apparitional, "images of reverie that appear like a flash, illuminating the space around, marking it off from mundane space as a nimbus marks off a supermundane presence", a type of inclination towards a "romantic-spiritual art". Significantly Kapur included the work of Swaminathan in the apparitional category. Here I think are two implicitly opposed views: one which assigns the fantastic to a creative but ambivalent overlap between reality and fiction, and one which attributes it to a marking off from reality, to a theology. Kapur shortly later moved to a call for an "objective partisanship" which did not "violate the subject that is already dispossessed with pity or satire", and which had regard for "historical facts as an imaginative summation of situations, lives, persons". This, contra Appasamy, led to a didacticism whose values were clear: "a social art is significant if it confirms the possibility of praxis."

Kapur had moved towards an implicitly didactic position in the exhibition she curated a year earlier, *Place for People*, 1981. In that catalogue she had linked views on mythic narration with an individual destiny which, by reference to the painting of Kitaj, found longer historical meaning through the dimension of epic. Personal integration is achieved by an affirmation springing from "fierce acts of the imagination", which "subverts any simplistic design of a future society in order to find such paradigms that can develop utopian alignments with ongoing history". Her critical position all but states that the artist should align with history, even if she opens up artistic affirmation to a less restricted series of dialectics than the Stalinist trivialisation.

Courtesy *Modern Indian Art: Some Literature and Problematics,*
School of Asian Studies, University of Sydney, 1994

"Contemporary Indian Art: A Question of Method" by Ajay J. Sinha

The urge to validate Indian art of the late 20th century places it at the boundary of interpretation with which [Homi] Bhabha is esteemed. I will map this boundary in the first part of the essay, hoping to redefine it in the second. Among South Asianists in US universities and museums who are increasingly pressed to consider this new and uncertain area of acquisition, the question of validating contemporary Indian art invites scepticism. In order to justify its avant-garde status, they search for its difference from progressive art movements in the West. Discouraged by its references to mainstream modernism, they inscribe it as derivative of that with which they are more familiar. Indian art criticism has offered two apologies to such a pervasive, Eurocentric view. One is made in terms of eclecticism, a pluralistic defense based on the principle of free borrowing and synthesis of various cultures, which in India includes Western art as well as India's own traditions. The second, more recent one claims the authenticity of India's contemporary art by discussing "alternative modernisms" thereby attempting to restore in India some of modernism's original edge as a homogeneous counterculture within Europe's bourgeois culture. In the age of postmodernism and multiculturalism, the search for India's authenticity has expanded beyond the nationalistic positions of Indian art criticism. In the United States, the pluralistic argument provides a new framework for interest in contemporary Indian art by adapting it to the discourse of minority cultures, which has gained ground in the United States with migration, the success of feminism, and US liberal politics.

Courtesy *Art Journal,* Fall 1999

"The Work of Art in These Past Few Decades" by Sudhir Patwardhan

In the modernist work, the elements were fully integrated. Each element spoke only as a part of the whole, without a separate voice. In the realist-narrative work, the second-order parts as we called them, had a life of their own, leading to a more open-ended and less autonomous structure. In the new collage-inspired works the elements are experienced as fragments, their internal relations strained, distanced, and at times uncanny. To bring such fragments together as parts of a work of art, the artist has to devise a structure of even greater openness. The structure has to have the resilience and breadth, and the wit, to somehow hold together the fragments of authentic meaning available to us today, without denying their reality as fragments....

The idea of autonomy demanded that art should be assessed by standards of its own, unique to itself. Such standards are now not easy to apply, nor are they favoured. At such a time it would be good to remind ourselves that openness of structure is not looseness of structure. The invasion of art by the outer world or the crowding of loaded signifiers into the work of art, cannot replace the artist's search for meaning, or his construction of meanings through the building of structures. If anything, the new openness makes this structuring more demanding, more difficult. The self, whether centered or decentered, is still structured, and the work of art is still a mirror image of the self. If I may be allowed one last expression of prejudice, for those of us to whom some form of wholeness – personal, social or spiritual, still beckons, the struggle is yet on to heal ourselves. For those who have made their peace with their pieces, the celebration has begun.

Courtesy *Embarkations,* Millennium show at Sakshi Gallery, Mumbai, January 2000

index

Page numbers in bold refer to captions